CAMBRIDGE
UNIVERSITY PRESS

Cambridge Lower Secondary
Mathematics

WORKBOOK 8

Greg Byrd, Lynn Byrd & Chris Pearce

CAMBRIDGE
UNIVERSITY PRESS

University Printing House, Cambridge CB2 8BS, United Kingdom

One Liberty Plaza, 20th Floor, New York, NY 10006, USA

477 Williamstown Road, Port Melbourne, VIC 3207, Australia

314–321, 3rd Floor, Plot 3, Splendor Forum, Jasola District Centre, New Delhi – 110025, India

103 Penang Road, #05-06/07, Visioncrest Commercial, Singapore 238467

Cambridge University Press is part of the University of Cambridge.

It furthers the University's mission by disseminating knowledge in the pursuit of education, learning and research at the highest international levels of excellence.

www.cambridge.org
Information on this title: www.cambridge.org/9781108746403

© Cambridge University Press 2021

First published 2014
Second edition 2021

20 19 18 17 16 15 14

Printed in India by Multivista Global Pvt Ltd

A catalogue record for this publication is available from the British Library

ISBN 978-1-108-74640-3 Paperback with Digital Access

⟩ Contents

Contents

› How to use this book

This workbook provides questions for you to practise what you have learned in class. There is a unit to match each unit in your Learner's Book. Each exercise is divided into three parts:

- **Focus:** these questions help you to master the basics

- **Practice:** these questions help you to become more confident in using what you have learned

- **Challenge:** these questions will make you think very hard.

You will also find these features:

Words you need to know.

Key words

factor tree
HCF
LCM
prime factor

Step-by-step examples showing how to solve a problem.

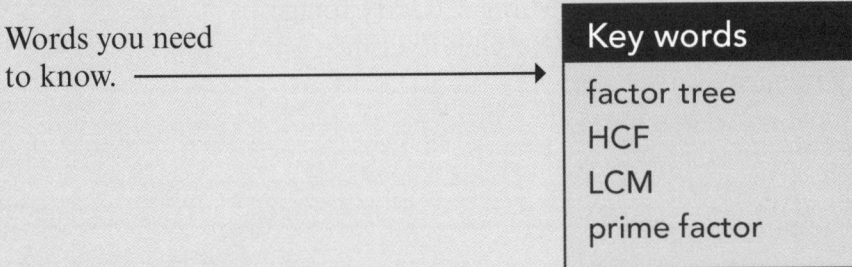

Worked example 2.5

You can use a flow chart like this to **solve** an equation.

Solve: $3x + 5 = 17$

Answer

$3x + 5 = 17$ x $\times 3$ $+5$ 17   Reverse the flow chart to work out the value of x.

So $x = 4$ 4 $\div 3$ 12 -5 17

Questions marked with this symbol help you to practise thinking and working mathematically.

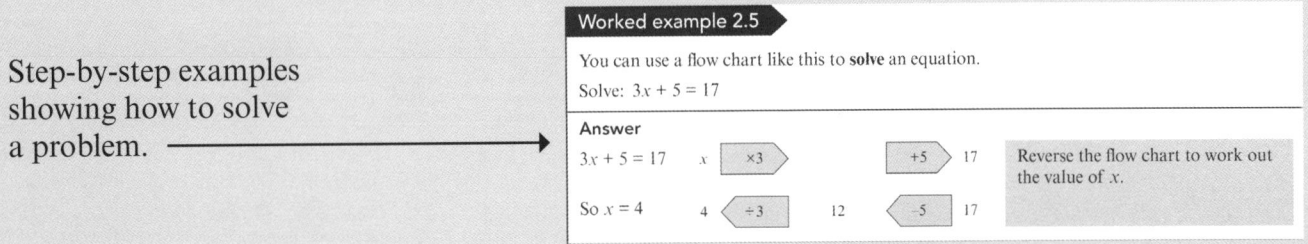

13   When $x = -4$, all of these expressions except one have the same value.
Which is the odd one out?

$x^2 - 7$ $(x+1)^2$ $-\dfrac{36}{x}$ $x-5$ $2x+17$ $5-x$

14   Write any values of x that make each pair of expressions equal.
   a $3x + 1$ and $3x^2 + 1$ b $4 - x$ and $x - 4$
   c $\dfrac{5x}{2} + 5$ and $\dfrac{2x}{5} + 5$ d $3(x + 2)$ and $2(x + 3)$

⟩ Acknowledgements

The authors and publishers acknowledge the following sources of copyright material and are grateful for the permissions granted. While every effort has been made, it has not always been possible to identify the sources of all the material used, or to trace all copyright holders. If any omissions are brought to our notice, we will be happy to include the appropriate acknowledgements on reprinting.

Thanks to the following for permission to reproduce images:

Cover Photo: ori-artiste/Getty Images

ROBERT BROOK/Getty Images; Michael Dunning/Getty Images; Liyao Xie/Getty Images; Richard Drury/Getty Images; Aaron Foster/ Getty Images; EyeEm/Getty Images; Tuomas Lehtinen/Getty Images; MirageC/Getty Images; yuanyuan yan/Getty Images; MirageC/Getty Images; Pongnathee Kluaythong/EyeEm/Getty Images; Pietro Recchia/EyeEm/ Getty Images; Yagi Studio/Getty Images

1 ▶ Integers

> 1.1 Factors, multiples and primes

Exercise 1.1

Key words

factor tree

highest common factor (HCF)

lowest common multiple (LCM)

prime factor

Focus

1   a   Draw a **factor tree** for 250 that starts with 2×125.

   b   Can you draw a different factor tree for 250 that starts with 2×125? Give a reason for your answer.

   c   Draw a factor tree for 250 that starts with 25×10.

   d   Write 250 as a product of its **prime factors**.

2   a   Draw a factor tree for 300.

   b   Draw a different factor tree for 300.

   c   Write 300 as a product of prime numbers.

3   a   Write as a product of prime numbers

      i   6   ii   30   iii   210

   b   What is the next number in this sequence? Why?

4   Work out

   a $2 \times 3 \times 7$ b $2^2 \times 3^2 \times 7^2$ c $2^3 \times 3^3 \times 7^3$

5   a   Draw a factor tree for 8712.

   b   Write 8712 as a product of prime numbers.

6   Write each of these numbers as a product of its prime factors.

   a   96   b   97   c   98   d   99

Practice

7   Write as a product of prime numbers

   a   70   b 70^2 c 70^3

8   a   Write each square number as a product of its prime factors.

      i   9   ii   36   iii   81

      iv   144   v   225   vi   576

      vii   625   viii   2401

b When a square number is written as a product of prime numbers, what can you say about the factors?

c $176\,400 = 2^4 \times 3^2 \times 5^2 \times 7^2$

Use this fact to show that $176\,400$ is a square number.

9 $315 = 3^2 \times 5 \times 7$ $\qquad$ $252 = 2^2 \times 3^2 \times 7$ $\qquad$ $660 = 2^2 \times 3 \times 5 \times 11$

Use these facts to find the **highest common factor** of

a 315 and 252 $\qquad$ **b** 315 and 660 $\qquad$ **c** 252 and 660

10 $60 = 2^2 \times 3 \times 5$ $\qquad$ $72 = 2^3 \times 3^2$ $\qquad$ $75 = 3 \times 5^2$

Use these facts to find the **lowest common multiple** of

a 60 and 72 $\qquad$ **b** 60 and 75 $\qquad$ **c** 72 and 75

11 **a** Write 104 as a product of its prime factors.

b Write 130 as a product of its prime factors.

c Find the **HCF** of 104 and 130.

d Find the **LCM** of 104 and 130.

12 **a** Write 135 as a product of prime numbers.

b Write 180 as a product of prime numbers.

c Find the HCF of 135 and 180.

d Find the LCM of 135 and 180.

Challenge

13 **a** Write 343 as a product of prime numbers.

b Write 546 as a product of prime numbers.

c Find the HCF of 343 and 546. $\qquad$ **d** Find the LCM of 343 and 546.

14 Find the LCM of 42 and 90.

15 **a** Find the HCF of 168 and 264.

b Find the LCM of 168 and 264.

16 **a** Show that the LCM of 48 and 25 is 1.

b Find the HCF of 48 and 25.

17 The HCF of two numbers is 6. The LCM of the two numbers is 72.

What are the two numbers?

> 1.2 Multiplying and dividing integers

Exercise 1.2

Focus

1 Copy this sequence of multiplications and add <u>three</u> more multiplications in the sequence.

$7 \times -4 = -28$ $5 \times -4 = -20$ $3 \times -4 = -12$ $1 \times -4 = -4$

2 Work out

   a -5×8 b -5×-8

   c -9×-11 d -20×-6

3 Put these multiplications into two groups.

A -12×-3	B $(-6)^2$	C -4×9
D 18×2	E 9×-4	F -4×-9

4 Copy and complete this multiplication table.

$\times$		-4	-9
-6			
5			-45
-8	-16		

5 Work out

   a $(3+4) \times 5$ b $(3+-4) \times 5$ c $(-3+-4) \times -5$ d $(3+-4) \times -5$

Practice

6 Estimate the answers by rounding numbers to the nearest integer.

   a -2.9×-8.15 b 10.8×-6.1 c $(-8.8)^2$ d $(-4.09)^2$

7 Show that $(-6)^2 + (-8)^2 - (-10)^2 = 0$

8 This is a multiplication pyramid.

Each number is the product of the two numbers below.
For example, $3 \times -2 = -6$

   a Copy and complete the pyramid.

   b Show that you can change the order of the numbers on the bottom row to make the top number 3456.

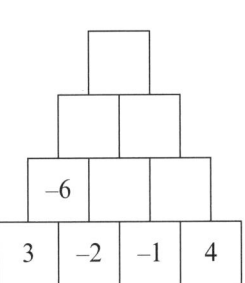

9 a The product of two **integers** is −6.

Find all the possible values of the two integers.

  b The product of two integers is 6.

Find all the possible values of the two integers.

10 a Here is a multiplication: $-9 \times -7 = 63$

Write it as a division in two different ways.

  b Here is a different multiplication: $12 \times -7 = -84$

Write it as a division in two different ways.

11 Work out

  a $42 \div -7$ b $-50 \div -10$ c $27 \div -3$ d $-52 \div -4$ e $60 \div -5$

12 Estimate the answers by rounding numbers to the nearest 10.

  a $92 \div -28.5$ b $-41 \div -18.9$ c $83.8 \div -11.6$ d $-77 \div 19$

Challenge

13 Copy and complete this multiplication pyramid.

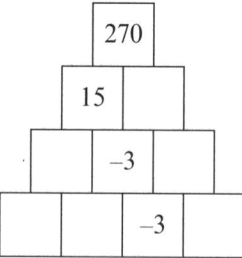

14 Find the value of y.

  a $-8 \times y = 48$ b $y \times -3 = -36$

  c $-10 \times y = 120$ d $y \times -5 = -40$

15 Find the value of z.

  a $z \div -4 = -8$ b $z \div -2 = 20$

  c $-36 \div z = 9$ d $30 \div z = -6$

 16 a Here is a statement: $-3 \times (-6 \times -4) = (-3 \times -6) \times -4$

Is it true or false? Give a reason to support your answer.

  b Here is a statement: $-24 \div (-4 \div -2) = (-24 \div -4) \div -2$

Is it true or false? Give a reason to support your answer.

> 1.3 Square roots and cube roots

Exercise 1.3

Focus

1 Work out
   a 14^2
   b $(-14)^2$
   c $(-20)^2$
   d $(-30)^2$

2 Work out
   a 4^3
   b $(-6)^3$
   c $(-10)^3$
   d $(-1)^2 + (-1)^3$

3 If possible, work out
   a $\sqrt{-64}$
   b $\sqrt[3]{-64}$
   c $\sqrt[3]{-125}$
   d $\sqrt[3]{-729}$

Practice

4 Solve each equation.
   a $x^2 = 25$
   b $x^2 = 225$
   c $x^2 - 81 = 0$
   d $x^2 + 121 = 0$

5 Solve each equation.
   a $x^3 = 216$
   b $x^3 = -216$
   c $x^3 + 1000 = 0$
   d $x^3 + 8000 = 0$

6 $23^2 = 529$ and $23^3 = 12\,167$

   Use these facts to solve the following equations.
   a $x^2 = 529$
   b $x^2 + 529 = 0$
   c $x^3 = 12\,167$
   d $x^3 + 12\,167 = 0$

7 Write whether each statement is true or false.
   a 9 is a **rational number**
   b -9 is a **natural number**
   c 99 is an integer
   d -999 is both an integer and a rational number
   e 9999 is both a natural number and a rational number

Challenge

8 a Copy and complete this table.

x	-3	-2	-1	0	1	2
$x^2 + x$				0		
$x^3 + x$				0		

   b Use the table to solve these equations.
   i $x^2 + x = 2$
   ii $x^3 + x = 2$

9 Here is an equation: $x^3 - x = 120$

    a Is $x = 5$ a solution? Give a reason for your answer.

    b Is $x = -5$ a solution? Give a reason for your answer.

10 a Write 64 as a product of its prime factors.

    b Show that 64 is a square number and a cube number.

    c Write 729 as a product of prime numbers.

    d Show that 729 is both a square number and a cube number.

    e Find another integer that is both a square number and a cube number.

 11 Look at the following solution of the equation $x^6 = 64$

$$x^6 = 64$$
$$\text{so} \quad x^3 = 8$$
$$\text{so} \quad x = 2$$

There is an error in this solution. Write a corrected version.

> 1.4 Indices

Exercise 1.4

Key words

index

power

Focus

1 Write as a single **power**

    a $3^2 \times 3$ **b** 7×7^3 **c** 12×12^5 **d** $15^4 \times 15$

2 Write as a single power

    a $6^3 \times 6^3$ **b** $10^5 \times 10^2$ **c** $3^6 \times 3^3$ **d** $14^3 \times 14^4$

 3 a Show that $2^0 + 2^1 + 2^2 + 2^3 = 2^4 - 1$

    b Can you find a similar expression for $2^0 + 2^1 + 2^2 + 2^3 + 2^4 + 2^5$?

    c Read what Zara says:

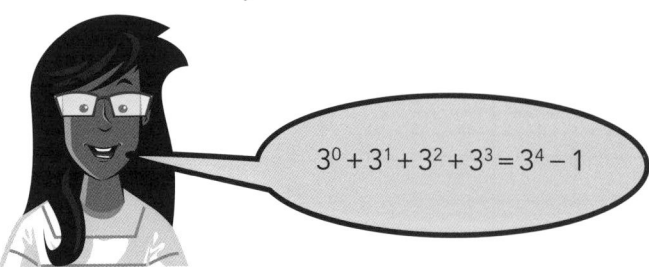

$$3^0 + 3^1 + 3^2 + 3^3 = 3^4 - 1$$

Is she correct? Give a reason for your answer.

Practice

4   Write as a single power

   a $\left(5^3\right)^2$ **b** $\left(15^3\right)^2$ **c** $\left(7^3\right)^3$ **d** $\left(3^4\right)^5$

5   **a**   Write 4 as a power of 2.   **b**   Write 4^3 as a power of 2.

   c   Write 9^3 as a power of 3.

6   $5^4 = 625$

   Write as a power of 5

   a 625^2 **b** 625^3 **c** 625^4

7   Find the missing power.

   a $4^2 \times 4^{\square} = 4^5$ **b** $7^4 \times 7^{\square} = 7^6$

   c $15^3 \times 15^{\square} = 15^6$ **d** $15^{\square} \times 15^4 = 15^4$

8   Work out and write the answer in **index** form.

   a $8^3 \div 8$ **b** $5^6 \div 5^2$ **c** $2^{10} \div 2^2$

   d $3^6 \div 3^3$ **e** $12^4 \div 12^4$

9   Find the missing power of 6.

   a $6^5 \div 6^{\square} = 6^2$ **b** $6^8 \div 6^{\square} = 6^4$

   c $6^{\square} \div 6^2 = 6^6$ **d** $6^{\square} \div 6^3 = 6^3$

Challenge

10   Work out and write the answer in index form.

   a $4^5 \div 2^3$ **b** $9^4 \div 3^5$ **c** $32^2 \div 2^6$ **d** $27^2 \div 3^6$

11   Write as a power of 5

   a   125   **b** 125^2 **c** 125^4

12   $12^4 = 20\,736$

   Write as a power of 12

   a $20\,736^2$ **b** $20\,736^3$ **c** $\sqrt{20\,736}$

13   Read what Marcus says:

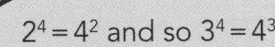

$2^4 = 4^2$ and so $3^4 = 4^3$

Is Marcus correct? Give a
reason to support your answer.

2 ▶ Expressions, formulae and equations

❭ 2.1 Constructing expressions

Exercise 2.1

Focus

Key words

equivalent
expression
unknown

You can write an algebraic **expression** by using a letter to represent an **unknown** number.

This bag contains x balls. Look at the different expressions that could be written about the bag.

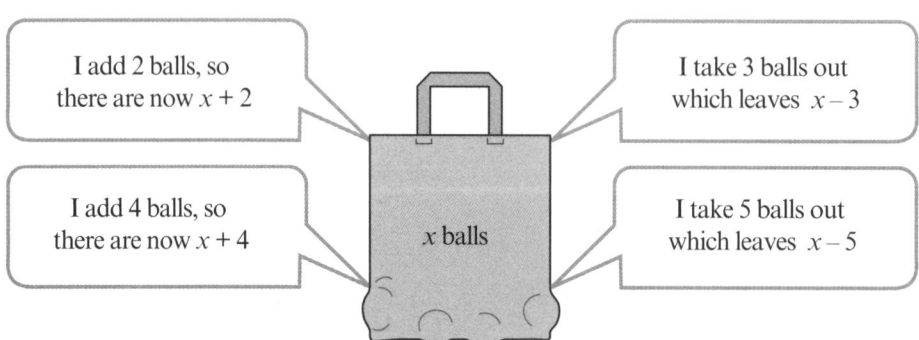

I add 2 balls, so there are now $x + 2$

I take 3 balls out which leaves $x - 3$

I add 4 balls, so there are now $x + 4$

x balls

I take 5 balls out which leaves $x - 5$

1 This bag contains y counters.
   Match each statement on the left with the correct expression on the right.
   The first one is done for you: **A and ii**

y counters

A	I add 1 counter to the bag, so there are now	i	$y - 8$
B	I take 1 counter out of the bag, which leaves	ii	$y + 1$
C	I add 5 counters to the bag, so there are now	iii	$y - 5$
D	I take 5 counters out of the bag, which leaves	iv	$y + 8$
E	I add 8 counters to the bag, so there are now	v	$y + 5$
F	I take 8 counters out of the bag, which leaves	vi	$y - 1$

2 This box contains some books.

I double the number of books in the box.

Copy and complete the working to show how many books are in the box now, when the box started with

When you double the number, you × by 2.

a 3 books: $3 \times 2 = \boxed{}$ **b** 5 books: $5 \times 2 = \boxed{}$

c 8 books: $8 \times \boxed{} = \boxed{}$ **d** x books: $x \times \boxed{} = 2x$

e y books: $y \times \boxed{} = \boxed{}$ **f** b books: $b \times \boxed{} = \boxed{}$

3 This tin contains some sweets.

I halve the number of sweets in the tin.

When you halve the number, you ÷ by 2.

Copy and complete the working to show how many sweets are in the tin now, when the tin started with

a 4 sweets: $4 \div 2 = \boxed{}$ **b** 10 sweets: $10 \div 2 = \boxed{}$

c 12 sweets: $12 \div \boxed{} = \boxed{}$ **d** x sweets: $x \div \boxed{} = \dfrac{x}{2}$

e y sweets: $y \div \boxed{} = \dfrac{\boxed{}}{2}$ **f** s sweets: $s \div \boxed{} = \dfrac{\boxed{}}{\boxed{}}$

4 Zalika has a box that contains c one-dollar coins.

Choose the correct expression from the cloud to show the total number of one-dollar coins in the box when

$\dfrac{c}{2}$

$c - 2$

$c + 2$

$2c$

a she takes 2 out

b she puts 2 more in

c she takes out half of the coins

d she doubles the number of coins in the box.

5 Match each description on the left with the correct expression on the right.

The first one is done for you: **A and v**

A	Multiply n by 3 and subtract 8	**i**	$3(n+8)$
B	Add 8 and n then multiply by 3	**ii**	$8(n+3)$
C	Multiply n by 3 and add 8	**iii**	$3(n-8)$
D	Add 3 and n then multiply by 8	**iv**	$8(n-3)$
E	Subtract 3 from n then multiply by 8	**v**	$3n-8$
F	Subtract 8 from n then multiply by 3	**vi**	$3n+8$

Practice

6 Shen thinks of a number, n.

Write an expression for the number Shen gets when he

   a   multiplies the number by 7 then adds 4

   b   divides the number by 6 then subtracts 8

   c   adds 4 to the number then divides by 5

   d   subtracts 4 from the number then divides by 5.

 7   a   Sort these cards into groups of **equivalent** expressions.

A $\dfrac{7 \times x}{8}$	B $\dfrac{x-7}{8}$	C $x + \dfrac{7}{8}$	D $\dfrac{7+x}{8}$	E $\dfrac{x}{8} \times 7$
F $\dfrac{7}{8} \times x$	G $\dfrac{7x}{8}$	H $\dfrac{7}{8} + x$	I $\dfrac{x+7}{8}$	J $\dfrac{7}{8}x$

   b   Which card is on its own?

 8   This is part of Kim's homework.

> Question
>
> Write an expression for
>
> a   one-fifth of x add 7   b   six subtract two-thirds of y
>
> Answers
>
> a $\dfrac{x+7}{5}$ b $6 - \dfrac{2y}{3}$

Are Kim's answers correct? If not, write the correct answers.

9   a   Write an expression for

   i   one-quarter of x add 5

   ii   three-fifths of x subtract two

   iii one add one-half of x

   iv   eleven subtract five-sixths of x.

   b   Describe in words each of these expressions.

   i $\dfrac{x}{2} - 9$ ii $\dfrac{2x}{3} + 10$ iii $25 - \dfrac{2x}{9}$ iv $12 + \dfrac{7x}{10}$

Challenge

10 Write an expression for the perimeter and an expression for the area of each rectangle.

Simplify each expression.

a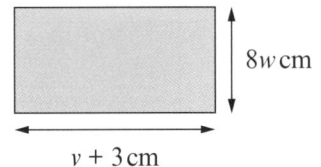

8*w* cm

v + 3 cm

b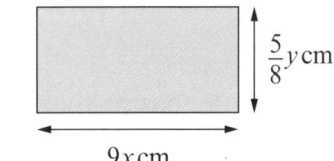

$\frac{5}{8}y$ cm

9*x* cm

11 The longest side of a triangle is *a* cm.

The second side is *b* cm shorter than the first side.

The third side is half as long as the second side.

Write an expression, in its simplest form, for the perimeter of the triangle.

> **Tip**
>
> Start by writing expressions for the second and third sides.

12 The price of one kilogram of lemons is $*l*.

The price of one kilogram of potatoes is $*p*.

The price of one kilogram of rice is $*r*.

Write an expression for the total cost of

a 1 kilogram of potatoes, 3 kilograms of lemons and 2 kilograms of rice

b 3 kilograms of potatoes and one-quarter of a kilogram of rice

c 200 grams of rice

d 600 grams of rice and 750 grams of lemons.

> **Tip**
>
> What fraction of 1 kg is 200 g?

13 Sion thinks of a number, *y*.

Choose the correct expression from the cloud for when Sion

a adds 3 to one-quarter of *y*, then multiplies by 8

b adds 8 to one-third of *y*, then multiplies by 4

c adds 4 to three-quarters of *y*, then multiplies by 8

d adds 3 to three-eighths of *y*, then multiplies by 4.

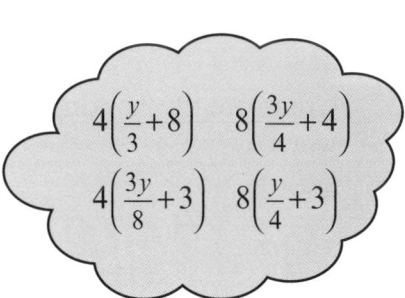

$4\left(\frac{y}{3}+8\right)$ $8\left(\frac{3y}{4}+4\right)$

$4\left(\frac{3y}{8}+3\right)$ $8\left(\frac{y}{4}+3\right)$

› 2.2 Using expressions and formulae

Exercise 2.2

Focus

A **formula** is a mathematical rule that connects two or more quantities. It can be written in letters or words. The plural of formula is **formulae**.

Before you start using formulae, you need to be able to **substitute** numbers into expressions.

1   Match each expression with its correct value when $x = 6$.

The first one is done for you: **A** and **iii**

A	$x + 3$	i	13	
B	$x - 5$	ii	4	
C	$7 + x$	iii	9	
D	$10 - x$	iv	12	
E	$2x$	v	3	
F	$\dfrac{x}{2}$	vi	1	

Tip

A is $x + 3 = 6 + 3 = 9$. This matches with **iii**.

Tip

$x + y = 4 + 3 = ?$

2   Work out the value of each expression when $x = 4$ and $y = 3$.

  a $x + y$ b $x - y$ c y^2

Tip

$y^2 = y \times y$

3   Complete the working to find the value of each expression when $x = 6$

  a $2x + 1$ (Work out the multiplication
      $2 \times x + 1 = 2 \times 6 + 1$ before the addition)
      $\qquad = 12 + 1$
      $\qquad = \boxed{}$

  b $3x - 1$ (Work out the multiplication
      $3 \times x - 1 = 3 \times 6 - 1$ before the subtraction)
      $\qquad = \boxed{} - 1$
      $\qquad = \boxed{}$

  c $2x^2$ (Work out the indices before
      $2 \times x^2 = 2 \times 6^2$ the multiplication)
      $\qquad = 2 \times 36$
      $\qquad = \boxed{}$

Tip

When you substitute numbers into an expression or formula, you must use the correct order of operations: brackets, indices, division, multiplication, addition, subtraction.

d $10 - \frac{x}{3}$ (Work out the division before the subtraction)

$10 - \frac{x}{3} = 10 - \frac{6}{3}$

$= 10 - \square$

$= \square$

e $2(x+4)$ (Work out the bracket before the multiplication)

$2 \times (x+4) = 2 \times (6+4)$

$= 2 \times \square$

$= \square$

4 Work out the value of the expression

a $a+3$ when $a=7$ **b** $b+6$ when $b=-4$

c $3c$ when $c=-3$ **d** $\frac{d}{5}$ when $d=-35$

e $a+b$ when $a=3$ and $b=-5$ **f** $c-d$ when $c=14$ and $d=7$

g $5e+2f$ when $e=3$ and $f=5$ **h** $2(g+h)$ when $g=9$ and $h=-20$

i $3x-7$ when $x=-5$ **j** $10(9-x)$ when $x=6$

k $\frac{x}{4}-10$ when $x=20$ **l** $\frac{x}{2}+\frac{y}{10}$ when $x=30$ and $y=-30$.

5 Use the formula $H=kv$ to work out the value of H when

a $k=9$ and $v=3$ **b** $k=8$ and $v=-2$.

Practice

6 Work out the value of the expression

a a^2-6 when $a=4$ **b** $30-b^2$ when $b=6$

c a^2+b^2 when $a=3$ and $b=4$ **d** c^2-d^2 when $c=5$ and $d=6$

e $3p^2$ when $p=4$ **f** $5q^2+1$ when $q=10$

g t^3 when $t=2$ **h** $10v^3$ when $v=4$

i z^3-2 when $z=2$ **j** $\frac{s^3}{10}$ when $s=10$

k $2(m^2+3)$ when $m=-4$ **l** $5(n^3+10)$ when $n=-2$.

> **Tip**
>
> $10v^3 = 10 \times v \times v \times v$

7 a Write a formula for the number of seconds in any number of minutes, using

     i words   **ii** letters.

b Use your formula from part **a** to work out the number of seconds in 30 minutes.

8 Use the formula $d=16t+38$ to work out d when $t=2$.

9 Harsha uses the formula $V = \frac{Ah}{3}$ to work out V when $A = 6$ and $h = 12$.
This is what she writes.

$$V = \frac{6 + 12}{3}$$
$$= \frac{18}{3}$$
$$= 6$$

a Explain the mistake she has made.

b Work out the correct answer.

10 Use the formula $A = \frac{(a+b)}{2} \times h$ to work out A when $a = 5$, $b = 7$ and $h = 4$.

 11 Pedro uses this formula to work out the volume of a
triangular-based pyramid:

$V = \frac{bhl}{6}$ where: V is the volume

b is the base

h is the height

l is the length.

> **Tip**
>
> Remember that bhl means $b \times h \times l$.

Pedro compares two pyramids.

Pyramid A has a base width of 4 cm, base length of 3 cm and height of 16 cm.

Pyramid B has a base width of 6 cm, base length of 4 cm and height of 8 cm.

Which pyramid has the larger volume? Show your working.

12 Make x the subject of each formula.

Write if **A**, **B** or **C** is the correct answer.

a $y = x - 8$
| **A** $x = y - 8$ | **B** $x = y + 8$ | **C** $x = 8y$ |

b $y = kx$
| **A** $x = ky$ | **B** $x = \frac{y}{k}$ | **C** $x = \frac{k}{y}$ |

c $y = x + w$
| **A** $x = y - w$ | **B** $x = y + w$ | **C** $x = w - y$ |

d $y = \frac{x}{r}$
| **A** $x = \frac{y}{r}$ | **B** $x = \frac{r}{y}$ | **C** $x = ry$ |

e $y = 2x + t$
| **A** $x = \frac{y+t}{2}$ | **B** $x = 2y + t$ | **C** $x = \frac{y-t}{2}$ |

Challenge

13 When $x = -4$, all of these expressions except one have the same value.

Which is the odd one out?

| $x^2 - 7$ | $(x+1)^2$ | $-\dfrac{36}{x}$ | $x-5$ | $2x+17$ | $5-x$ |

14 Write any values of x that make each pair of expressions equal.

    a $3x + 1$ and $3x^2 + 1$ **b** $4 - x$ and $x - 4$

    c $\dfrac{5x}{2} + 5$ and $\dfrac{2x}{5} + 5$ **d** $3(x + 2)$ and $2(x + 3)$

15 **a** Use the formula $D = wp + 4$ to work out the value of D when $w = 2.5$ and $p = 6$.

    b Rearrange the formula $D = wp + 4$ to make p the subject.

    c Use your formula to work out the value of p when $D = 100$ and $w = 12$.

16 The formula below is used to calculate the distance travelled by an object.

$s = ut + \dfrac{1}{2}at^2$ where: s = distance

                            u = starting speed

                            a = acceleration

                            t = time

> **Tip**
>
> $\dfrac{1}{2}at^2$ means
>
> $\dfrac{1}{2} \times a \times t^2$

Work out the distance travelled by an object when

    a $u = 0$, $a = 6$ and $t = 5$ **b** $u = 30$, $a = -4$ and $t = 10$

> 2.3 Expanding brackets

Exercise 2.3

Focus

You can use a box method to multiply numbers, like this:

$3 \times 14 = 3 \times (10 + 4)$

×	10	4
3	30	12

$3 \times 14 = 30 + 12 = 42$

1 Copy and complete the boxes to work out the answers.

a 4×18

×	10	8
4		

$4 \times 18 = \square + \square = \square$

b 3×21

×	20	1
3		

$3 \times 21 = \square + \square = \square$

2 Copy and complete the boxes to show two different ways to multiply 6 by 58.

a $6 \times 58 = 6 \times (50 + 8)$

×	50	8
6		

$6 \times 58 = \square + \square = \square$

b $6 \times 58 = 6 \times (60 - 2)$

×	60	−2
6		

$6 \times 58 = \square + \square = \square$

3 Copy and complete the boxes to simplify these expressions. Some have been started for you.

a $3(x + 5)$

×	x	5
3	$3x$	

$3(x + 5) = 3x + \square$

b $2(x + 9)$

×	x	9
2		

$2(x + 9) = \square + \square$

c $5(y - 1)$

×	y	−1
5		−5

$5(y - 1) = \square - 5$

d $4(y - 8)$

×	y	−8
4		

$4(y - 8) = \square - \square$

Key words

brackets
expand

Tip

$3 \times (10 + 4)$ can be written as $3(10 + 4)$.

You use the table to **expand** the **bracket** $3(10 + 4)$ to get $3 \times 10 + 3 \times 4$.

Tip

Your answers to **a** and **b** should be the same.

4   Copy and complete the boxes to simplify these expressions. Some
    have been started for you.

a $3(2x+1)$

×	2x	1
3	6x	

$3(2x+1)=6x+\square$

b $5(4x+9)$

×	4x	9
5		

$5(4x+9)=\square+\square$

c $2(3y-7)$

×	3y	−7
2		−14

$2(3y-7)=\square-14$

d $5(8y-5)$

×	8y	−5
5		

$5(8y-5)=\square-\square$

5   Expand the brackets.

a $6(a+6)$ b $5(b+7)$ c $7(c-8)$

d $6(d-9)$ e $5(8+e)$ f $7(7+f)$

g $6(6-g)$ h $5(7-h)$

Practice

6   Expand the brackets.

a $7(8i+9)$ b $6(8+7j)$ c $5(6k-7)$

d $7(8-9l)$ e $6(9a+8m)$ f $5(7b+6n)$

g $7(7c-8x)$ h $6(9px+8y)$

7   Read what Marcus says.

If I expand $4(a-7)$ and $4(7-a)$ I will get the same answer, as both expressions have exactly the same terms in them.

Is Marcus correct?

Explain your answer.

8   Expand and simplify each expression.

a $6(a+7)+8(a+9)$ b $8(b+7)+6(5b+6)$

c $7(c+8)+9(8+7c)$ d $7(8d+9)-8(d+7)$

e $6(5+6e)-7(8e+9)$ f $9(8f+7g)-6(5g-6f)$

> **Tip**
>
> Part **d** =
> $56d+63-8d-56$
> = ...

9 Expand each expression. Three of them have been started for you.

a $a(a+1) = a \times a + a \times 1 = a^2 + \boxed{}$

b $b(b-5)$ **c** $c(3c+6)$ **d** $e(4e+9)$

e $i(3i+7x) = i \times 3i + i \times 7x = 3i^2 + \boxed{}$

f $j(3a-7j)$ **g** $k(3k-6x)$ **h** $3m(m+3x)$

i $3r(3r-x-3) = 3r \times 3r - 3r \times x - 3r \times 3 = 9r^2 - \boxed{} - \boxed{}$

j $2a(3+2a+b)$ **k** $3x(-z-y-x)$

 10 Here are some expression cards.

Sort the cards into groups of equivalent expressions.

A $8y(5+6y)$	**B** $4y(5y+6y^2)$
C $2y(24y+20)$	**D** $2y^2(10+12y)$
E $4(10y+12y^2)$	**F** $4y^2(6y+5)$
G $y^2(20+24y)$	**H** $y(40+48y)$

Challenge

11 Write down and then simplify an expression for the area of each rectangle.

a $(2x+1)\,\text{cm}$

 $4\,\text{cm}$

b $(3y-2)\,\text{cm}$

 $2y\,\text{cm}$

12 Expand and simplify each expression.

a $a(a+3)+a(a+4)$ **b** $b(b+3)+b(4b+5)$

c $c(3c+4)+c(5c+6)$ **d** $d(3d+4)-d(d+5)$

e $e(3+4e)-e(5e-6)$ **f** $f(3f+4g)-5f(6f-7g)$

13 This is part of Sofia's homework.
She has made a mistake in every question.

> *Question*
> Expand and simplify each expression.
> 1. $3(a + 5) - 3(3a + 5)$
> 2. $p(4q + r) + q(2r - 4p)$
> 3. $5b(b + 3a) + a(4a + 6b)$
>
> *Answer*
> 1. $3(a + 5) - 3(3a + 5) = 3a + 15 - 9a - 15 = 6a + 30$
> 2. $p(4q + r) + q(2r - 4p) = 4pq + pr + 2qr - 4pq$
> $$= 3pr + pq = 4p^2qr$$
> 3. $5b(b + 3a) + a(4a + 6b) = 5b^2 + 15ab + 4a^2 + 6ab$
> $$= 4a^2 + 5b^2 + 11ab$$

a Explain what she has done wrong.

b Work out the correct answers.

14 Write down and then simplify an expression for
the area of this compound shape.

$(2x - 1)$ cm

$5x$ cm

$3x$ cm

$(3x + 4)$ cm

15 Fill in the missing numbers and letters in these expressions.
Use all the numbers and letters from the cloud.

a $4(3x + \boxed{}) = \boxed{}x + 28$

b $3x(2x - \boxed{}) = 6\boxed{} - 3x$

c $6(\boxed{} - 3) = 30x - \boxed{}$

d $\boxed{}x(9 - \boxed{}) = 45x - 5x^2$

e $2(\boxed{}x + 4) + 3(4x - \boxed{}) = 16x - 16$

f $x(4x + 1) - \boxed{}(x - 5) = 2x^2 + \boxed{}x$

1	2	5
7	8	11
12	18	x
$2x$	$5x$	x^2

> 2.4 Factorising

Exercise 2.4

Focus

Key words

factorisations

factorise

term

When you **factorise** an expression, you do the opposite to expanding a bracket.

Expanding: $3(x + 8) = 3x + 24$ Factorising: $3x + 24 = 3(x + 8)$

1 Expand these brackets. Use the boxes to help if you want to.
The first one is done for you.

a $2(x + 6)$

×	x	6
2	$2x$	12

$2(x + 6) = 2x + 12$

b $3(x + 5)$

×	x	5
3		

$3(x + 5) = \boxed{} + \boxed{}$

c $5(y - 3)$

×	y	−3
5		

$5(y - 3) = \boxed{} - \boxed{}$

d $4(y - 7)$

×	y	−7
4		

$4(y - 7) = \boxed{} - \boxed{}$

2 Factorise these expressions. Use your answers to Question 1.
The first one is done for you.

a $2x + 12 = 2(x + 6)$

b $3x + 15 = \boxed{}$

c $5y - 15 = \boxed{}$

d $4y - 28 = \boxed{}$

3 Copy and complete these **factorisations**.

All the numbers you will need are in the cloud.

a $2x + 8 = 2(x + \boxed{})$
b $3x + 9 = 3(x + \boxed{})$

c $5y - 25 = 5(y - \boxed{})$
d $7y - 14 = 7(\boxed{} - \boxed{})$

$\begin{matrix} 2 & & 3 \\ & 4 & & 5 \end{matrix}$

4 Expand these brackets.

a $3(2x + 1) = 6x + \boxed{}$
b $4(3x + 1) = \boxed{} + \boxed{}$

c $2(5y - 1) = \boxed{} - \boxed{}$
d $6(4y - 1) = \boxed{} - \boxed{}$

5 Use your answers to Question **4** to factorise these expressions.

a $6x + 3 = \boxed{}$
b $12x + 4 = \boxed{}$

c $10y - 2 = \boxed{}$
d $24y - 6 = \boxed{}$

Practice

6 Copy and complete these factorisations.

All the numbers you will need are in the cloud.

a $4x + 6 = 2(2x + \boxed{})$
b $6x - 15 = 3(2x - \boxed{})$

c $35y + 10 = 5(\boxed{}y + \boxed{})$
d $28y - 63 = 7(\boxed{}y - \boxed{})$

$\begin{matrix} 2 & & 3 & & 4 \\ & 5 & & 7 & & 9 \end{matrix}$

7 Factorise each expression.

Make sure you use the highest common factor.

a $5z + 15$
b $2y - 14$
c $20x + 4$
d $9w - 3$

e $6v + 8$
f $14a - 21$
g $12 - 6b$
h $14 + 21d$

8 Each expression on a grey card has been factorised to give an expression on a white card.

Match each grey card with the correct white card.

A	$3x^2 + 15x$	i	$5x(3x + 1)$
B	$4x^2 + 12x$	ii	$2x(2x + 5)$
C	$4x^2 + 10x$	iii	$3x(x + 5)$
D	$15x^2 + 5x$	iv	$4x(x + 3)$

9 Factorise each expression.

a $7m^2 + m$
b $5a^2 - 15a$
c $t^2 + 9t$

d $8h - 4h^2$
e $3y + 12y^2$
f $12y - 16y^2$

g $16e^2 + 8e$
h $15e + 6i$

10 Copy and complete these factorisations.

a $14cd - 7c = 7c(2d - \boxed{})$
b $12a + 8ab = 4a(\boxed{} + 2b)$

c $21g + 15gh = 3g(\boxed{} + \boxed{})$
d $30w - 15tw = 15w(\boxed{} - \boxed{})$

11 Copy and complete each factorisation.

  a $2a + 4h + 8 = 2(a + 2h + \boxed{})$ **b** $5b - 25 + 5j = 5(b - \boxed{} + j)$

  c $12tu + 16u - 20 = 4(3tu + \boxed{} - 5)$ **d** $3e^2 + 4e + ef = e(3e + \boxed{} + \boxed{})$

  e $7k - k^2 - ak = k(\boxed{} - \boxed{} - \boxed{})$

  f $6n^2 - 9n + 3mn = 3n(\boxed{} - \boxed{} + \boxed{})$

Challenge

 12 a Copy and complete this spider diagram.

The four expressions around the edge are all equivalent to the expression in the middle.

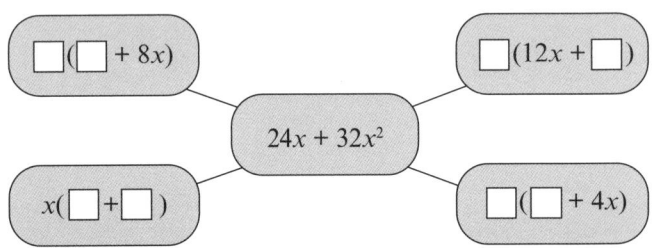

  b Which expression around the edge is the correct fully factorised expression?

13 a Expand and simplify $4(2x + 3) + 5(x - 4) + 3(5 - 2x)$

  b Factorise your answer to part **a**.

14 Read what Zara says.

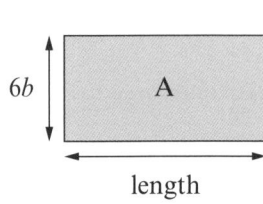

When I expand $5(3x - 2) - 5(2 + x)$, then collect like **terms** and finally factorise the result, I get the expression $20(x - 1)$.

Show that Zara is wrong.

Explain the mistake she has made.

15 Awen expands an expression, collects like terms and factorises the result.

Work out the missing terms.

$2a(\boxed{} + 4) - 4(a^2 + \boxed{}) + 6a(a - 8) = 8(a^2 - \boxed{} - 2)$

16 The diagram shows a rectangle.

The area of the rectangle is $12b^2 - 30b$

Write an expression for

  a the length of the rectangle

  b the perimeter of the rectangle.

$6b$ A   length

› 2.5 Constructing and solving equations

Exercise 2.5

Key words
solve
variable

Focus

1 Write if each of the following is a formula, an expression or an equation.

   a $ab + 7c$

   b $m = 2b - 3g^2$

   c $8(x - 8)$

   d $2x + 5 = 13$

Remember that:	Examples
A **formula** is a rule that shows the relationship between two or more quantities (**variables**). It must have an equals sign.	$F = ma$ $v = u + 10t$
An **expression** is a statement that involves one or more variables, but does not have an equals sign.	$3x - 7$ $a^2 + 2b$
An **equation** contains an unknown number, it must have an equals sign, and it can be solved to find the value of the unknown number.	$3x - 7 = 14$ $4 = 6y + 22$

> **Worked example 2.1**

You can use a flow chart like this to **solve** an equation.

Solve $3x + 5 = 17$

Answer

$3x + 5 = 17$

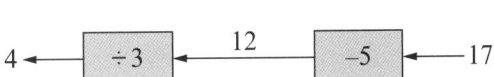

Reverse the flow chart to work out the value of x.

So $x = 4$

2 Complete these flow charts to work out the value of x.

a $2x + 1 = 11$

$x = \boxed{}$

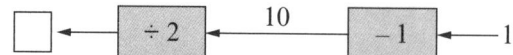

b $5x - 2 = 18$

$x = \boxed{}$

c $3(x + 4) = 21$

$x = \boxed{}$

d $\dfrac{x}{4} - 1 = 5$

$x = \boxed{}$

3 The diagram shows a rectangle.

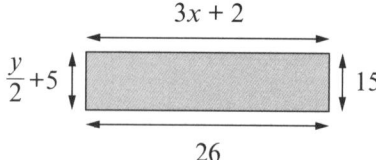

Complete the workings to find the values of x and y.

$3x + 2 = 26$

$x = \boxed{}$

$\dfrac{y}{2} + 5 = 15$

$y = \boxed{}$

Tips

The lengths of the rectangle are the same, so $3x + 2 = 26$.

The widths of the rectangle are the same, so $\dfrac{y}{2} + 5 = 15$.

4   The diagram shows a rectangle.

Complete the workings to find the values of x and y.

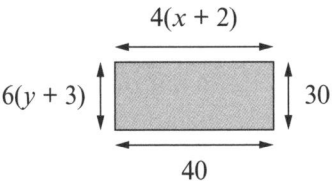

$4(x+2)=40$

$x=\square$ $\square \longleftarrow \boxed{-2} \longleftarrow \boxed{} \longleftarrow \boxed{\div 4} \longleftarrow 40$

$6(y+3)=30$ $y \longrightarrow \boxed{+3} \longrightarrow \boxed{\times 6} \longrightarrow 30$

$y=\square$ $\square \longleftarrow \boxed{} \longleftarrow \boxed{} \longleftarrow \boxed{} \longleftarrow 30$

Tips

The lengths of the rectangle are the same, so $4(x+2)=40$.

The widths of the rectangle are the same, so $6(y+3)=30$.

Sometimes, you may have to solve an equation that has the same letter on both sides of the $=$ sign.

Worked example 2.2

Solve $5x+8=3x+20$

Answer

Subtract $3x$ from both sides: $5x-3x+8=3x-3x+20$

$2x+8=20$

Subtracting $3x$ from both sides leaves no x on the right.

Then use a flow chart to solve $2x+8=20$

$x=6$ $6 \longleftarrow \boxed{\div 2} \overset{12}{\longleftarrow} \boxed{-8} \longleftarrow 20$

5   Complete the workings to simplify these equations. Then solve the equations by drawing a flow chart.

a $4x+5=x+17$ Subtract x from both sides: $4x-x+5=x-x+17$

$3x+\square=\square$

b $7x+2=2x+27$ Subtract $2x$ from both sides: $7x-2x+2=2x-2x+27$

$\square x+\square=\square$

c $10x-4=8x+12$ Subtract $8x$ from both sides: $10x-8x-4=8x-8x+12$

$\square x-\square=\square$

Practice

6 For each of these students

   i   Write an equation to represent what they say.

   ii Solve your equation to find the value of x.

The first one is started for you.

a

> My sister is 20 years old.
> My Dad is x years old.
> Half of my Dad's age plus 1 is the same as my sister's age.
> How old is my Dad?

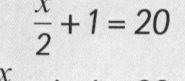

$$\frac{x}{2} + 1 = 20$$
$$\frac{x}{2} + 1 - 1 = 20 - 1$$
$$\frac{x}{2} = \square$$
$$x = \square \times 2$$
$$x = \square$$

b

> My brother is 9 years old.
> My Mum is x years old.
> One third of my Mum's age minus 2 is the same as my brother's age.
> How old is my Mum?

c

> My friend is 16 years old.
> My Gran is x years old.
> One quarter of my Gran's age minus 8 is the same as my friend's age.
> How old is my Gran?

7 Work out the value of the algebraic unknown in each isosceles triangle.
   All measurements are in centimetres. Show how you can check your answers are correct.

a

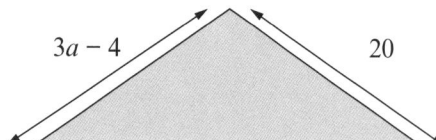

$3a - 4$ 20

b

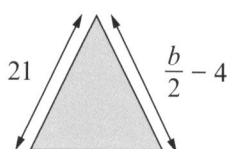

21 $\frac{b}{2} - 4$

c

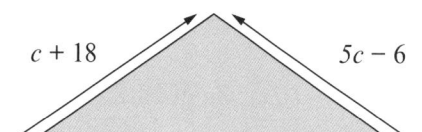

$c + 18$ $5c - 6$

d

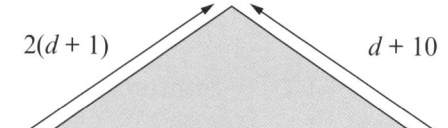

$2(d + 1)$ $d + 10$

8 Work out the value of x in each isosceles trapezium.

All measurements are in centimetres. Show how you can check
your answers are correct.

a $7(x-2)$ 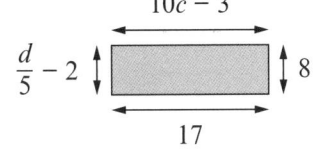 $3x+6$

b $3x+6$ 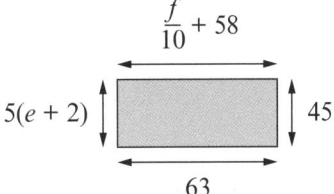 $6(x-1)$

c $2(x+6)$ 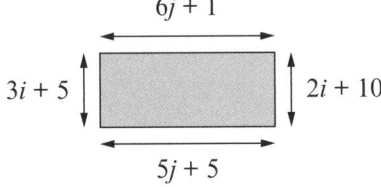 $9(x-1)$

9 Work out the value of the letters in each diagram.

All measurements are in centimetres.

a

$10c-3$

$\dfrac{d}{5}-2$ 8

17

b

$\dfrac{f}{10}+58$

$5(e+2)$ 45

63

c

$6j+1$

$3i+5$ $2i+10$

$5j+5$

10 For each part of this question

   i   Write an equation to represent the problem.

   ii   Solve the equation.

a Arti thinks of a number. He divides it by 2 then subtracts 9.
The answer is 5.

What number did Arti think of?

b Han thinks of a number. She multiplies it by 4 then subtracts 1.
The answer is the same as 3 times the number plus 6.

What number did Han think of?

c Danni thinks of a number. She subtracts 2 then multiplies the
result by 8. The answer is the same as subtracting 5 from the
number then multiplying by 16.

What number did Danni think of?

Challenge

11 The total area of this rectangle is 52 cm².

   a   Write an equation to represent the problem.

   b   Solve the equation to work out the value of y.

   c   Show how you can check your answer is correct.

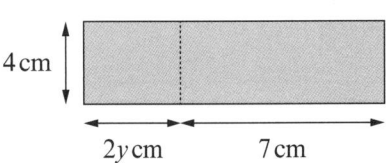

4 cm

$2y$ cm   7 cm

12 A square has a side length of 7 cm.

A rectangle has a length of $\frac{y}{8} - 3$ cm and a width of 4 cm.

The square has the same perimeter as the rectangle.

Work out the value of y. Show all your working.

13 a Complete the workings to solve this equation.

$$\frac{x+4}{6} = 3$$
$$x + 4 = 3 \times 6$$
$$x + 4 = 18$$
$$x = \boxed{}$$

b Solve these equations.

i $\quad \frac{x+2}{7} = -4$
        ii $\quad \frac{3x-1}{2} = 7$

14 Solve these equations.

a $\quad \frac{4}{5}y = 32$
        b $\quad \frac{5}{7}z - 3 = 7$

c $\quad 2(5n - 4) = 12$
        d $\quad 4\left(\frac{2}{3}m - 3\right) = 20$

15 Here is a secret code box.

8	11	8	3	7	4	5	2	9

Solve each equation below.

Use your answers to fill in the letters in the code box to find the name of a Winter Olympic sport.

L	$4(x - 5) = 8$
H	$2(x + 3) = 3x - 3$
O	$\frac{x-5}{6} = 1$
I	$5x + 3 - 2x - 1 = 17$

G	$2(2x + 3) + 5x = 24$
E	$12 + 3(x + 4) = 36$
S	$30 = 6(2x - 1)$
B	$2(x - 5) = 3(2x - 14)$

> 2.6 Inequalities

Exercise 2.6

Focus

Key word
inequality

Remember: < means 'is less than'   ⩽ means 'is less than or equal to'
> means 'is greater than'   ⩾ means 'is greater than or equal to'

1   Write True (**T**) or False (**F**) for each statement. Part **a** is done for you.

   a $4 < x < 9$ means 'x is greater than 4 and less than 9'   **T**

   b $4 \leqslant x < 9$ means 'x is greater than 4 and less than or equal to 9'

   c $4 < x \leqslant 9$ means 'x is greater than 4 and less than or equal to 9'

   d $4 \leqslant x \leqslant 9$ means 'x is greater than or equal to 4 and less than 9'

2   Match each **inequality** with the correct meaning.

   The first one is done for you: **A** and **iii**

A	$0 \leqslant x \leqslant 5$	i	x is greater than or equal to 0 and less than 5
B	$0 \leqslant x < 5$	ii	x is greater than 0 and less than or equal to 5
C	$0 < x < 5$	iii	x is greater than or equal to 0 and less than or equal to 5
D	$0 < x \leqslant 5$	iv	x is greater than 0 and less than 5

3   Write each statement as an inequality. Part **a** is done for you.

   a x is greater than or equal to 8 and less than 12 $8 \leqslant x < 12$

   b y is greater than 1 and less than 7

   c m is greater than or equal to 0 and less than or equal to 5

   d n is greater than 0 and less than or equal to 5

4   Write in words what each inequality means. Part **a** is done for you.

   a $7 < x \leqslant 15$ x is greater than 7 and less than or equal to 15

   b $10 < y < 20$

   c $0 \leqslant x \leqslant 5$

   d $50 \leqslant y < 100$

5 Match each inequality with the correct number line.

Remember that:

- an open circle (O) is for the < inequality
- a closed circle (●) is for the ≤ inequality.

The first one is done for you: **A** and **iii**

A	$2 \leqslant x < 7$	i	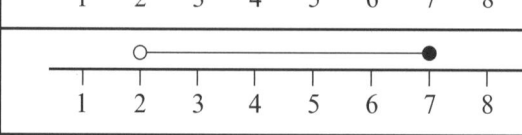
B	$2 < x < 7$	ii	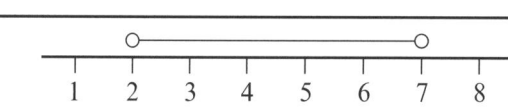
C	$2 < x \leqslant 7$	iii	
D	$2 \leqslant x \leqslant 7$	iv	

Practice

6 Copy each number line. Show each inequality on its number line.

a $5 < x < 9$

| 4 | 5 | 6 | 7 | 8 | 9 | 10 |

b $12 < x \leqslant 15$

| 11 | 12 | 13 | 14 | 15 | 16 | 17 |

c $-6 < x \leqslant -2$

| −7 | −6 | −5 | −4 | −3 | −2 | −1 |

d $-1 \leqslant x \leqslant 4$

| −2 | −1 | 0 | 1 | 2 | 3 | 4 | 5 |

7 Write the inequality shown by each number line. Use the letter x.

a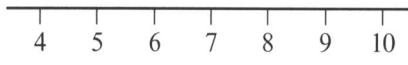

b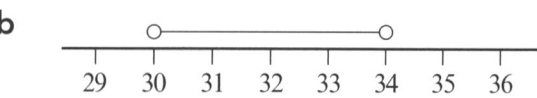

c

d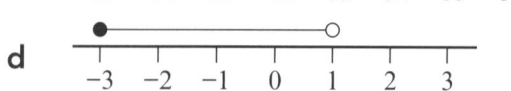

8   Copy and complete these equivalent inequalities.

   a $x > 4$ is equivalent to $2x > \boxed{}$

   b $x < 9$ is equivalent to $\boxed{}x < 63$

   c $y \geqslant 1$ is equivalent to $y + 9 \geqslant \boxed{}$

   d $y \leqslant 1$ is equivalent to $y - 5 \leqslant \boxed{}$

9   This is part of Lori's homework.

> Question
>
> Use the inequality $-3 < x < 3$ to write
>
> i   the smallest integer x could be
>
> ii   the largest integer x could be
>
> iii   a list of the integer values x could be.
>
> Answer
>
> i   smallest integer is -3
>
> ii   largest integer is 3
>
> iii x could be $-3, -2, -1, 0, 1, 2, 3$

Explain the mistakes Lori has made and write the correct solutions.
Make sure you correct all of Lori's mistakes.

10   For each inequality, write

   i   the smallest integer y could be

   ii   the largest integer y could be

   iii   a list of the integer values y could be.

   a $32 < y < 38$

   b $24 < y \leqslant 27$

   c $40 \leqslant y < 44$

   d $-12 \leqslant y \leqslant -9$

11   Write true (**T**) or false (**F**) for each statement.
    The first one is done for you.

   a $8 > y > 2$ means the same as $2 < y < 8$ **T**

   b $10 > y \geqslant 0$ means the same as $0 \leqslant y < 10$

   c $1 \geqslant y \geqslant -4$ means the same as $1 \leqslant y \leqslant -4$

   d $3 \geqslant y > -3$ means the same as $-3 \leqslant y < 3$

Challenge

12 This is part of Raj's homework.

> Question
> a Show the inequality $5\frac{1}{5} < n \le 8\frac{3}{4}$ on a number line.
> b Write
>   i   the smallest integer n could be
>   ii the greatest integer n could be
>   iii a list of the integer values n could be.
>
> Answer
> a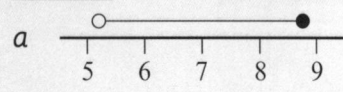
>   5 6 7 8 9
>
> b i   smallest integer is 5
>   ii largest integer is 9
>   iii n could be 5, 6, 7, 8, 9

    a   Raj has made three mistakes. What are the mistakes he has made?

    b   For each inequality, write

        i   the smallest integer n could be   **ii**   the greatest integer n could be

        iii   a list of the integer values n could be.

        A $6\frac{1}{3} \le n < 10\frac{4}{5}$ **B** $-7\frac{3}{8} < n \le -3\frac{7}{9}$

13 Match each inequality with:

    a   the correct smallest integer   **b**   the correct largest integer

    c   the correct list of integers.

Inequality	Smallest integer	Largest integer	List of integers
A $1.9 \le x \le 5.5$	**i** 0	**P** 5	**W** 1, 2, 3, 4, 5, 6
B $0.2 < x < 6.1$	**ii** 2	**Q** 7	**X** 0, 1, 2, 3, 4
C $-0.5 < x \le 4.9$	**iii** 3	**R** 6	**Y** 2, 3, 4, 5
D $2.95 \le x < 7.85$	**iv** 1	**S** 4	**Z** 3, 4, 5, 6, 7

14 Copy each number line. Show each inequality on its number line.

   a $0.75 < x \leqslant 3.25$

                   0   1   2   3   4

   b $10.6 \leqslant x < 13.4$

                   10   11   12   13   14

15 Write the inequality shown by each number line. Use the letter y.

   a

           22   23   24   25   26

   b

           0   1   2   3   4

16 Arun and Marcus are discussing inequalities.
Read what they say.

The inequalities $y \leqslant 14$ and $y > 2$ can be written together as $2 < y \leqslant 14$.

The inequalities $y \leqslant 14$ and $y > 2$ can be written together as $14 \geqslant y > 2$.

Write each pair of inequalities as one inequality using

    i   Arun's method   **ii**   Marcus's method.

   a $y < 18$ and $y > 12$ **b** $y \leqslant 4$ and $y \geqslant 0$

   c $x > 7$ and $x \leqslant 25$ **d** $x \geqslant 10$ and $x < 38$

3 ▶ Place value and rounding

❯ 3.1 Multiplying and dividing by 0.1 and 0.01

Exercise 3.1

Focus

Key words

decimal places
inverse operation

Look at the rule in this cloud.

×0.1 is the same as ÷10 → e.g. $60 \times 0.1 = 60 \div 10 = 6$

1 Copy and complete the workings.

a $20 \times 0.1 = 20 \div 10 = \square$
b $70 \times 0.1 = 70 \div \square = \square$
c $80 \times 0.1 = 80 \div \square = \square$
d $75 \times 0.1 = 75 \div \square = \square$

×0.01 is the same as ÷100 → e.g. $600 \times 0.01 = 600 \div 100 = 6$

2 Copy and complete the workings.

a $300 \times 0.01 = 300 \div 100 = \square$
b $500 \times 0.01 = 500 \div \square = \square$
c $800 \times 0.01 = 800 \div \square = \square$
d $650 \times 0.01 = 650 \div \square = \square$

3 Work out these.
All the answers are in the rectangle.

| 0.12 | 1.2 | 12 | 120 |

a 120×0.1 b 12×0.1
c $12\,000 \times 0.01$ d 12×0.01

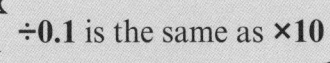 $\div 0.1$ is the same as $\times 10$ → e.g. $6 \div 0.1 = 6 \times 10 = 60$

4 Copy and complete the workings.

a $4 \div 0.1 = 4 \times 10 = \square$ b $7 \div 0.1 = 7 \times \square = \square$
c $20 \div 0.1 = 20 \times \square = \square$ d $25 \div 0.1 = 25 \times \square = \square$

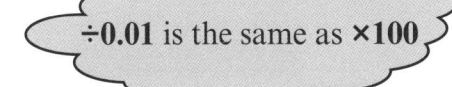 $\div 0.01$ is the same as $\times 100$ → e.g. $6 \div 0.01 = 6 \times 100 = 600$

5 Copy and complete the workings.

a $2 \div 0.01 = 2 \times 100 = \square$ b $5 \div 0.01 = 5 \times \square = \square$
c $30 \div 0.01 = 30 \times \square = \square$ d $12 \div 0.01 = 12 \times \square = \square$

6 Work out these.
All the answers are in the rectangle.

| 1.6 | 16 | 160 | 1600 |

a $16 \div 0.1$ b $0.16 \div 0.1$
c $0.16 \div 0.01$ d $16 \div 0.01$

Practice

7 Work out

a 33×0.1 b 999×0.1 c 30×0.1 d 8.7×0.1
e 77×0.01 f 70×0.01 g 700×0.01 h 7×0.01

8 Work out

a $5 \div 0.1$ b $5.6 \div 0.1$ c $55.6 \div 0.1$ d $0.55 \div 0.1$
e $5 \div 0.01$ f $5.6 \div 0.01$ g $55.6 \div 0.01$ h $0.55 \div 0.01$

9 Work out the answers to these questions.
Use **inverse operations** to check your answers.

a 27×0.1 b 27.9×0.01 c $0.2 \div 0.1$ d $2.7 \div 0.01$

10 Which symbol, $\times$ or $\div$, goes in each box?

a $55 \,\square\, 0.1 = 550$ b $46 \,\square\, 0.01 = 0.46$ c $3.7 \,\square\, 0.1 = 37$
d $208 \,\square\, 0.01 = 2.08$ e $0.19 \,\square\, 0.1 = 1.9$ f $505 \,\square\, 0.01 = 5.05$

11 What goes in the box, 0.1 or 0.01?

a $44 \times \boxed{} = 4.4$ 　　　b $4.4 \div \boxed{} = 44$ 　　　c $0.40 \times \boxed{} = 0.004$

d $4 \div \boxed{} = 40$ 　　　e $44.4 \times \boxed{} = 0.444$ 　　　f $44 \div \boxed{} = 4400$

 12 Which calculation, **A**, **B**, **C** or **D**, gives a different answer to the other three?
Show your working.

| **A** $0.096 \div 0.1$ | **B** 96×0.01 | **C** 9.6×0.1 | **D** $96 \div 0.01$ |

Challenge

13 A tiler works out the area of the wall he is going to tile.

The tiler uses this formula to work out the extra area of tiles he must order due to **wastage**.

> $E = 0.1A$ 　where: 　E is the extra area
>
> 　　　　　　　　　A is the area of the wall

The diagram shows the dimensions of the wall he is going to tile.

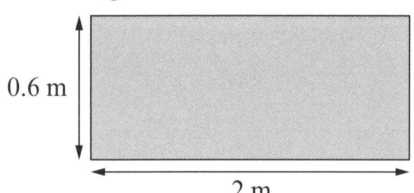

Tip

Wastage is the pieces of tiles that cannot be used because they are broken or the wrong size after cutting.

a Work out the extra area of tiles he must order due to wastage.

The tiler gets a small discount on the cost of the tiles.

He uses this formula to work out the discount.

> $D = 0.01C$ 　where: 　D is the discount 　C is the cost of the tiles

b Work out the discount when the cost of the tiles is $195.

14 The diagram shows a triangle of height 0.1 m.

The area of the triangle is 1.16 m².

The formula for the area of a triangle is $A = \dfrac{1}{2}bh$

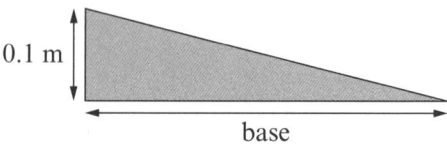

a Rearrange the formula to make b the subject.

b Use your formula to work out the base length of the triangle.

 15 Alicia thinks of a number.

Alicia divides her number by 0.01, and then multiplies the answer by 0.1.

Alicia then divides this answer by 0.01 and gets a final answer of 2340.

What number does Alicia think of first?

Explain how you worked out your answer.

16 This is part of Ceri's homework.

> Question
> 'When you multiply a number with one decimal place by 0.01 you will always get an answer smaller than zero.'
>
> Write one example to show this statement is not true.
>
> Answer
> $345.8 \times 0.01 = 3.458$ and 3.458 is not smaller than zero so the statement is not true.

For each of these statements, write one example to show the statement is not true.

a When you divide a number with one decimal place by 0.1 you will always get an answer bigger than 1.

b When you multiply a number with two **decimal places** by 0.01 you will always get an answer greater than 0.01

> 3.2 Rounding

Exercise 3.2

Focus

Erin uses this method to **round** 35 680 to 1 **significant figure**.

> Draw a line after the first s.f. and circle the next digit 3|⑤6 8 0
> The circled digit is a 5, so round the 3 up to 4 and 4 0 0 0 0
> replace all the other digits with zeros.
> So 35 680 rounded to 1 s.f. is 40 000.

Key words
accurate
degree of accuracy
round
significant figures (s.f.)

1 Use Erin's method to round each number to 1 significant figure.

   a 213   b 4823   c 23 850   d 185 255

2 Round each number to 2 significant figures.

   a 213   b 4823   c 23 850   d 185 255

Tip
Draw a line after the second s.f. and circle the next digit.

3 Round each number to 3 significant figures.

    a   4729   **b**   66 549   **c**   2 355 244

> **Tip**
>
> Draw a line after the third s.f. and circle the next digit.

Paolo uses this method to round 0.002 432 to 1 significant figure.

> Draw a line after the first s.f. and circle the next digit.   0.002 | ④3 2
>
> The circled digit is a 4, so leave the 2 as it is. Do not write the 4, 3 or 2 but remember to write all the zeros before the 2.   0.002
>
> So 0.002 432 rounded to 1 s.f. is 0.002.

4 Use Paolo's method to round each number to 1 significant figure.

    a   0.0231   **b**   0.005 671   **c**   0.000 038 1   **d**   0.688

5 Round each number to 2 significant figures.

    a   0.0231   **b**   0.005 671   **c**   0.000 038 1   **d**   0.688

Practice

6 Round each number to one significant figure (1 s.f.).

    Choose the correct answer: **A**, **B** or **C**.

		A		**B**		**C**	
a	468	**A**	5	**B**	50	**C**	500
b	9.02	**A**	10	**B**	9	**C**	0.9
c	5686	**A**	6000	**B**	5000	**C**	6
d	0.0035	**A**	4	**B**	0.04	**C**	0.004

7 Round each number to two significant figures (2 s.f.).

    All the answers are in the circle.

    a   358   **b**   0.361   **c**   3572

    d   0.003 560 1   **e**   35.99   **f**   3.6009

> 0.0036 0.36
> 3.6 36
> 360 3600

8 This is part of Li's homework.

> <u>Question</u>
>
> Round each number to 3 s.f.
>
>   a 2 374 650   b 0.002 058 84
>
> <u>Answer</u>
>
>   a 237   b 0.002

Li has rounded one large number and one small number to three significant figures.

Both answers are wrong.

    a   Explain the mistakes Li has made.

    b   Write the correct answers.

9   Round each number to the given number of significant figures (s.f.).

    a   2468.15 (1 s.f.)   **b**   759.233 (2 s.f.)   **c**   5.3691 (3 s.f.)

    d   0.0781 (1 s.f.)   **e**   0.1954 (2 s.f.)   **f**   6.03888 (3 s.f.)

    g   964 (1 s.f.)   **h**   0.899 (2 s.f.)   **i**   19.985 (3 s.f.)

10   Which is the correct answer in each case, A, B, C or D?

    a   567 rounded to 1 s.f.

        A   5   **B**   6   **C**   500   **D**   600

    b   15.493 rounded to 2 s.f.

        A   15   **B**   16   **C**   15.49   **D**   15.50

    c   0.07887 rounded to 3 s.f.

        A   0.078   **B**   0.079   **C**   0.0789   **D**   0.0790

    d   0.00777777 rounded to 4 s.f.

        A   0.0077   **B**   0.0078   **C**   0.007777   **D**   0.007778

    e   0.03963 rounded to 2 s.f.

        A   0.040   **B**   0.04   **C**   0.4   **D**   0.030

11   **a**   Use a calculator to work out the answer to $\dfrac{24.2^2 \times \sqrt{83}}{7}$

        Write all the numbers on your calculator display.

    b   Round your answer to part **a** to the stated number of significant figures (s.f.).

        i   1 s.f.   **ii**   2 s.f.   **iii**   3 s.f.

        iv   4 s.f.   **v**   5 s.f.   **vi**   6 s.f.

12   Gina drove from her house in Madrid to a friend's house in Paris, a distance of 1275.3 km.

    Gina then drove to another friend's house in Rome, a distance of 1445.2 km.

    How far did Gina drive altogether?

    Give your answer correct to two significant figures (2 s.f.).

13   Round the number 530.403977 to the stated number of significant figures (s.f.).

    a   1 s.f.   **b**   2 s.f.   **c**   3 s.f.

    d   4 s.f.   **e**   5 s.f.   **f**   6 s.f.

Challenge

14 The instructions on a packet of rice say you should cook 75 g per person.
Yuang carefully weighed out 75 g of rice.
He counted the grains and found he had 2896 grains of rice.
Work out the average (mean) mass of a single grain of rice.
Give your answer correct to three significant figures (3 s.f.).

15 Gerry's electric toothbrush rotates the brush 125 times per second.
Gerry brushes her teeth for two minutes, twice a day.
How many rotations does her electric toothbrush make in one week?
Give your answer correct to one significant figure (1 s.f.).

16 A football club sells, on average, 23 000 tickets per match.
In one season they play, on average, 46 matches.
How many tickets do they sell, on average, each season?
Round your answer to an appropriate **degree of accuracy**.

17 This formula is often used in science.

$$v = u + at$$

Work out the value of a when $v = 5.2$, $u = 1.4$ and $t = 72$.
Round your answer to an appropriate degree of accuracy.

> **Tip**
>
> Change the subject of the formula first.

18 Complete these steps for each calculation.

   i Work out an estimate of the answer by rounding each number to one significant figure.

   ii Use a calculator to work out the **accurate** answer.
   Give this answer correct to three significant figures (3 s.f.).

   iii Compare your estimate with the accurate answer to decide if your accurate answer is correct.

a 0.6292×189.3

b $782.5 \div 1.95$

c 21.4×590

d $\dfrac{0.7951 \times 206}{1.96}$

e $\dfrac{9732 - 3176}{6.816}$

f $\dfrac{48.22 + 9.81}{20.05}$

g $\dfrac{158.2}{0.1956 \times 43.5}$

h $\dfrac{2.104 \times 11.795}{7.887 - 3.109}$

i $\dfrac{78\,500 \times 0.02}{0.235 \times 388}$

4 ▶ Decimals

> 4.1 Ordering decimals

Exercise 4.1

Focus

Key words

compare
decimal number
order

1 Complete the workings to write these numbers in **order** of size,
starting with the smallest.

| 5.51 | 5.08 | 5.21 | 5.17 |

All the numbers have the same whole number part, so you only need
to **compare** the decimal parts.

Step 1: Write the decimal parts only: 51, 08, 21, 17

Step 2: Now write in order the decimal parts only: 08, 17, ☐, ☐

Step 3: Now write the complete numbers in order: 5.08, ☐, ☐, ☐

2 Use the same method as in Question **1** to write these **decimal numbers**
in order of size, starting with the smallest.

   a   4.29, 4.16, 4.95, 4.91

      Write the decimal parts only: ☐ ☐ ☐ ☐

      Write in order the decimal parts only: ☐ ☐ ☐ ☐

      Write the complete numbers in order: ☐ ☐ ☐ ☐

   b   8.94, 8.49, 8.95, 8.47

      Write the decimal parts only: ☐ ☐ ☐ ☐

      Write in order the decimal parts only: ☐ ☐ ☐ ☐

      Write the complete numbers in order: ☐ ☐ ☐ ☐

   c   0.19, 0.15, 0.13, 0.01

      Write the decimal parts only: ☐ ☐ ☐ ☐

      Write in order the decimal parts only: ☐ ☐ ☐ ☐

      Write the complete numbers in order: ☐ ☐ ☐ ☐

3 Write the correct sign, < or >, between each pair of numbers.

   a   7.27 ☐ 7.23   **b**   9.71 ☐ 9.83

   c   20.17 ☐ 20.09   **d**   3.9 ☐ 3.65

4 Write the correct sign, < or >, between each pair of numbers.
Use the number line to help you.

   a   −5.2 ☐ −5.7

   b   −6.5 ☐ −6.2

   c   −7.2 ☐ −7.5

   d   −8.8 ☐ −8.9

> **Tip**
>
> In each part, the whole numbers are the same. So you only need to compare the decimal parts. In Q3a, 27 > 23 so 7.27 > 7.23.

5 Write the correct sign, < or >, between each pair of measurements.
Copy and complete the working.

   a   3.5 g ☐ 380 mg $3.5\,g = 3.5 \times 1000 = 3500\,mg$ 3500 mg ☐ 380 mg

   b   0.4 t ☐ 845 kg $0.4\,t = 0.4 \times 1000 = $ ☐ kg   ☐ kg ☐ 845 kg

   c   2.5 cm ☐ 48 mm $2.5\,cm = 2.5 \times 10 = $ ☐ mm   ☐ mm ☐ 48 mm

   d   950 g ☐ 0.08 kg $0.08\,kg = 0.08 \times 1000 = $ ☐ g   950 g ☐ ☐ g

   e   2500 m ☐ 1.9 km $1.9\,km = 1.9 \times 1000 = $ ☐ m   2500 m ☐ ☐ m

   f   250 cm ☐ 6.5 m $6.5\,m = 6.5 \times 100 = $ ☐ cm   250 cm ☐ ☐ cm

Practice

6 Write the decimal numbers in each set in order of size, starting
with the smallest.

   a   45.454, 45.545, 45.399, 45.933

   b   5.183, 5.077, 5.044, 5.009

   c   31.425, 31.148, 31.41, 31.14

   d   7.502, 7.052, 7.02, 7.2

7 Write the correct sign, = or ≠, between each pair of measurements.

   a   205.5 cm ☐ 255 mm   **b**   0.125 g ☐ 125 mg

   c   500 g ☐ 0.05 kg   **d**   10.5 t ☐ 1050 kg

   e   0.22 kg ☐ 220 g   **f**   1.75 km ☐ 175 m

> **Tip**
>
> Start by converting one of the measurements so that both measurements are in the **same units**.

8 Write the correct sign, < or >, between each pair of numbers.

   a   9.1 ☐ 9.03   **b**   56.4 ☐ 56.35

   c   0.66 ☐ 0.606   **d**   3.505 ☐ 3.7

   e   0.77 t ☐ 806 kg   **f**   7800 m ☐ 0.8 km

   g   3.5 kg ☐ 375 g   **h**   156.3 cm ☐ 1234 mm

9   Write the measurements in each set in order of size, starting with
    the smallest.

    a   4.3 cm, 27 mm, 0.2 cm, 7 mm

    b   34.5 cm, 500 mm, 29 cm, 19.5 mm

    c   2000 g, 75.75 kg, 5550 g, 3 kg

    d   1.75 kg, 1975 g, 0.9 kg, 1800 g

    e   0.125 g, 100 mg, 0.2 g, 150 mg

    f   25 km, 2750 m, 0.05 km, 999 m

> **Tip**
>
> Make sure all the measurements are in the same units before you start to order them.

10 Write the correct sign, < or >, between each pair of numbers.

    a   −2.3 ☐ −2.4   b   −7.23 ☐ −7.29

    c   −0.15 ☐ −0.08   d   −11.02 ☐ −11.5

11 Write these decimal numbers in order of size, starting with
    the smallest.

    a   −8.34, −8.06, −8.28, −8.8   b   −1.425, −1.78, −1.03, −1.5

> **Tip**
>
> Draw a number line to help if you want to.

Challenge

12 Frank and Sarina run around a park every day.

    They keep a record of the distances they run each day for 10 days.

    These are the distances Frank runs each day.

400 m	2.4 km	0.8 km	3200 m	32 km	1.2 km
1.6 km	2000 m	3.6 km	1200 m		

    a   Which distance do you think Frank has written down
        incorrectly? Explain your answer.

    These are the distances Sarina runs each day.

2 km	4000 m	0.75 km	3.5 km	1000 m	3000 m
1.25 km	0.5 km	3250 m	1.75 km		

    b   Sarina says the longest distance she ran is almost ten times the
        shortest distance she ran.

        Is Sarina correct? Explain your answer.

    Frank and Sarina run in different parks.

    The distance round one of the parks is 250 m. The distance round
    the other park is 400 m.

    Frank and Sarina always run a whole number of times around
    their park.

    c   Who do you think runs in each park? Explain how you made
        your decision.

13 Each card describes a sequence of decimal numbers.

| A | First term: −7.5 | Term-to-term rule: 'add 0.3' |

| B | First term: −1.71 | Term-to-term rule: 'multiply by 2' |

| C | First term: −9.95 | Term-to-term rule: 'add 1.5' |

a Work out the third term of each sequence.

b Write the numbers from part **a** in order of size, starting with the smallest.

 14 *y* is a number with two decimal places, and $-1.43 \leq y < -1.38$

Write all the possible numbers that *y* could be.

 15 The formula to convert a temperature in degrees Centigrade (*C*) to degrees Fahrenheit (*F*) is

$$F = C \times 1.8 + 32$$

a Use a calculator to work out *F* when $C = -38.6$

b Which is colder, a temperature of −38.6 °C or −38.6 °F? Explain your answer.

> 4.2 Multiplying decimals

You already know that multiplying a number by 0.1 is the same as dividing the number by 10.

Key word

estimation

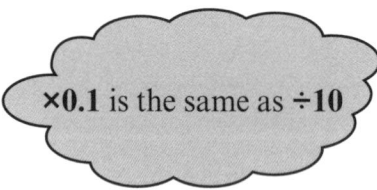

×0.1 is the same as ÷10

Exercise 4.2

Focus

1 Look at these rules.

×0.2 is the same as ÷10 and ×2
OR ×2 and ÷10

×0.3 is the same as ÷10 and ×3
OR ×3 and ÷10

Follow the pattern to complete these rules.

a $\times 0.4$ is the same as $\div 10$ and $\times \boxed{}$

  OR $\times \boxed{}$ and $\div 10$

b $\times 0.6$ is the same as $\div 10$ and $\times \boxed{}$

  OR $\times \boxed{}$ and $\div 10$

2 To multiply a number by 0.2

- divide the number by 10, then multiply by 2 **OR**
- multiply the number by 2, then divide by 10.

Copy and complete the workings.

> e.g. 60×0.2
> $60 \div 10 = 6$ and $6 \times 2 = 12$
> OR $60 \times 2 = 120$ and $120 \div 10 = 12$

a 30×0.2 $30 \div 10 = 3$ and $3 \times 2 = \boxed{}$

b -40×0.2 $-40 \div \boxed{} = \boxed{}$ and $\boxed{} \times 2 = \boxed{}$

c 12×0.2 $12 \times 2 = 24$ and $\boxed{} \div 10 = \boxed{}$

d -8×0.2 $-8 \times 2 = \boxed{}$ and $\boxed{} \div \boxed{} = \boxed{}$

3 To multiply a number by 0.3

- divide the number by 10, then multiply by 3 **OR**
- multiply the number by 3, then divide by 10.

Copy and complete the workings.

a 30×0.3 $30 \div 10 = 3$ and $\boxed{} \times 3 = \boxed{}$

b -50×0.3 $-50 \div \boxed{} = \boxed{}$ and $\boxed{} \times 3 = \boxed{}$

c 15×0.3 $15 \times 3 = 45$ and $45 \div 10 = \boxed{}$

d -9×0.3 $-9 \times 3 = \boxed{}$ and $\boxed{} \div \boxed{} = \boxed{}$

4 To multiply a number by 0.02

- divide the number by 100, then multiply by 2 **OR**
- multiply the number by 2, then divide by 100.

Copy and complete the workings.

a 500×0.02 $500 \div 100 = 5$ and $5 \times 2 = \boxed{}$

b -600×0.02 $-600 \div \boxed{} = \boxed{}$ and $\boxed{} \times 2 = \boxed{}$

c 25×0.02 $25 \times 2 = 50$ and $50 \div 100 = \boxed{}$

d -4×0.02 $-4 \times 2 = \boxed{}$ and $\boxed{} \div \boxed{} = \boxed{}$

5 To multiply a number by 0.03

- divide the number by 100, then multiply by 3 **OR**
- multiply the number by 3, then divide by 100.

Copy and complete the workings.

a 500×0.03 $500 \div 100 = 5$ and $5 \times 3 = \boxed{}$

b -700×0.03 $-700 \div \boxed{} = \boxed{}$ and $\boxed{} \times 3 = \boxed{}$

c 12×0.03 $12 \times 3 = 36$ and $36 \div 100 = \boxed{}$

d -3×0.03 $-3 \times 3 = \boxed{}$ and $\boxed{} \div \boxed{} = \boxed{}$

Practice

6 Work out

    a 0.1×-9 **b** 0.3×5 **c** 0.5×-12

    d 0.7×6 **e** 0.9×-8

7 Work these out.

    All the answers are in the cloud.

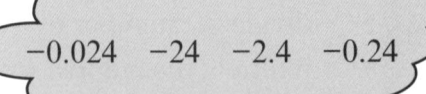

    a -6×0.04 **b** -12×0.2 -0.024 -24 -2.4 -0.24

    c -24×0.001 **d** -800×0.03

8 Here are five calculation cards.

A $\quad -24 \times 0.52$	**B** $\quad 0.07 \times -180$
C $\quad 0.03 \times -430$	**D** $\quad -20 \times 0.65$
E $\quad 0.9 \times -15$	

    a Work out the answer to each calculation.

    b Write the answers in order of size, starting with the smallest.

9 **a** Copy and complete these patterns.

        i $\quad 3 \times 3 = 9$ **ii** $\quad 4 \times 7 = 28$

             $0.3 \times 3 = \square$ $0.4 \times 7 = \square$

             $0.3 \times 0.3 = \square$ $0.4 \times 0.7 = \square$

             $0.3 \times 0.03 = \square$ $0.4 \times 0.07 = \square$

             $0.3 \times 0.003 = \square$ $0.4 \times 0.007 = \square$

    b Work out

        i $\quad 0.1 \times 0.05$ **ii** $\quad 0.4 \times 0.6$

        iii $\quad 0.08 \times 0.3$ **iv** $\quad 0.02 \times 0.08$

        v $\quad 0.12 \times 0.4$ **vi** $\quad 0.04 \times 0.15$

 10 **a** Sort these cards into groups of equal value.

        You should have one card left over.

A $\quad 0.04 \times 0.03$	**B** $\quad 0.8 \times 0.02$
C $\quad 0.03 \times 0.06$	**D** $\quad 0.002 \times 0.9$
E $\quad 0.001 \times 16$	**F** $\quad 0.05 \times 0.4$
G $\quad 0.6 \times 0.002$	**H** $\quad 0.012 \times 0.1$
I $\quad 0.04 \times 0.4$	**J** $\quad 0.18 \times 0.01$

    b Write a different card that could go in the same group as the card that is left over.

11 a   Work out 234×56

    b   Use your answer to part **a** to write the answers to these calculations.

       i 23.4×56 ii 234×5.6

       iii 23.4×5.6 iv 2.34×5.6

       v 23.4×0.56 vi 2.34×0.056

Challenge

12 Work out these multiplications. Show how to check your answers.

    a 7.2×8.3 b 0.24×4.5

    c 0.87×6.35 d 0.61×0.742

> **Tip**
>
> Use **estimation** to check your answers by rounding all the numbers in the question to one significant figure.

13 This is part of Tom's homework.

> Question
> Work out
>
> a 0.23×6.9 b 82×0.003 c 0.078×0.005
>
> Answers
>
> a 1.587   b 0.0246   c 0.0039

Use estimation to check if Tom's answers could be correct.

If you think they are incorrect, explain why.

14 A chainsaw uses petrol and oil.

The instructions for the chainsaw are:

> Mix 31.25 mL of oil with 1 litre of petrol.

    a   Work out an estimate of the volume of oil (mL) that are needed to mix with 2.4 litres of petrol.

    b   Calculate the accurate volume of oil (mL) that is needed to mix with 2.4 litres of petrol.

15 Jay is mixing concrete. She has 32.5 kg of concrete. She uses an additive to make the concrete waterproof.

The instructions for the concrete mixture are:

> Mix 0.03 litres of additive with 1 kg concrete.

    a   Work out an estimate of the volume of additive, in litres, that Jay needs.

    b   Calculate the accurate volume of additive, in litres, that Jay needs.

> **Tip**
>
> An **additive** is an ingredient added to something in small amounts to improve it in some way.

16 The formula to convert a temperature in degrees Centigrade (C) to degrees Fahrenheit (F) is

$$F = C \times 1.8 + 32$$

a Work out F when

   i $C = -15$ ii $C = -20$

b Read what Marcus says.

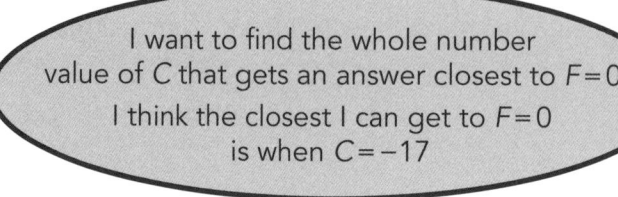

I want to find the whole number value of C that gets an answer closest to $F = 0$
I think the closest I can get to $F = 0$ is when $C = -17$

Is Marcus correct? Explain your answer.

> 4.3 Dividing by decimals

When you divide a number by a decimal, use the **place value** of the decimal to work out an easier **equivalent calculation**. An easier equivalent calculation is to divide by a whole number instead of a decimal.

For example, you can write $6.3 \div 0.7$ as $\frac{6.3}{0.7}$

Multiplying the numerator and denominator of the fraction by 10

gives $\frac{6.3 \times 10}{0.7 \times 10} = \frac{63}{7}$

This makes an equivalent calculation that is much easier to do, because dividing by 7 is much easier than dividing by 0.7.

Key words
equivalent calculation
place value
reverse calculation
short division
term-to-term rule

Exercise 4.3

Focus

1 Copy and complete these divisions.

   a $1.6 \div 0.4 = \frac{1.6}{0.4}$ $\frac{1.6 \times 10}{0.4 \times 10} = \frac{\square}{\square} = \square$

   b $4.5 \div 0.9 = \frac{4.5}{0.9}$ $\frac{4.5 \times 10}{0.9 \times 10} = \frac{\square}{\square} = \square$

c $\quad -24 \div 0.3 = \dfrac{-24}{0.3}$ $\qquad \dfrac{-24 \times 10}{0.3 \times 10} = \dfrac{\square}{\square} = \square$

d $\quad -21 \div 0.7 = \dfrac{-21}{0.7}$ $\qquad \dfrac{-21 \times 10}{0.7 \times 10} = \dfrac{\square}{\square} = \square$

> **Tip**
>
> **Remember:**
>
> positive ÷ positive = positive
>
> negative ÷ positive = negative

2 Match each grey card with the correct white answer card.

A	$1.8 \div 0.2$
B	$2.1 \div 0.3$
C	$2.5 \div 0.5$
D	$2.4 \div 0.6$
E	$7.2 \div 0.9$

i	7
ii	4
iii	9
iv	8
v	5

3 Copy and complete these divisions.

a $\quad 2 \div 0.4 = \dfrac{2}{0.4}$ $\qquad \dfrac{2 \times 10}{0.4 \times 10} = \dfrac{\square}{\square} = \square$

b $\quad 3 \div 0.5 = \dfrac{3}{0.5}$ $\qquad \dfrac{3 \times 10}{0.5 \times 10} = \dfrac{\square}{\square} = \square$

c $\quad -6 \div 0.2 = \dfrac{-6}{0.2}$ $\qquad \dfrac{-6 \times 10}{0.2 \times 10} = \dfrac{\square}{\square} = \square$

d $\quad -4 \div 0.8 = \dfrac{-4}{0.8}$ $\qquad \dfrac{-4 \times 10}{0.8 \times 10} = \dfrac{\square}{\square} = \square$

> **Tip**
>
> You can use exactly the same method as in Question **1**.

4 This is part of Mia's homework.
Mia has made a mistake in her solution.
  a Explain the mistake she has made.
  b Work out the correct answer.

> _Question_
> Work out $40 \div 0.5$
>
> _Answer_
> $40 \div 0.5 = \dfrac{40}{0.5}$
>
> $\dfrac{40}{0.5 \times 10} = \dfrac{40}{5} = 8$

5 Which of these calculation cards is the odd one out?
Explain why.

A	$60 \div 0.5$		B	$24 \div 0.2$		C	$44 \div 0.4$		D	$12 \div 0.1$		E	$36 \div 0.3$

Practice

6 Work out

    a $0.78 \div 0.3$

    b $6.56 \div 0.4$

    c $-984 \div 0.8$

    d $-189 \div 0.7$

> **Tip**
>
> Follow these steps.
>
> **1** Write the division as a fraction.
>
> **2** Multiply the numerator and denominator by 10.
>
> **3** Use **short division** to work out the answer.

7 Harry pays \$2.58 for a piece of ribbon 0.6 m long.

Harry uses this formula to work out the cost of the ribbon per metre.

$$\text{cost per metre} = \frac{\text{price of piece}}{\text{length of piece}}$$

What is the cost of the ribbon per metre?

8 For each division, work out

    i   an estimate of the answer

    ii the accurate answer.

    a $49.5 \div 0.3$ **b** $-936 \div 0.4$

    c $31.5 \div 0.5$ **d** $-351 \div 0.6$

    e $58.94 \div 0.7$ **f** $-3808 \div 0.8$

> **Tip**
>
> Remember to round the number you are dividing: to one significant figure, e.g.
> $276 \div 3 \approx$
> $300 \div 3 = 100$
> **OR**
> to a number that is easier to divide, e.g. $502 \div 7 \approx$
> $490 \div 7 = 70$

9 **a** Complete the table below showing the 13 times table.

1	2	3	4	5	6	7	8	9
13	26	39						

    b Use the table to help you work out $75.53 \div 1.3$

    c Show how to check your answer to part **b** is correct.
Use estimation and a **reverse calculation**.

10 **a** Complete the table below showing the 19 times table.

1	2	3	4	5	6	7	8	9
19	38	57						

> **Tip**
>
> Your rounded answer to Question 9 part **b** × 13 should equal about 755.

    b Ana buys a piece of metal for \$47.12.
The piece of metal is 1.9 m long.
Work out the cost per metre of the metal.

    c Show how to check your answer to part **b** is correct.
Use estimation and a reverse calculation.

> **Tip**
>
> In Question 10 part **b**, you can use the same formula as in Question 7.

Challenge

11 Work with a partner to answer this question.

    a Elin works out that $654 \times 32 = 20\,928$

       Use Elin's calculation to work out

       i $20\,928 \div 32$ **ii** $20\,928 \div 654$

       iii $20\,928 \div 3.2$ **iv** $20\,928 \div 65.4$

    b Explain the method you used to work out the answers to part **a**.

    c Use Elin's calculation to work out

       i $2092.8 \div 3.2$ **ii** $209.28 \div 3.2$

       iii $20.928 \div 3.2$ **iv** $2.0928 \div 3.2$

    d Explain the method you used to work out the answers to part **c**.

12 Work out. Give each answer to the degree of accuracy shown.

    a $2.97 \div 0.7$ (1 d.p.)   **b** $76.94 \div 1.3$ (2 d.p.)

    c $-5479 \div 1.8$ (3 d.p.)

> **Tip**
>
> You only need to work out the division to one decimal place **more than** the degree of accuracy you need.

13 The diagram shows a triangle with an area of $8.84\,\text{m}^2$.

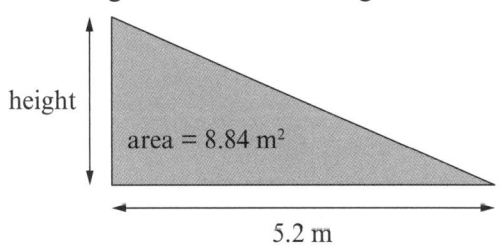

The base length of the triangle is 5.2 m.

Meghan works out that the height of the triangle is 3.64 m.

    a Show that Meghan is wrong.

    b Work out the correct height of the triangle. Show all your working.

> **Tip**
>
> Remember, the formula for the area of a triangle is area = $\frac{1}{2}$ × base × height

14 The diagram shows a compound shape.

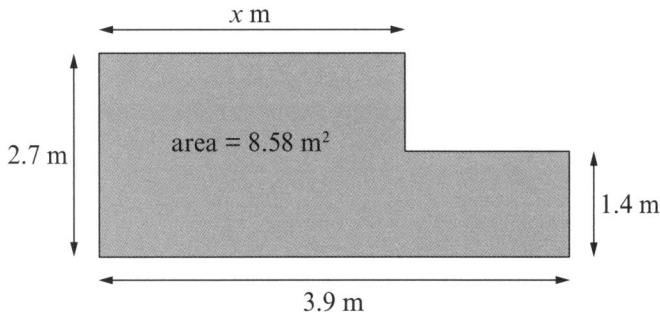

The area of the shape is $8.58\,\text{m}^2$.

Work out the length x m.

Explain how you worked out your answer.

Show all your working.

15 Carlos makes this number sequence, but he has spilled tea on his work.

> This is my number sequence:
>
> | 1st term | 2nd term | 3rd term | 4th term |
> |---|---|---|---|
> | | 7.2 | 8.64 | |
>
> My term-to-term rule is: multiply by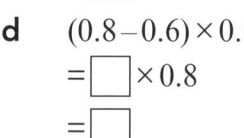

Carlos thinks the **term-to-term** rule is multiply by 0.8.

a Is Carlos correct? Explain your answer.

b Work out the missing numbers under the tea.
Explain how you worked out your answers.

> 4.4 Making decimal calculations easier

Exercise 4.4

Focus

Key word
factor

1 Copy and complete the workings for these questions.
All the answers are in the rectangle.

| 0.54 |
| 0.06 |
| 0.16 |
| 0.12 |

a $(0.2 + 0.1) \times 0.4$
$= \boxed{} \times 0.4$
$= \boxed{}$

b $(0.9 - 0.7) \times 0.3$
$= \boxed{} \times 0.3$
$= \boxed{}$

c $(0.4 + 0.5) \times 0.6$
$= \boxed{} \times 0.6$
$= \boxed{}$

d $(0.8 - 0.6) \times 0.8$
$= \boxed{} \times 0.8$
$= \boxed{}$

2 Copy and complete the workings to make these calculations easier.
All the missing numbers are in the trapezium.

a 60×0.9
$= 60 \times (1 - 0.1)$
$= 60 \times 1 - 60 \times 0.1$
$= 60 - 6$
$= \boxed{}$

b 42×0.9
$= 42 \times (1 - 0.1)$
$= 42 \times 1 - 42 \times 0.1$
$= \boxed{} - \boxed{}$
$= \boxed{}$

21.6	1.8	42
37.8	54	24
2.4	4.2	18
16.2		

c 18×0.9
$= 18 \times (1 - 0.1)$
$= 18 \times 1 - 18 \times 0.1$
$= \boxed{} - \boxed{}$
$= \boxed{}$

d 24×0.9
$= 24 \times (1 - 0.1)$
$= 24 \times 1 - 24 \times 0.1$
$= \boxed{} - \boxed{}$
$= \boxed{}$

3 Work out the answers to these calculations.
Look for different ways to make the calculations easier.
They have all been started for you.

a $2.5 \times 5.7 \times 4$
$2.5 \times 4 = 10$
$10 \times 5.7 = \boxed{}$

b $2.5 \times 24.1 \times 4$
$2.5 \times 4 = \boxed{}$
$\boxed{} \times 24.1 = \boxed{}$

c $8 \times 1.2 \times 2.5$
$8 \times 2.5 = 20$
$20 \times 1.2 = 2 \times 10 \times 1.2$
$\qquad = 2 \times 12$
$\qquad = \boxed{}$

d $\dfrac{0.3 \times 1.3}{0.1}$
$\dfrac{0.3}{0.1} = 0.3 \times 10 = \boxed{}$
$\boxed{} \times 1.3 = \boxed{}$

e $(42 + 18) \times 0.8$
$42 + 18 = 60$
$60 \times 0.8 = 60 \div 10 \times 8$
$\qquad = \boxed{} \times 8$
$\qquad = \boxed{}$

f $(23 + 27) \times 0.7$
$23 + 27 = \boxed{}$
$\boxed{} \times 0.7 = \boxed{} \div 10 \times \boxed{}$
$\qquad = \boxed{} \times \boxed{}$
$\qquad = \boxed{}$

g $(530 - 230) \times 0.08$
$530 - 230 = 300$
$300 \times 0.08 = 300 \div 100 \times 8$
$\qquad = \boxed{} \times 8$
$\qquad = \boxed{}$

h $(670 - 270) \times 0.03$
$670 - 270 = \boxed{}$
$\boxed{} \times 0.03 = \boxed{} \div 100 \times \boxed{}$
$\qquad = \boxed{} \times \boxed{}$
$\qquad = \boxed{}$

4 Complete the workings. Use **factors** to make these calculations easier.

a 16×0.35

$= 16 \times 0.5 \times 0.7$

$= 8 \times 0.7$

$= \square \times 7 \div 10$

$= \square \div 10$

$= \square$

b 12×0.45

$= 12 \times 0.5 \times 0.9$

$= \square \times 0.9$

$= \square \times 9 \div 10$

$= \square \div 10$

$= \square$

c 18×0.15

$= 18 \times 0.5 \times 0.3$

$= \square \times 0.3$

$= \square \times 3 \div 10$

$= \square \div 10$

$= \square$

d 26×0.35

$= 26 \times 0.5 \times 0.7$

$= \square \times 0.7$

$= \square \times 7 \div 10$

$= \square \div 10$

$= \square$

Practice

5 Work out. Use the same method as in Question **1**.

a $(0.5 + 0.1) \times 0.4$

b $(0.3 + 0.5) \times 0.7$

c $(0.9 - 0.3) \times 1.1$

d $(1.7 - 1.3) \times 1.2$

6 Work out. Use the same method as in Question **2**.

a 16×0.9 **b** 36×0.9 **c** 5.2×0.9

7 The diagram shows a rectangle.

The width is 0.9 m and the length is 8.7 m.

Work out the area of the rectangle.

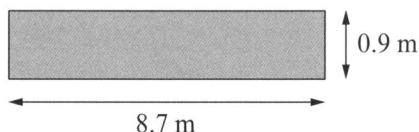

0.9 m

8.7 m

8 Work out

a 48×9.9

b 48×0.99

c 1.2×9.9

d 1.2×0.99

Tip

$48 \times 9.9 = 48 \times (10 - 0.1)$

$48 \times 0.99 = 48 \times (1 - 0.01)$

9 The diagram shows a square of side length 0.99 m.

The formula for the perimeter of a square is

> perimeter $= 4 \times$ side length

Work out the perimeter of the square.

0.99 m

10 The diagram shows an equilateral triangle of side length 9.9 m.

The formula for the perimeter of an equilateral triangle is

> perimeter $= 3 \times$ side length

Work out the perimeter of the equilateral triangle.

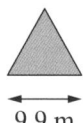

9.9 m

11 Work out. Look for different ways to make the calculations easier.

    a $2.5 \times 26.5 \times 4$ **b** $8 \times 63.4 \times 2.5$

    c $\dfrac{0.4 \times 1.6}{0.1}$ **d** $\dfrac{0.6 \times 4.21}{0.1}$

    e $(280 + 170) \times 0.3$ **f** $(980 - 580) \times 0.03$

12 Work out. Use the same method as in Question **4**.

    a 70×0.15 **b** 124×0.35

Challenge

13 A formula used in maths is

$$S = \frac{a}{1-r}$$

    a Work out the value of S when $a = 5.6$ and $r = 0.6$

    b Work out the value of a when $S = 36$ and $r = 0.8$

14 The diagram shows a square of side length 9.9 m.

Work out

    a the perimeter of the square

    b the area of the square.

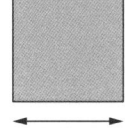

9.9 m

15 A formula used in science is

$$F = ma$$

    a Work out the value of F when $m = 26$ and $a = 0.45$

    b Work out the value of m when $F = 20.8$ and $a = 0.4$

> **Tip**
>
> Remember that ma means $m \times a$

16 Work out using the factor method.

    a 350×0.16 (use $0.16 = 0.2 \times 0.8$)

    b 130×0.21 (use $0.21 = 0.3 \times 0.7$)

17 Here are four formula cards.

Use the cards to work out the value of e when $a = 425$

$e = \dfrac{(d - 28) \times 0.03}{0.4}$ $d = c \times 0.45$

$c = 4 \times (b + 33) \times 2.5$ $b = a \times 0.12$

5 ▶ Angles and constructions

▶ 5.1 Parallel lines

Exercise 5.1

Focus

1 Explain why **vertically opposite angles** are equal.

2   **a**   Look at this diagram.
State why x and y are equal.
Copy the diagram.

    b   Mark all the angles that are corresponding to x.

    c   Mark, in a different way, all the angles that are alternate to y.

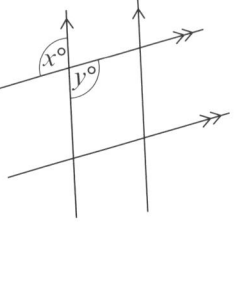

> **Key words**
>
> alternate angles
> corresponding angles
> vertically opposite angles

3   Find the values of a, b, c and d.

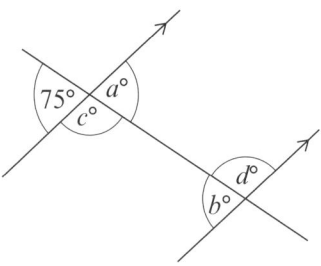

Give a reason for each angle.

Practice

4   Look at the diagram.

    a   Which angles are 68° because they are **corresponding angles**?

    b   Which angles are 68° because they are **alternate angles**?

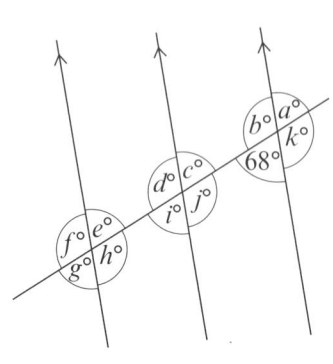

5 **a** Complete these sentences.

   i Two alternate angles are *ABG* and _____.

   ii Another two alternate angles are *CBE* and _____.

   iii Two corresponding angles are *GEF* and _____.

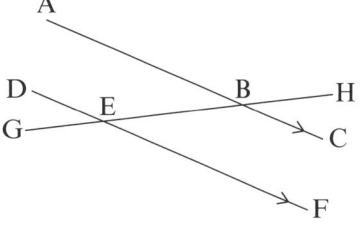

b Read what Sofia says:

HBC and *DEG* are alternate angles.

Is Sofia correct?

Explain your answer.

6 Explain why only two of the lines *l*, *m* and *n* are parallel.

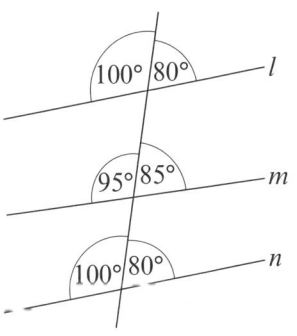

7 Calculate the values of *x* and *y*. Give reasons for your answers.

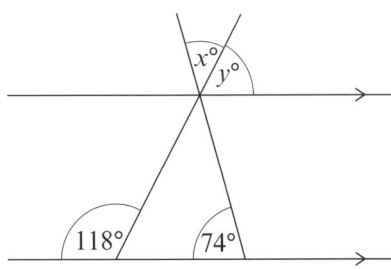

8 Give a reason why *t* must be 120°.

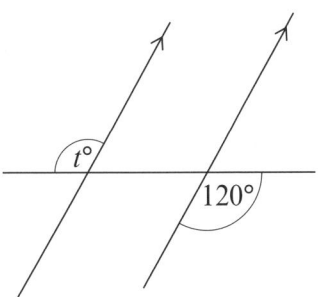

9 Are lines l_1 and l_2 parallel?
   Give a reason for your answer.

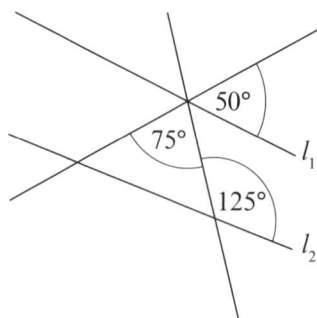

Challenge

10 Explain why the sum of a and b must be 180°.

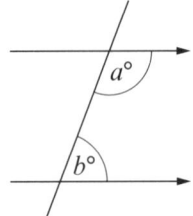

11 Use this diagram to show that the angle sum of triangle
    XYZ is 180°.

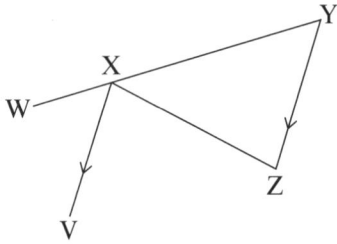

12 Look at the diagram.
    Copy and complete the explanation that the angle
    sum of triangle ABC is 180°.
    Write the reason for each line.

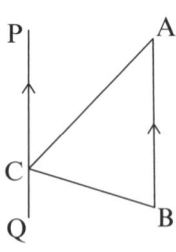

1) Angle A of the triangle = angle PCA
    _____

2) Angle B of the triangle = angle QCB
    _____

3) Angle PCA + angle C of the triangle + angle
    QCB = 180° _____

    Hence angle A + angle B + angle C = 180°

13 *A*, *B*, *C* and *D* are the four angles of a parallelogram.

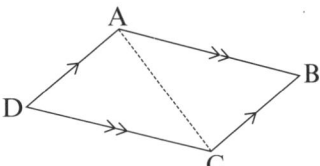

Tip

Use alternate angles.

    a   Show that angle *A* = angle *C*.
    b   Show that angle *B* = angle *D*.

› 5.2 The exterior angle of a triangle

Exercise 5.2

Focus

Key word

exterior angle of a triangle

1   How big is each **exterior angle** of an equilateral triangle?

2   One of the exterior angles of an isosceles triangle is 30°.
How big are the other two exterior angles?

3   Find the values of *x* and *y*.

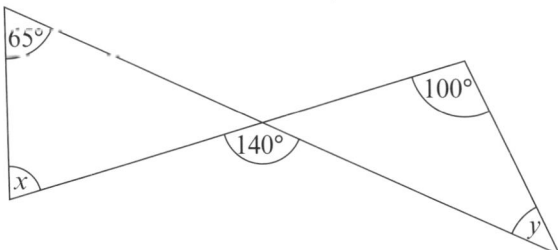

4   Work out angles *a* and *b*.

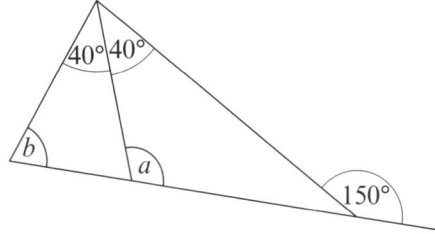

Practice

5   Show that the interior angles of this shape add up to 360°.

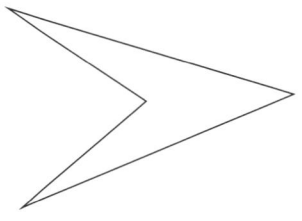

6 Use exterior angles to show that the angle sum of quadrilateral *PQRS* is 360°.

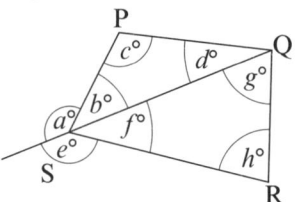

7 *ABCD* is a four-sided shape but two of the sides cross.

    a Explain why the sum of the angles at *A*, *B*, *C* and *D* must be less than 360°.

    b Find the sum of the angles at *A*, *B*, *C* and *D*. Give a reason for your answer.

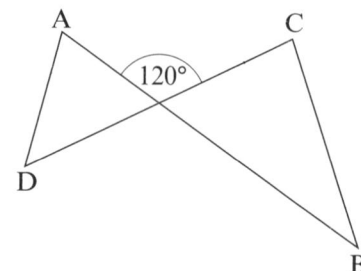

Challenge

8 Explain why $x + y + z = 360°$.

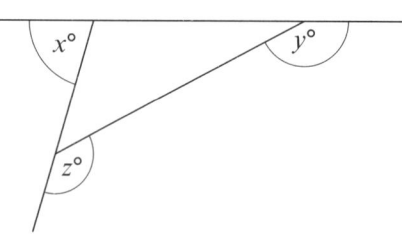

9 Calculate the values of *a*, *b* and *c*. Give a reason for each answer.

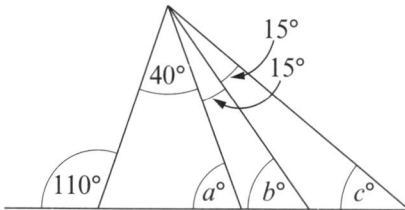

10 a Work out angle *a*.

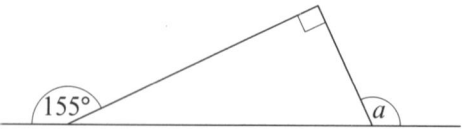

    b Show that $x + y = 270°$

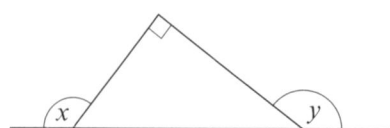

11 a The exterior angles of a triangle are 105°, 115° and 140°.
Calculate the three interior angles of the triangle.

b Zara draws a different triangle.
Look at what Zara says:

> I have drawn a triangle. The exterior angles are 100°, 120° and 130°.

Show that this is impossible.

> 5.3 Constructions

Exercise 5.3

Focus

1 a Construct this triangle.
b Measure the length of the third side.

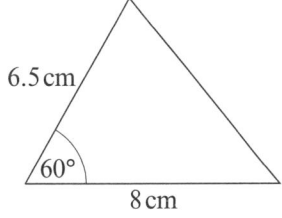

Key words
bisector
hypotenuse

2 a Construct this triangle.
b Measure the shortest side.

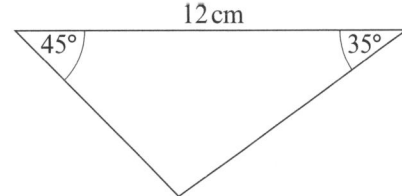

3 a Construct triangle *ABC*.
b Measure angle *B*.
c Measure *BC*.

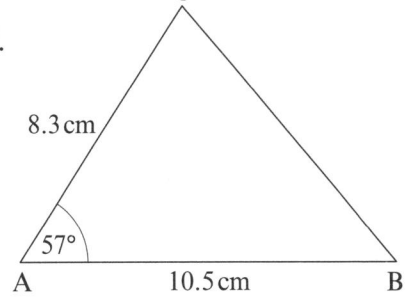

Practice

4 a Draw a triangle where two angles are 85° and 50° and the side between them is 9.2 cm.

b Measure the longest side of the triangle.

5   **a**   Draw a triangle with side lengths 10.5 cm, 7.5 cm and 6.5 cm.

   b   Measure the largest angle of the triangle.

6   **a**   The two shorter sides of a right-angled triangle are 9 cm and 6 cm.

      i   Draw the triangle.   **ii**   Measure the **hypotenuse**.

   b   The hypotenuse of a right-angled triangle is 9 cm and another side is 6 cm.

      i   Draw the triangle.   **ii**   Measure the third side.

7   **a**   Make an accurate copy of this shape.

   b   The length BD should be 19.0 cm. Use this fact to check the accuracy of your drawing.

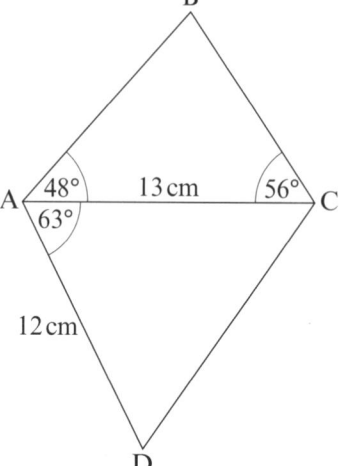

8   **a**   Draw a triangle with side lengths 8.4 cm, 10.5 cm and 6.3 cm.

   b   This should be a right-angled triangle. Use this fact to check the accuracy of your drawing.

Challenge

9   **a**   Draw triangle *ABC*.

   b   Use compasses to draw the perpendicular **bisector** of *BC*. Show your construction lines on your drawing.

   c   Check the accuracy of your drawing with a protractor and a ruler.

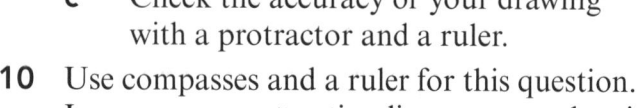

10   Use compasses and a ruler for this question. Leave your construction lines on your drawing.

   a   Make an accurate drawing of triangle *XYZ*.

   b   Draw the bisector of angle *X*.

   c   The bisector at angle *X* meets *YZ* at *W*. Mark *W* on your drawing and measure *YW*.

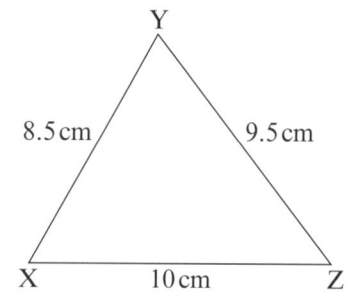

11   Show all your construction lines in this question.

   a   Make an accurate drawing of triangle *ABC*.

   b   Draw the bisector of angle *A*.

   c   The bisector of angle *A* meets *BC* at *D*. Measure *BD*.

   d   Draw another copy of triangle *ABC*.

   e   The perpendicular bisector of *AB* meets *BC* at *E*. Find the length of *BE*.

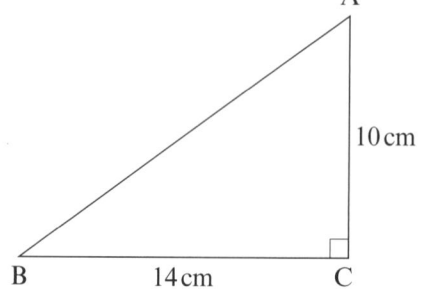

6 ▷ Collecting data

⟩ 6.1 Data collection

Exercise 6.1

Focus

1 Your school has a record of personal data about you.

Suggest a piece of information that might be in your record that is

a categorical data   b discrete data

c continuous data.

2 Here are two questions about homework.

- How much homework do learners do each night?
- On which subject do learners spend most time?

a What data do you need to collect to answer these questions?

b You decide to collect data from a sample of learners in your school.

How will you choose the sample?

3 When babies are born, their gender, length and mass are recorded.

a What type of data is this?

b Write three statistical questions you could answer using this data.

c How could you choose a sample of babies to collect data to answer your questions?

Practice

4 Here are three questions about customers at a large hotel.

- Why do people choose this hotel?
- What are they here for?
- How long do they stay?

a What data do you need to collect to answer these questions?

b How can you collect the data you need?

5 It is healthy to eat vegetables. Look at these statements.

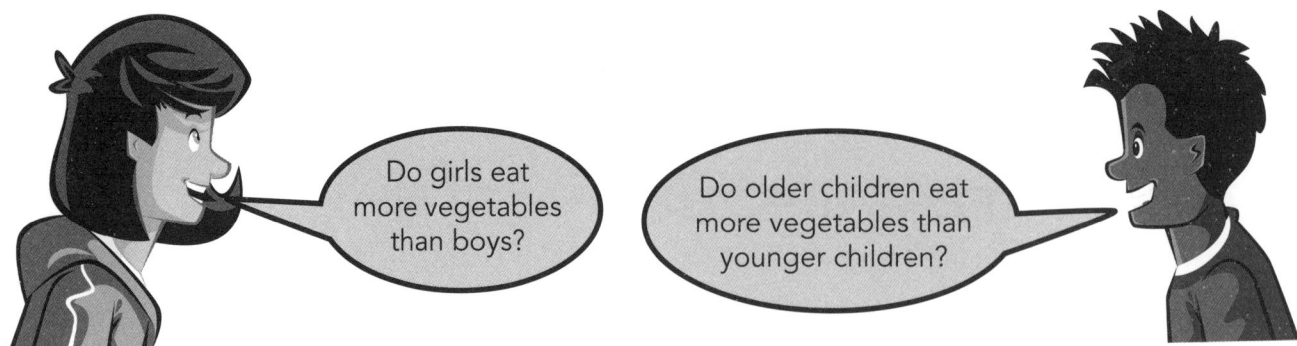

Do girls eat more vegetables than boys?

Do older children eat more vegetables than younger children?

    a What data do you need to answer these questions?

    b How can you collect the data you need?

6 Sudoku is a popular puzzle. Here are two questions:

- Are girls better than boys at Sudoku?
- Are 11-year-olds better than 14-year-olds at Sudoku?

    a What data do you need to collect to answer these questions?

    b How can you collect the data you need?

Challenge

 7 You want to answer this question.

> Are words in other languages longer than words in English?

You can choose a language to test.

    a What data do you need to collect to answer this question?

    b How can you collect the data you need?

    c Test your data collection method on a small sample.

    d Was your data collection method satisfactory? Can you think of a way to improve it?

 8 Here is a statistical question:

> Do books for children have shorter sentences than books for adults?

To answer this question, you are going to collect some data.

    a What data do you need to collect?

    b Describe a method of choosing a sample of sentences from a book.

    c Choose a book and try your sampling method.

    d Were there any problems with your sampling method?

       Do you want to change your sampling method?

9   **Arm span** is the distance between your fingertips when you spread your arms.

The **femur** is the bone in your thigh.

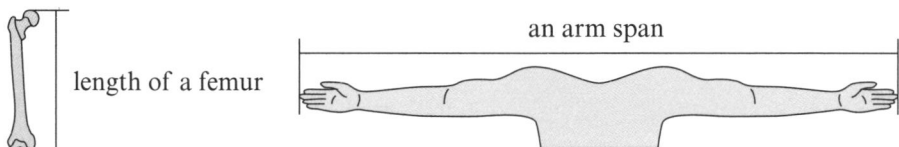

length of a femur   an arm span

Here are two statements.

- A person's arm span and height are roughly the same length.
- The length of a person's femur is about one-quarter of their height.

You are going to test these statements by measuring a sample of people.

What factors do you need to think about when you are planning your sample?

> **Tip**
>
> Think about differences between people that might affect the measurements.

> 6.2 Sampling

Exercise 6.2

Focus

1   There are 850 students in a college.

a   Describe three ways to choose a sample of 40 students.

b   Give an advantage and a disadvantage of each method.

2   Zara wants to give a questionnaire to 100 people who travel on a bus route.

a   Describe an advantage of this method.

b   Describe two disadvantages of this method.

c   Describe a method that overcomes the disadvantages you identified in part **b**.

d   Describe one disadvantage of your method in part **c**.

I will give a questionnaire to the first 100 passengers who get on the bus after 10:00 tomorrow.

3   A supermarket has a car park.

Here is a conjecture: Cars park for longer in the morning than in the afternoon.

This chart shows the results of a survey of the parking time for 100 cars in the morning and 100 cars in the afternoon. The survey was done on a Tuesday.

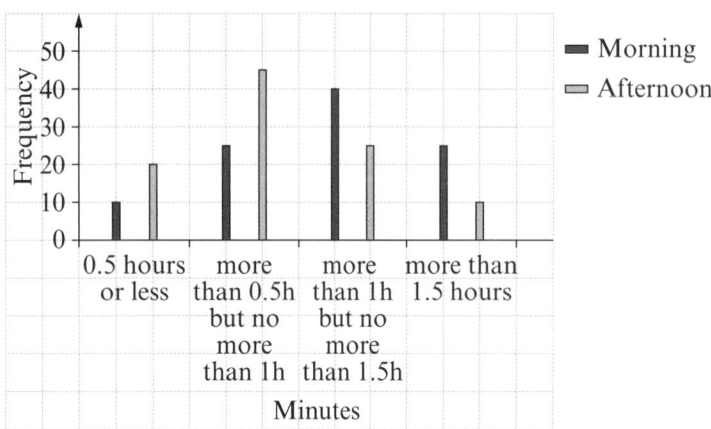

a   Does the data support the conjecture? Give a reason for your answer.

b   Write down one way to improve the survey.

Practice

 4   Men and women of different ages visit a coffee shop.

The owner wants to give a survey to a sample of 50 customers.

The owner says, 'I will interview all the customers who come to the coffee shop between 10:00 and 12:00 tomorrow morning.'

a   Write one disadvantage of this method of choosing a sample.

b   Describe a better way to choose a sample. Justify your answer.

 5   A survey records the speeds of cars on a road.

The survey measures the speed of every car that passes in two hours; between 08:00 and 09:00 and between 17:00 and 18:00 on one Wednesday.

a   Why are two separate time periods better than one?

b   Describe a disadvantage of this method.

c   Suggest two ways to improve the survey.

6 The guests at two hotels are asked to give a score for *quality of service*, on a scale of 1 to 5.

1 is poor and 5 is excellent.

This chart shows the results.

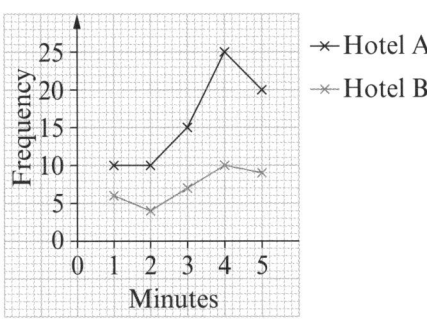

Here is a conjecture: Hotel A provides better service than hotel B.

a Does the data support the conjecture? Give a reason for your answer.

b Write down one way to improve the survey.

Challenge

7 One way to choose a sample is to call people on the telephone and ask them to complete a questionnaire.

a How can you make sure you get a representative sample?

b Describe an advantage of this method.

c Describe a disadvantage of this method.

8 Here is a question:

> How many questions are there in the exercises in this book?

It would take a long time to look at every exercise in the book. Instead, you can answer this question by looking at a sample of exercises.

Here are two ways of choosing a sample.

A Look at all the exercises in the first three units.

B Choose three units by picking numbers from a hat. Look at all the exercises in those units.

a Try each of these methods. Record the number of questions in each exercise in a chart so you can compare the two methods.

b Think of a third way to choose a sample. Try your method and record the results.

c Compare the three methods of choosing a sample.

Tip

You could talk about advantages and disadvantages. Is one method better than the others? Why?

Fractions

> 7.1 Fractions and recurring decimals

Exercise 7.1

Focus

Key words

equivalent
decimal

improper fraction

mixed number

recurring decimal

terminating
decimal

unit fraction

1 Match each **unit fraction** with the correct **equivalent decimal**.
   Write if the fraction is a **terminating decimal** or a **recurring decimal**.

   One is done for you: $\frac{1}{6} = 0.1\dot{6}$, recurring decimal

$\frac{1}{2}$	$\frac{1}{3}$	$\frac{1}{4}$	$\frac{1}{5}$	$\frac{1}{6}$	$\frac{1}{7}$	$\frac{1}{8}$	$\frac{1}{9}$	$\frac{1}{10}$

$0.1\dot{6}$	0.25	$0.\dot{3}$	0.5	0.2	$0.\dot{1}$	0.1	$0.\dot{1}4285\dot{7}$	0.125

2 Copy and complete the workings to convert each fraction into
   a decimal.
   Write if the fraction is a terminating or recurring decimal.
   The first two have been done for you.

Tip

Remember, you
may need to carry
on the division
for more than two
decimal places.

a $\frac{2}{5}$
$$\begin{array}{r} 0\ .\ 4 \\ 5\overline{)2\ .\ {}^{2}0} \end{array}$$
$\frac{2}{5} = 0.4$
terminating decimal

b $\frac{2}{3}$
$$\begin{array}{r} 0\ .\ 6\ 6\ 6\ \dots \\ 3\overline{)2\ .\ {}^{2}0\ {}^{2}0\ {}^{2}0} \end{array}$$
$\frac{2}{3} = 0.\dot{6}$
recurring decimal

c $\frac{3}{4}$
$$\begin{array}{r} 0\ . \\ 4\overline{)3\ .\ {}^{3}0\ 0} \end{array}$$

d $\frac{3}{5}$
$$\begin{array}{r} 0\ . \\ 5\overline{)3\ .\ {}^{3}0\ 0} \end{array}$$

e $\frac{5}{6}$
$$\begin{array}{r} 0\ . \\ 6\overline{)5\ .\ {}^{5}0\ 0} \end{array}$$

f $\frac{2}{7}$
$$\begin{array}{r} 0\ . \\ 7\overline{)2\ .\ {}^{2}0\ 0} \end{array}$$

g $\frac{3}{8}$
$$\begin{array}{r} 0\ . \\ 8\overline{)3\ .\ {}^{3}0\ 0} \end{array}$$

h $\frac{4}{9}$
$$\begin{array}{r} 0\ . \\ 9\overline{)4\ .\ {}^{4}0\ 0} \end{array}$$

i $\frac{7}{10}$
$$\begin{array}{r} 0\ . \\ 10\overline{)7\ .\ {}^{7}0\ 0} \end{array}$$

j $\frac{2}{11}$
$$\begin{array}{r} 0\ . \\ 11\overline{)2\ .\ {}^{2}0\ 0} \end{array}$$

3   Use your answers to Question **2** to write these fractions in order of size, starting with the smallest.

$\dfrac{7}{10}, \dfrac{3}{5}, \dfrac{3}{8}, \dfrac{4}{9}, \dfrac{2}{11}$

Practice

 4   Here are five fraction cards.

A $\boxed{\dfrac{7}{8}}$ B $\boxed{\dfrac{4}{5}}$ C $\boxed{\dfrac{3}{10}}$ D $\boxed{\dfrac{3}{20}}$ E $\boxed{\dfrac{8}{25}}$

   a   Without doing any calculations, do you think these fractions are terminating or recurring decimals? Explain why.
   b   Use a written method to convert each fraction to a decimal.
   c   Write the fractions in order of size, starting with the smallest.

5   Here are five fraction cards.

A $\boxed{\dfrac{5}{9}}$ B $\boxed{\dfrac{1}{3}}$ C $\boxed{\dfrac{5}{12}}$ D $\boxed{\dfrac{4}{11}}$ E $\boxed{\dfrac{8}{15}}$

   a   Without doing any calculations, do you think these fractions are terminating or recurring decimals? Explain why.
   b   Use a written method to convert each fraction to a decimal.
   c   Write the fractions in order of size, starting with the smallest.

6   Read what Marcus says:

I know that $\dfrac{1}{6}$ and $\dfrac{2}{6}$ are recurring decimals. This means that any fraction with a denominator of 6 is also a recurring decimal.

> **Tip**
>
> Remember, when several digits repeat in a decimal, you only put a dot over the first and last repeating digits, e.g. $\dfrac{1}{7} = 0.\dot{1}4285\dot{7}$

   Is Marcus correct? Explain your answer.

7   Use a calculator to convert each fraction to a decimal.

   a $\dfrac{8}{9}$ b $\dfrac{17}{20}$ c $\dfrac{4}{15}$ d $\dfrac{27}{40}$

8   Use a calculator to convert these fractions to decimals.

   a $\dfrac{6}{7}$ b $\dfrac{11}{13}$ c $\dfrac{5}{21}$

9 This is part of Su's homework.

> *Question*
> *Write these fractions as decimals.*
> i $\frac{7}{24}$ ii $\frac{8}{11}$ iii $\frac{11}{18}$ iv $\frac{5}{39}$
> *Answer*
> i $\frac{7}{24} = 0.29\dot{1}\dot{6}$ ii $\frac{8}{11} = 0.7\dot{2}$ iii $\frac{11}{18} = 0.1\dot{6}$ iv $\frac{5}{39} = 0.128205\dot{1}$

    a   Use a calculator to check Su's homework.

    b   Explain any mistakes she has made and write the correct answers.

 10 Read what Zara says.

I worked out on my calculator that $7 \div 9 = 0.7777777778$. This means that seven ninths is not a recurring decimal as the sevens don't go on for ever: there's an eight on the end.

Do you think Zara is correct?

Explain your answer.

Challenge

11 There are 27 students in a class. 22 of them are right-handed.
What fraction of the students are left-handed?
Write your answer as a decimal.

12 Write these numbers in order of size, starting with the smallest.
$0.56, \frac{4}{7}, 0.6, \frac{7}{13}, 58.2\%, \frac{18}{27}, 55\%, 0.5$

13 Without using a calculator, write each fraction as a decimal.

    a $\frac{5}{3}$ **b** $\frac{13}{4}$ **c** $\frac{29}{9}$ **d** $\frac{35}{8}$

14 Write each length of time, in hours, as

       i   a mixed number   **ii**   a decimal.

    a   3 hours 30 minutes   **b**   2 hour 45 minutes

    c   1 hour 10 minutes   **d**   4 hours 20 minutes

    e   9 hours 12 minutes   **f**   11 hours 25 minutes

> **Tips**
>
> Start by converting the fractions and percentages to decimals.
>
> Change the **improper fractions** into **mixed numbers** first.

15 Read what Arun says.

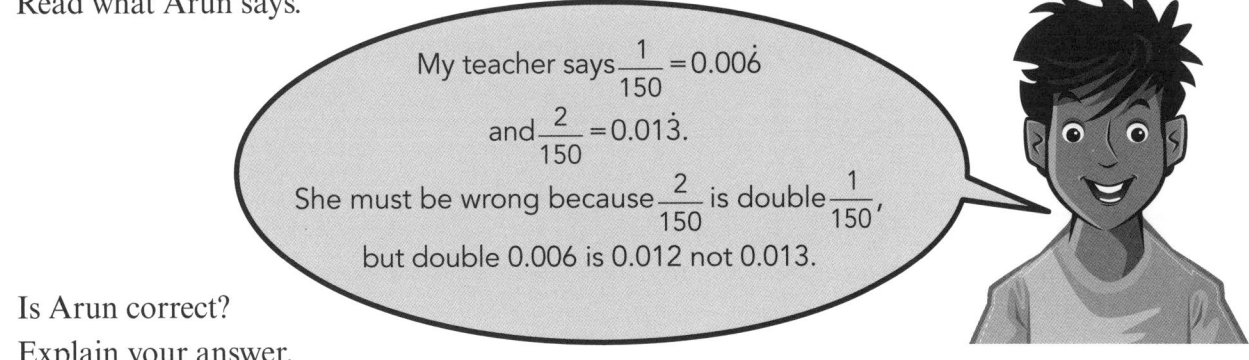

My teacher says $\frac{1}{150} = 0.00\dot{6}$
and $\frac{2}{150} = 0.01\dot{3}$.
She must be wrong because $\frac{2}{150}$ is double $\frac{1}{150}$,
but double 0.006 is 0.012 not 0.013.

Is Arun correct?
Explain your answer.

› 7.2 Ordering fractions

Exercise 7.2

Focus

For questions **1** to **4**, use the common denominator method.

1 Write the correct sign, = or ≠, between each pair of fractions.
They have all been started for you.

a $\frac{13}{4} \square 3\frac{2}{8}$ $\frac{13}{4} = 3\frac{\square}{4} = 3\frac{\square}{8}$

b $\frac{40}{9} \square 4\frac{1}{3}$ $\frac{40}{9} = 4\frac{\square}{9}$ and $4\frac{1}{3} = 4\frac{\square}{9}$

c $-\frac{9}{6} \square -1\frac{1}{2}$ $-\frac{9}{6} = -1\frac{\square}{6} = -1\frac{\square}{\square}$

d $-4\frac{3}{5} \square -\frac{47}{10}$ $-\frac{47}{10} = -4\frac{7}{10}$ and $-4\frac{3}{5} = -4\frac{\square}{10}$

> **Tip**
>
> Change the improper fractions to mixed numbers first, then use a common denominator to compare the fraction parts.

2 Write the correct symbol, < or >, between each pair of fractions.
They have all been started for you.

a $\frac{7}{2} \square 3\frac{3}{4}$ $\frac{7}{2} = 3\frac{1}{2} = 3\frac{\square}{4}$

b $\frac{13}{3} \square 4\frac{1}{6}$ $\frac{13}{3} = 4\frac{\square}{3} = 4\frac{\square}{6}$

c $8\frac{2}{5} \square \frac{83}{10}$ $\frac{83}{10} = 8\frac{\square}{10}$ and $8\frac{2}{5} = 8\frac{\square}{10}$

d $\frac{22}{3} \square 7\frac{2}{5}$ $\frac{22}{3} = \square\frac{\square}{3} = \square\frac{\square}{15}$ and $7\frac{2}{5} = 7\frac{\square}{15}$

> **Tip**
>
> Use the same method as in Question **1**.

3 Write the correct symbol, < or >, between each pair of fractions.
They have all been started for you. Use the number lines to help.

a $-\dfrac{5}{4}\,\square\,-1\dfrac{1}{2}$ $-\dfrac{5}{4}=-1\dfrac{\square}{4}$ and $-1\dfrac{1}{2}=-1\dfrac{\square}{4}$

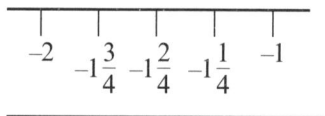

b $-\dfrac{8}{3}\,\square\,-2\dfrac{5}{6}$ $-\dfrac{8}{3}=-2\dfrac{\square}{3}=-2\dfrac{\square}{6}$

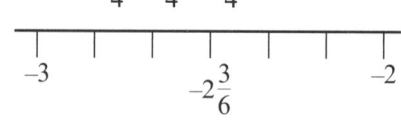

c $-\dfrac{27}{5}\,\square\,-5\dfrac{4}{15}$ $-\dfrac{27}{5}=-5\dfrac{\square}{5}=-5\dfrac{\square}{15}$

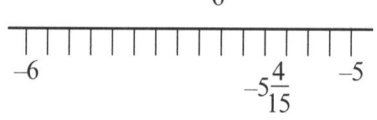

d $-\dfrac{17}{6}\,\square\,-2\dfrac{3}{4}$ $-\dfrac{17}{6}=-2\dfrac{\square}{6}=-2\dfrac{\square}{12}$ and $-2\dfrac{3}{4}=-2\dfrac{\square}{12}$

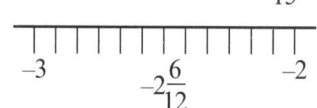

4 Work out which is larger.

a $-\dfrac{11}{4}$ or $-2\dfrac{5}{8}$ **b** $-\dfrac{23}{10}$ or $-2\dfrac{2}{5}$ **c** $-7\dfrac{3}{4}$ or $-\dfrac{23}{3}$

5 a Complete the workings to write each fraction as a decimal.
Work out the **first four** decimal places.

i $-\dfrac{17}{7}=-2\dfrac{3}{7}$

$$7\,\overline{)\,3\,.\,{}^30\ \ {}^20\ \ {}^60\ \ 0\ }^{0\ .\ 4\ \ 2}$$

$\dfrac{3}{7}=0.42\,\square$ $-2\dfrac{3}{7}=-2.42\,\square$

ii $-\dfrac{22}{9}=-2\dfrac{4}{9}$

$$9\,\overline{)\,4\,.\,{}^40\ \ {}^40\ \ 0\ \ 0\ }^{0\ .\ 4}$$

$\dfrac{4}{9}=\square$ $-2\dfrac{4}{9}=\square$

iii $-\dfrac{27}{11}=-2\dfrac{5}{11}$

$$11\,\overline{)\,5\,.\,{}^50\ \ {}^60\ \ 0\ \ 0\ }^{0\ .\ 4}$$

$\dfrac{5}{11}=\square$ $-2\dfrac{5}{11}=\square$

b Write the fractions $-\dfrac{17}{7}$, $-\dfrac{22}{9}$ and $-\dfrac{27}{11}$ in order of size, starting with the smallest.

Practice

6 Write the missing word from each of these sentences.
Use either the word 'larger' or 'smaller'.

a When you compare two fractions with the same denominator, the larger the numerator the .... the fraction.

b When you compare two fractions with the same numerator, the larger the denominator the .... the fraction.

7 Write the correct symbol, < or >, between each pair of fractions.

   a $\dfrac{2}{9} \square \dfrac{7}{9}$ **b** $\dfrac{15}{8} \square \dfrac{19}{8}$ **c** $\dfrac{7}{11} \square \dfrac{7}{13}$ **d** $\dfrac{4}{5} \square \dfrac{4}{3}$

8 Put these fraction cards in order of size, starting with the smallest.

   A $\boxed{-4\dfrac{1}{5}}$ **B** $\boxed{-\dfrac{14}{3}}$ **C** $\boxed{-\dfrac{22}{5}}$ **D** $\boxed{-4\dfrac{1}{3}}$

9 Three friends sat a Spanish test on the same day.

Amina scored $\dfrac{18}{25}$, Ben scored $\dfrac{37}{50}$, and Cynthia scored 73%.

Who had the highest percentage score?

> **Tip**
>
> Change the fractions into percentages by writing equivalent fractions with a denominator of 100.

10 Two swimming clubs compare the percentage of girl members.

In the Dolphins club, 42 out of 60 members are girls.

In the Seals club, 68% of members are girls.

Which club has the higher percentage of girl members?

Show how you worked out your answer.

Challenge

11 Write these fractions in order of size, starting with the smallest.

   $-\dfrac{49}{6}$ $-\dfrac{61}{7}$ $-8\dfrac{7}{8}$ $-\dfrac{107}{12}$

> **Tip**
>
> Use the division method.

12 One day, a baker sells 87% of his loaves of bread.

The following day, he sells 30 out of 34 loaves.

Use a calculator to work out on which day he sold the greater percentage of bread loaves.

13 In a drugs trial, two different drugs are tested on some patients.

145 patients are given drug A, and it helps 112 of them.

180 patients are given drug B, and it helps 137 of them.

Use a calculator to work out which drug helped the greater percentage of patients.

14 Arun has three fraction cards. He puts them in order, starting with the smallest.

   $\boxed{-\dfrac{8}{9}}$ $\boxed{-\dfrac{29}{36}}$ $\boxed{-\dfrac{13}{18}}$

> I think that on a number line $-\dfrac{29}{36}$ is exactly halfway between $-\dfrac{8}{9}$ and $-\dfrac{13}{18}$

Read what Arun says.

   a Is Arun correct?
Explain your answer.

   b On a number line, work out which fraction is exactly halfway between $-1\dfrac{3}{4}$ and $-\dfrac{11}{6}$.

> 7.3 Subtracting mixed numbers

Exercise 7.3

Focus

1 Copy and complete the steps in each subtraction.

a $4\frac{2}{3} - 3\frac{1}{3}$

$\dfrac{14}{3} - \dfrac{10}{3}$

$\dfrac{14}{3} - \dfrac{10}{3} = \dfrac{\square}{3}$

$\dfrac{\square}{3} = 1\dfrac{\square}{3}$

b $3\frac{2}{9} - 1\frac{7}{9}$

$\dfrac{29}{9} - \dfrac{16}{9}$

$\dfrac{29}{9} - \dfrac{16}{9} = \dfrac{\square}{9}$

$\dfrac{\square}{9} = 1\dfrac{\square}{9}$

c $7\frac{1}{5} - 5\frac{2}{5}$

$\dfrac{\square}{5} - \dfrac{\square}{5}$

$\dfrac{\square}{5} - \dfrac{\square}{5} = \dfrac{\square}{5}$

$\dfrac{\square}{5} = 1\dfrac{\square}{5}$

d $5\frac{3}{7} - 2\frac{6}{7}$

$\dfrac{\square}{7} - \dfrac{\square}{7}$

$\dfrac{\square}{7} - \dfrac{\square}{7} = \dfrac{\square}{7}$

$\dfrac{\square}{7} = 2\dfrac{\square}{7}$

2 Work out these subtractions. Show all the steps in your working.

a $2\frac{3}{5} - 1\frac{1}{5}$ **b** $4\frac{3}{11} - 2\frac{7}{11}$ **c** $3\frac{2}{7} - 1\frac{4}{7}$ **d** $6\frac{1}{9} - 3\frac{2}{9}$

3 Copy and complete each subtraction.

a $4\frac{1}{2} - 2\frac{3}{4}$

$\dfrac{9}{2} - \dfrac{11}{4}$

$\dfrac{18}{4} - \dfrac{11}{4} = \dfrac{\square}{4}$

$\dfrac{\square}{4} = 1\dfrac{\square}{4}$

b $3\frac{1}{8} - 1\frac{1}{4}$

$\dfrac{\square}{8} - \dfrac{5}{4}$

$\dfrac{\square}{8} - \dfrac{10}{8} = \dfrac{\square}{8}$

$\dfrac{\square}{8} = 1\dfrac{\square}{8}$

c $5\frac{3}{5} - 2\frac{3}{10}$

$\dfrac{28}{5} - \dfrac{\square}{10}$

$\dfrac{56}{10} - \dfrac{\square}{10} = \dfrac{\square}{10}$

$\dfrac{\square}{10} = 3\dfrac{\square}{10}$

d $6\frac{1}{3} - 2\frac{1}{6}$

$\dfrac{\square}{3} - \dfrac{\square}{6}$

$\dfrac{\square}{6} - \dfrac{\square}{6} = \dfrac{\square}{6}$

$\dfrac{\square}{6} = 4\dfrac{\square}{6}$

4 Work out these subtractions. Show all the steps in your working.

a $5\frac{5}{6}-\frac{11}{12}$ b $4\frac{3}{4}-1\frac{15}{16}$ c $10\frac{3}{10}-8\frac{4}{5}$ d $6\frac{1}{4}-3\frac{5}{12}$

5 One of these cards gives a different answer to the other two.

A $\boxed{4\frac{19}{20}-2\frac{7}{10}}$ B $\boxed{5\frac{14}{15}-3\frac{3}{5}}$ C $\boxed{5\frac{4}{7}-3\frac{5}{21}}$

Which one is it? Show all your working.

Practice

6 Bim and Yolander have been out for a training run.

Bim ran for $8\frac{5}{8}$ kilometres. Yolander ran for $10\frac{3}{4}$ kilometres.

a estimate, then b calculate, the answers to these questions.

   i What is the difference between the distances run by Bim and Yolander?

   ii How far in total did Bim and Yolander run?

7 Silvie has a piece of wood $4\frac{1}{8}$ m long.

She wants to make some shelves.

She cuts two pieces of wood, each $1\frac{3}{4}$ m long, from the piece she has.

How long is the piece of wood Silvie has left?

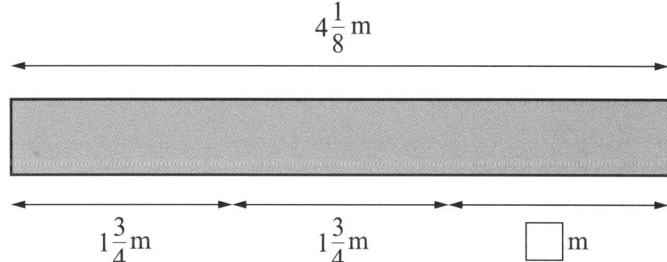

8 Copy and complete this subtraction.

$8\frac{1}{4}-3\frac{9}{10}$

Step 1: $\frac{33}{4}-\frac{39}{10}$

Step 2: $\frac{33}{4}-\frac{39}{10}=\frac{\square}{20}-\frac{\square}{20}=\frac{\square}{20}$

Step 3: $\frac{\square}{20}=\square\frac{\square}{20}$

9 Work out these subtractions. Show all the steps in your working.

a $7\frac{1}{2}-3\frac{3}{5}$ b $5\frac{2}{9}-3\frac{5}{6}$ c $4\frac{3}{4}-1\frac{5}{6}$ d $10\frac{1}{8}-5\frac{2}{10}$

10 Xao is a plumber.

He has two pieces of pipe.

The first piece is $3\frac{2}{5}$ m long; the second is

$4\frac{3}{4}$ m long.

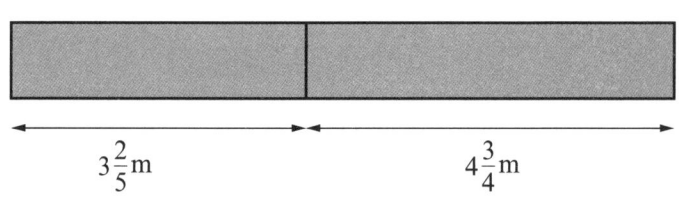

$3\frac{2}{5}$ m $4\frac{3}{4}$ m

He fixes them together, as shown in the diagram.

a   **i**   estimate, then

     ii   calculate the total length of the two pipes.

Xao wants a pipe that is $10\frac{1}{4}$ m long.

b   How much more pipe does he need?

 11 The table shows the distances that Nia drives on Monday to Friday one week.

Day	Monday	Tuesday	Wednesday	Thursday	Friday
Distance (km)	$126\frac{1}{2}$	$187\frac{3}{4}$	$105\frac{3}{8}$	$95\frac{7}{10}$	$157\frac{1}{4}$

Nia works out that the **range** of the distances she travels is $91\frac{19}{20}$ km.

Is Nia correct? Explain your answer.

Show all your working.

Challenge

 12 This is part of Beth's homework. She has made a mistake in her solution.

> <u>Question</u>
> Work out $3\frac{4}{9} - 1\frac{3}{4}$
> <u>Answer</u>
> $3\frac{4}{9} = 3\frac{16}{36}$ and $1\frac{3}{4} = 1\frac{27}{36}$
> $3\frac{16}{36} - 1\frac{27}{36} = 2\frac{11}{36}$

a   Explain the mistake Beth has made.

b   Work out the correct answer.

13 The diagram shows two statues. Each statue is made from three parts.
    The height of each part, in metres, is shown.

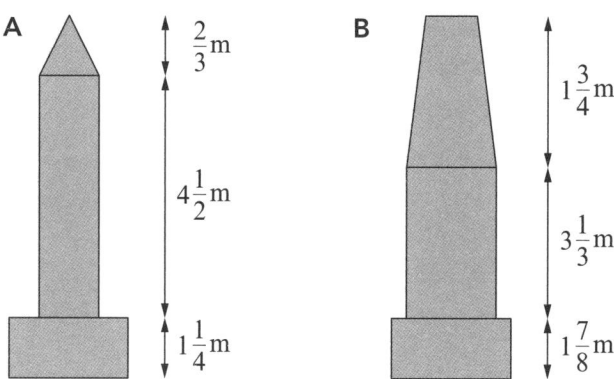

A
$\frac{2}{3}$ m

$4\frac{1}{2}$ m

$1\frac{1}{4}$ m

B
$1\frac{3}{4}$ m

$3\frac{1}{3}$ m

$1\frac{7}{8}$ m

a   Which statue is taller? Show your working.

b   What is the difference in height between the two statues?

14 The area of this compound shape is $15\frac{2}{3}$ m².

    The area of one rectangle is $9\frac{4}{7}$ m².

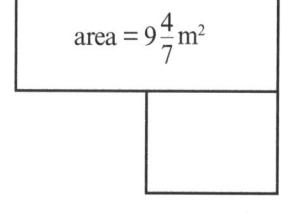

area = $9\frac{4}{7}$ m²

    a   estimate, then   b   calculate the area of the other rectangle.

15 Read what Arun says.

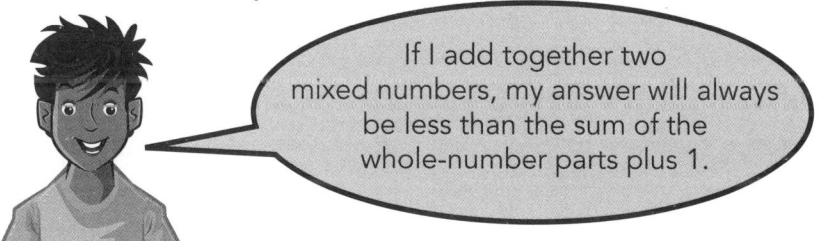

If I add together two mixed numbers, my answer will always be less than the sum of the whole-number parts plus 1.

Tip

A counter-example is any example that shows a statement is false.

    Use at least two **counter-examples** to show that Arun's statement is not true.

16 The diagram shows four mixed numbers **linked** by lines.

    a   Work out the total of any two of the linked mixed numbers.

    b   Without working out all the answers, explain how you can decide which two mixed numbers give the greatest total?

        What is this total? Write your answer in its simplest form.

    c   Work out the difference between any two of the linked mixed numbers.

    d   Without working out all the answers, explain how you can decide which two mixed numbers give the smallest difference?

        What is this difference? Write your answer in its simplest form.

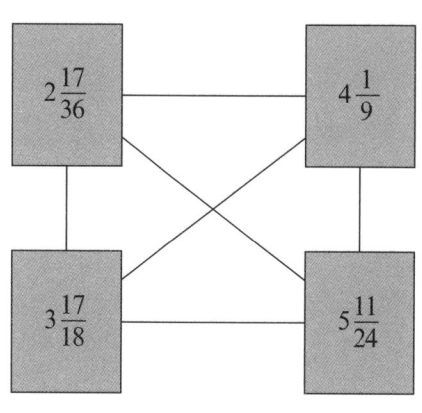

$2\frac{17}{36}$

$4\frac{1}{9}$

$3\frac{17}{18}$

$5\frac{11}{24}$

> 7.4 Multiplying an integer by a mixed number

Exercise 7.4

Focus

1 Copy and complete each multiplication.

a $2\frac{1}{2} \times 6 = 2 \times 6 + \frac{1}{2} \times 6$

$= \boxed{} + 3$

$= \boxed{}$

b $3\frac{1}{4} \times 8 = 3 \times 8 + \frac{1}{4} \times 8$

$= \boxed{} + \boxed{}$

$= \boxed{}$

c $5\frac{1}{3} \times 9 = 5 \times 9 + \frac{1}{3} \times 9$

$= \boxed{} + \boxed{}$

$= \boxed{}$

d $4\frac{1}{5} \times 15 = 4 \times 15 + \frac{1}{5} \times 15$

$= \boxed{} + \boxed{}$

$= \boxed{}$

2 This rectangle has a length of $12\,\text{m}$ and a width of $2\frac{1}{4}\,\text{m}$.

$2\frac{1}{4}\,\text{m}$

$12\,\text{m}$

Work out

a   an estimate for the area of the rectangle

b   the accurate area of the rectangle.

3 Copy and complete each multiplication.

a $3\frac{2}{3} \times 12 = 3 \times 12 + \frac{2}{3} \times 12$

$= \boxed{} + 8$

$= \boxed{}$

b $2\frac{3}{4} \times 8 = 2 \times 8 + \frac{3}{4} \times 8$

$= \boxed{} + \boxed{}$

$= \boxed{}$

c $3\frac{2}{5} \times 10 = 3 \times 10 + \frac{2}{5} \times 10$

$= \boxed{} + \boxed{}$

$= \boxed{}$

d $1\frac{5}{6} \times 18 = 1 \times 18 + \frac{5}{6} \times 18$

$= \boxed{} + \boxed{}$

$= \boxed{}$

4 Archie uses this formula in a science lesson.

$F = m \times a$

a Estimate the value of F when $m = 21$ and $a = 3\frac{2}{3}$.

When $m = 21$ and $a = 3\frac{2}{3}$, Archie works out that $F = 77$.

b **i** Use your answer to part **a** to help you decide if Archie could be correct.

ii Work out the value of F to help you decide if Archie is correct.

5 Copy and complete each multiplication.

a $3\frac{1}{2} \times 7 = 3 \times 7 + \frac{1}{2} \times 7$

$= \boxed{} + \frac{7}{2}$

$= \boxed{} + 3\frac{1}{2}$

$= \boxed{}\frac{\boxed{}}{\boxed{}}$

b $4\frac{1}{4} \times 9 = 4 \times 9 + \frac{1}{4} \times 9$

$= \boxed{} + \frac{9}{4}$

$= \boxed{} + 2\frac{\boxed{}}{4}$

$= \boxed{}\frac{\boxed{}}{\boxed{}}$

c $6\frac{2}{3} \times 5 = 6 \times 5 + \frac{2}{3} \times 5$

$= \boxed{} + \frac{\boxed{}}{\boxed{}}$

$= \boxed{} + \boxed{}\frac{\boxed{}}{\boxed{}}$

$= \boxed{}\frac{\boxed{}}{\boxed{}}$

d $4\frac{3}{5} \times 8 = 4 \times 8 + \frac{3}{5} \times 8$

$= \boxed{} + \frac{\boxed{}}{\boxed{}}$

$= \boxed{} + \boxed{}\frac{\boxed{}}{\boxed{}}$

$= \boxed{}\frac{\boxed{}}{\boxed{}}$

Practice

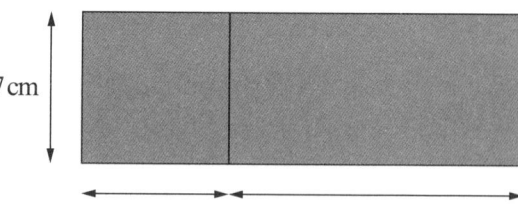

7 cm

7 cm

$11\frac{3}{4}$ cm

6 The diagram shows a square joined to a rectangle.

Show that the total area of the shape is $131\frac{1}{4}$ cm².

7 Rosa buys carpet for her bedroom floor.

The floor is a rectangle with length $4\frac{5}{8}$ m and width 3 m.

a Rosa estimates that the area of her bedroom floor is 12 m².
Is Rosa correct? Explain your answer.

b Work out the area of her bedroom floor.

Rosa buys carpet that costs $15 per square metre.

She can only buy a whole number of square metres.

Rosa works out that the carpet will cost her more than $200.

c Is Rosa correct? Explain your answer.

8 Which is greater, $3\frac{2}{3} \times 25$ or $4\frac{2}{5} \times 21$?

Show all your working.

9 Write these cards in order of size, starting with the smallest.

A $\boxed{8 \times 4\frac{5}{6}}$ B $\boxed{12 \times 3\frac{1}{5}}$ C $\boxed{5 \times 7\frac{5}{7}}$

10 For each of these calculations, work out

    i an estimate   **ii** the accurate answer.

Write each answer in its simplest form.

a $2\frac{5}{8} \times 12$ **b** $6\frac{3}{4} \times 10$ **c** $3\frac{1}{12} \times 15$

Challenge

11 Alec works in a factory. His job is to pack boxes.

It takes him $3\frac{3}{4}$ minutes to pack one box.

How long will it take him to pack 60 boxes?
Give your answer in hours and minutes.

12   Work out
   a   an estimate for the area of the grey section of this rectangle
   b   the accurate area of the grey section of this rectangle.

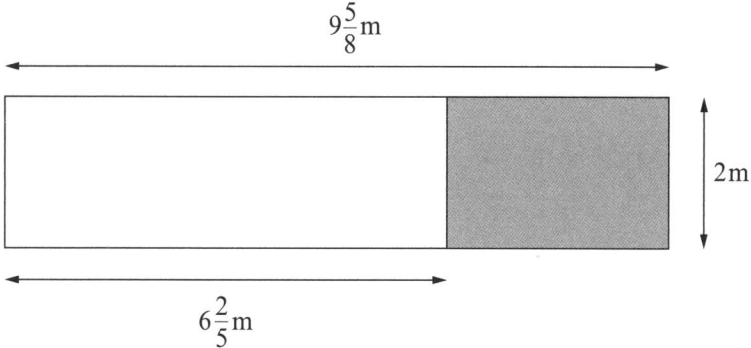

13   a   Work out the value of each of these cards.
         Write each answer in its simplest form.

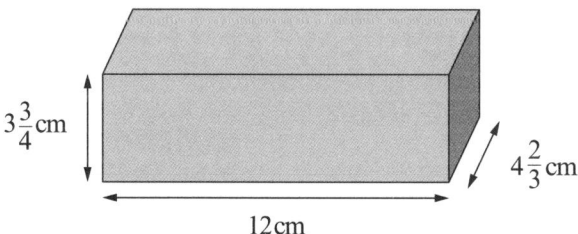

   b   Write down the **median** value.
   c   Work out the range of the values.

14   The diagram shows a cuboid.

> **Tip**
>
> Remember, the median is the middle value when the numbers are arranged in order of size.

The length, width and height of the cuboid are shown on the diagram.
   a   Estimate the volume of the cuboid.
   b   Raj works out that the volume of the cuboid is 210 cm³.
       Is Raj correct? Show your working.

15 a This is part of Helena's homework.

> <u>Question</u>
> x is an integer. Work out the value of x when $x \times 5\frac{4}{9} = 65\frac{1}{3}$
>
> <u>Answer</u>
> Try $x = 10$ $10 \times 5\frac{4}{9} = 10 \times 5 + 10 \times \frac{4}{9} = 50 + \frac{40}{9} = 50 + 4\frac{4}{9} = 54\frac{4}{9}$
>
> $54\frac{4}{9} < 65\frac{1}{3}$ so try a bigger value for x
>
> Try $x = 14$ $14 \times 5\frac{4}{9} = 14 \times 5 + 14 \times \frac{4}{9} = 70 + \frac{56}{9} = 70 + 6\frac{2}{9} = 76\frac{2}{9}$
>
> $76\frac{2}{9} > 65\frac{1}{3}$ so try a smaller value for x

        Carry on with Helena's homework to find the correct value for x.

b y is an integer.

        Use the same method as Helena to work out the value of y when $y \times 7\frac{5}{8} = 99\frac{1}{8}$

> 7.5 Dividing an integer by a fraction

Exercise 7.5

Focus

Key word
reciprocal

1 a Work out the answer to each calculation. Use the diagrams to help you.

    i $1 \div \frac{1}{2}$ **ii** $2 \div \frac{1}{2}$

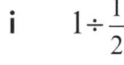

    iii $3 \div \frac{1}{2}$ **iv** $4 \div \frac{1}{2}$

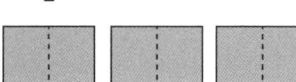
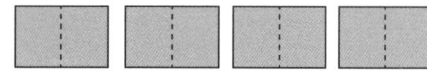

b Write the answers to

   i $\quad 5 \div \dfrac{1}{2}$ **ii** $\quad 6 \div \dfrac{1}{2}$

   iii $\quad 7 \div \dfrac{1}{2}$ **iv** $\quad 8 \div \dfrac{1}{2}$

2 a Work out the answer to each calculation. Use the diagrams to help you.

   i $\quad 1 \div \dfrac{1}{3}$ **ii** $\quad 2 \div \dfrac{1}{3}$

   iii $\quad 3 \div \dfrac{1}{3}$ **iv** $\quad 4 \div \dfrac{1}{3}$

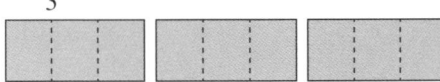 

b Write the answers to

   i $\quad 5 \div \dfrac{1}{3}$ **ii** $\quad 6 \div \dfrac{1}{3}$ **iii** $\quad 7 \div \dfrac{1}{3}$ **iv** $\quad 8 \div \dfrac{1}{3}$

3 a Work out the answer to each calculation. Use the diagrams to help you.

   i $\quad 1 \div \dfrac{1}{4}$ **ii** $\quad 2 \div \dfrac{1}{4}$

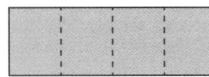 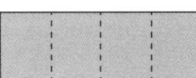

b Write the answers to

   i $\quad 3 \div \dfrac{1}{4}$ **ii** $\quad 4 \div \dfrac{1}{4}$

   iii $\quad 7 \div \dfrac{1}{4}$ **iv** $\quad 10 \div \dfrac{1}{4}$

4 Work out the answer to each calculation. Draw diagrams to help if you want to.

   a $\quad 1 \div \dfrac{1}{5}$ **b** $\quad 3 \div \dfrac{1}{6}$ **c** $\quad 2 \div \dfrac{1}{8}$

5 This is what Sofia says about dividing an integer by a unit fraction.

> The quick way to divide an integer by a unit fraction is to multiply the integer by the denominator of the fraction.

Use Sofia's method to work out

   a $\quad 11 \div \dfrac{1}{2}$ **b** $\quad 20 \div \dfrac{1}{5}$ **c** $\quad 12 \div \dfrac{1}{9}$

Practice

6 Work out the answer to each calculation. Use the diagrams to help you.

a $2 \div \frac{2}{3}$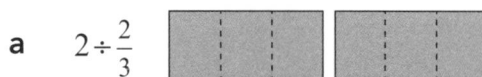

b $2 \div \frac{2}{5}$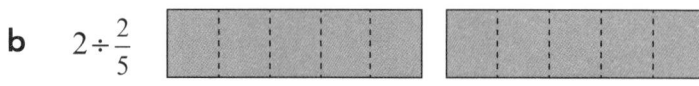

c $3 \div \frac{3}{4}$

> **Tip**
>
> Think of the questions as
>
> 'How many $\frac{2}{3}$ are in 2?'
>
> 'How many $\frac{2}{5}$ are in 2?'
>
> 'How many $\frac{3}{4}$ are in 3?'

7 Work out the answer to each calculation.
Use the **reciprocal** method.
The first two have been started for you.

a $8 \div \frac{3}{5} = 8 \times \frac{5}{3} = \frac{40}{3} = \square \frac{\square}{\square}$

b $7 \div \frac{3}{4} = 7 \times \frac{4}{3} = \frac{\square}{\square} = \square \frac{\square}{\square}$

c $9 \div \frac{4}{7}$

d $12 \div \frac{5}{8}$

e $6 \div \frac{7}{9}$

8 Work out the answer to each calculation.
Give each answer as a mixed number in its lowest terms.

a $4 \div \frac{2}{7}$

b $3 \div \frac{9}{10}$

c $10 \div \frac{4}{5}$

d $8 \div \frac{14}{15}$

9 The area of a rectangle is $18\,\text{m}^2$.

The width of the rectangle is $\frac{4}{5}\,\text{m}$.

What is the length of the rectangle?

Give your answer as a mixed number in its lowest terms.

> **Tip**
>
> length =
> area ÷ width

10 Jaq uses this formula in a science lesson.

$$s = u \times t$$

a Work out the value of s when $u = \frac{3}{5}$ and $t = 12$.

b Work out the value of t when $s = 22$ and $u = \frac{4}{9}$.

> **Tip**
>
> Rearrange the
> formula $s = u \times t$ to
> get $t = \square$

Challenge

11 Which of these two calculation cards gives the greater answer?

A $25 \div \dfrac{6}{7}$ B $25 \div \dfrac{3}{8}$

Explain how you made your decision.

12 Which of these two calculation cards gives the smaller answer?

A $32 \div \dfrac{13}{15}$ B $35 \div \dfrac{13}{15}$

Explain how you made your decision.

13 The answers to these three calculation cards are the first three terms in a sequence.

$2 \div \dfrac{12}{31}$ $3 \div \dfrac{6}{11}$ $5 \div \dfrac{6}{7}$

Work out

a the first term of the sequence

b the term-to-term rule of the sequence

c the next three terms in the sequence

d the 10th term in the sequence.

14 A straight line graph has the equation $y = \dfrac{3}{4}x$

a Copy and complete this table of values.

x	0	2	4	6	8
y					

b Draw a coordinate grid going from 0 to 8 on the x-axis and on the y-axis.

Plot the points from the table above. Draw the line $y = \dfrac{3}{4}x$ from $x = 0$ to $x = 8$.

> **Tip**
>
> Remember,
> $y = \dfrac{3}{4}x$ means
> $y = \dfrac{3}{4} \times x$, so you
> need to work out
> $\dfrac{3}{4} \times 0$, $\dfrac{3}{4} \times 2$, etc.

15   The diagram shows a triangle.

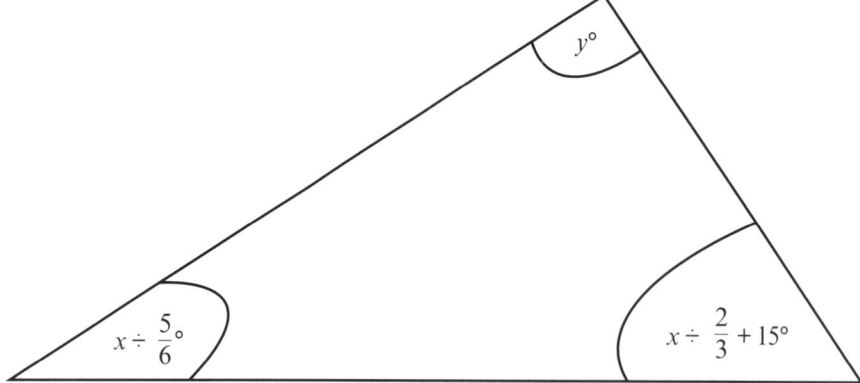

   a   Work out the value of y when $x = 30°$
   b   Work out the value of y when $x = 43°$
   c   Explain why it is not possible for x to be 65°.

> 7.6 Making fraction calculations easier

Exercise 7.6

Focus

In this exercise, work out as many of the answers as you can mentally.
Write each answer in its simplest form and as a mixed number when appropriate.

1   Work out each addition.

   Some working has been shown to help you.

   a $\dfrac{1}{5} + \dfrac{1}{10} = \dfrac{2}{10} + \dfrac{1}{10} = \dfrac{\square}{10}$

   b $\dfrac{1}{9} + \dfrac{1}{3} = \dfrac{1}{9} + \dfrac{\square}{9} = \dfrac{\square}{9}$

   c $\dfrac{1}{8} + \dfrac{3}{4} = \dfrac{1}{8} + \dfrac{\square}{8} = \dfrac{\square}{\square}$

   d $\dfrac{1}{4} + \dfrac{1}{12} = \dfrac{\square}{12} + \dfrac{1}{12} = \dfrac{\square}{12} = \dfrac{\square}{\square}$

2 Work out each subtraction.
Some working has been shown to help you.

a $\dfrac{1}{3}-\dfrac{1}{6}=\dfrac{2}{6}-\dfrac{1}{6}=\dfrac{\Box}{6}$

b $\dfrac{1}{4}-\dfrac{1}{8}=\dfrac{\Box}{8}-\dfrac{1}{8}=\dfrac{\Box}{8}$

c $\dfrac{2}{3}-\dfrac{1}{9}=\dfrac{\Box}{9}-\dfrac{1}{9}=\dfrac{\Box}{\Box}$

d $\dfrac{7}{10}-\dfrac{1}{5}=\dfrac{7}{10}-\dfrac{\Box}{10}=\dfrac{\Box}{\Box}=\dfrac{\Box}{\Box}$

3 Work out each addition.
Some working has been shown to help you.

a $\dfrac{1}{2}+\dfrac{1}{5}=\dfrac{1\times5+1\times2}{2\times5}=\dfrac{5+2}{10}=\dfrac{\Box}{10}$

b $\dfrac{1}{3}+\dfrac{1}{7}=\dfrac{1\times7+1\times3}{3\times7}=\dfrac{\Box+\Box}{21}=\dfrac{\Box}{21}$

c $\dfrac{2}{3}+\dfrac{1}{4}=\dfrac{2\times4+1\times3}{3\times4}=\dfrac{\Box+\Box}{12}=\dfrac{\Box}{12}$

d $\dfrac{1}{6}+\dfrac{3}{5}=\dfrac{1\times5+3\times6}{6\times5}=\dfrac{\Box+\Box}{\Box}=\dfrac{\Box}{\Box}$

4 Work out each subtraction.
Some working has been shown to help you.

a $\dfrac{1}{2}-\dfrac{1}{7}=\dfrac{1\times7-1\times2}{2\times7}=\dfrac{7-2}{14}=\dfrac{\Box}{14}$

b $\dfrac{2}{3}-\dfrac{1}{5}=\dfrac{2\times5-1\times3}{3\times5}=\dfrac{\Box-\Box}{15}=\dfrac{\Box}{15}$

c $\dfrac{3}{5}-\dfrac{2}{7}=\dfrac{3\times7-2\times5}{5\times7}=\dfrac{\Box-\Box}{35}=\dfrac{\Box}{35}$

d $\dfrac{5}{6}-\dfrac{3}{5}=\dfrac{5\times5-3\times6}{6\times5}=\dfrac{\Box-\Box}{\Box}=\dfrac{\Box}{\Box}$

5 In a tennis club, $\dfrac{1}{3}$ of the members are women,
$\dfrac{2}{5}$ of the members are men and the rest are children.
What fraction of the members are children?

> **Tip**
>
> Work out $\dfrac{1}{3}+\dfrac{2}{5}$ first, then subtract your answer from 1. Remember, $1=\dfrac{15}{15}$.

Practice

6 Work out these additions and subtractions.
Use the same method as in Questions **1** and **2**.

a $\dfrac{1}{2}+\dfrac{1}{4}$
    b $\dfrac{1}{4}+\dfrac{3}{8}$
    c $\dfrac{4}{5}+\dfrac{1}{10}$
    d $\dfrac{1}{3}+\dfrac{4}{9}$

e $\dfrac{1}{4}+\dfrac{7}{12}$
    f $\dfrac{2}{15}+\dfrac{2}{5}$
    g $\dfrac{2}{3}-\dfrac{1}{9}$
    h $\dfrac{3}{4}-\dfrac{1}{8}$

i $\dfrac{1}{5}-\dfrac{1}{20}$
    j $\dfrac{2}{5}-\dfrac{1}{10}$
    k $\dfrac{7}{9}-\dfrac{1}{3}$
    l $\dfrac{11}{15}-\dfrac{3}{5}$

7 Work out these additions and subtractions.

Use the same method as in Questions **3** and **4**.

a $\dfrac{1}{4}+\dfrac{1}{5}$ **b** $\dfrac{1}{3}+\dfrac{1}{8}$ **c** $\dfrac{1}{9}+\dfrac{1}{5}$ **d** $\dfrac{1}{4}+\dfrac{2}{9}$

e $\dfrac{5}{11}+\dfrac{1}{2}$ **f** $\dfrac{2}{9}+\dfrac{3}{4}$ **g** $\dfrac{1}{2}-\dfrac{1}{5}$ **h** $\dfrac{3}{5}-\dfrac{1}{4}$

i $\dfrac{6}{7}-\dfrac{1}{3}$ **j** $\dfrac{3}{4}-\dfrac{2}{5}$ **k** $\dfrac{7}{11}-\dfrac{2}{5}$ **l** $\dfrac{7}{9}-\dfrac{2}{7}$

8 In a bag of mixed fruits, $\dfrac{2}{7}$ are lemons, $\dfrac{3}{8}$ are strawberries and the rest are bananas.

What fraction of the fruits in the bag are bananas?

9 **a** Work out.

Some working has been shown to help you with the first two.

i $6\div\dfrac{3}{4}=6\times4\div3=\square$ **ii** $9\div\dfrac{3}{5}=9\times5\div3=\square$ **iii** $7\div\dfrac{1}{2}$

iv $8\div\dfrac{2}{7}$ **v** $12\div\dfrac{3}{5}$ **vi** $20\div\dfrac{4}{5}$

b Use a calculator to check your answers to part **a**.

c Did you get the answers to part **a** correct? If not, what mistakes did you make?

10 The diagram shows a rectangle.

The area of the rectangle is $15\,\text{m}^2$.

The width of the rectangle is $\dfrac{5}{8}\,\text{m}$.

What is the length of the rectangle?

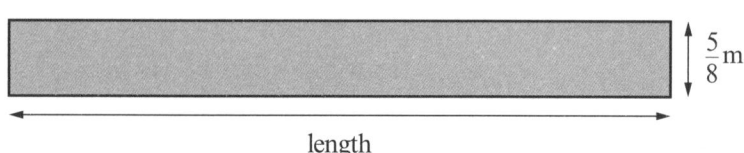

$\dfrac{5}{8}\,\text{m}$

length

Challenge

 11 This is how Arun mentally works out $14\div\left(\dfrac{7}{10}-\dfrac{1}{2}\right)$

> First, I work out $\dfrac{7}{10}-\dfrac{1}{2}$ which equals $\dfrac{1}{5}$
>
> Then I work out $14\div\dfrac{1}{5}$, which equals $\dfrac{14}{5}=2\dfrac{4}{5}$

a Explain the mistake Arun has made.

b Work out the correct answer.

12 Work out.

If you cannot do a calculation mentally, write down some workings to help you.

Tip

Remember the correct order of operations: brackets, indices, division and multiplication, addition and subtraction

a $\quad 10 \times \left(\dfrac{4}{5} - \dfrac{1}{5} \right)$

b $\quad 3 \div \left(\dfrac{1}{6} + \dfrac{1}{6} \right)$

c $\quad \dfrac{14}{15} - \left(\dfrac{3}{5} - \dfrac{1}{3} \right)$

d $\quad \dfrac{7}{12} - \left(\dfrac{1}{4} + \dfrac{1}{3} \right)$

13 Here are two calculation cards.

A $\quad \left(\dfrac{1}{3} + \dfrac{1}{6} \right) \times \left(\dfrac{5}{8} - \dfrac{3}{8} \right)$

B $\quad \left(3\dfrac{1}{4} + 2\dfrac{3}{4} \right) \div \left(\dfrac{2}{7} + \dfrac{3}{14} \right)$

Read what Sofia says.

The answer to card **B** divided by the answer to card **A** is 96.

Is Sofia correct?

Show all your working.

14 Here are three formula cards.

$$b = \dfrac{18}{a}$$

$$c = b \times \left(2\dfrac{1}{3} - 1\dfrac{5}{6} \right)$$

$$d = 3 \left(c - 11\dfrac{3}{4} \right)$$

Work out the value of d when $a = \dfrac{2}{3}$

Explain the method you used.

8 > Shapes and symmetry

> 8.1 Quadrilaterals and polygons

Remember

The number of sides of a **regular polygon** is equal to the number of **lines of symmetry**.

The number of sides of a regular polygon is equal to the order of **rotational symmetry**.

Key words

hierarchy
lines of symmetry
quadrilateral
regular polygon
rotational symmetry

Exercise 8.1

Focus

1   For each regular polygon, give the correct name and number of sides.
    The first one is done for you.

    a 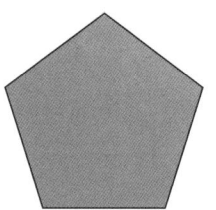   b 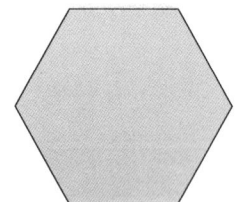   c    d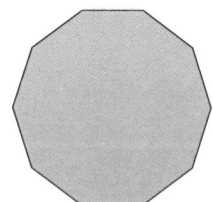

    pentagon, 5 sides

2   Look at square *ABCD*.

    Copy and complete these sentences using the options in the box.

    | *BC* | length | *DC* | 90 |

    a   All sides are the same ....

    b   *AB* is parallel to .... and *AD* is
        parallel to ....

    c   All the angles are ....°.

    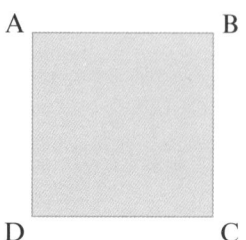

3 Look at rectangle *EFGH*.

Copy and complete these sentences using the options in the box.

| HG | opposite | 90 | FG |

a .... sides are the same length.

b *EH* is parallel to .... and *EF* is
parallel to ....

c All the angles are ....°.

4 Look at kite *IJKL*.

Copy and complete these sentences using the options in the box.

| IL | equal | not | parallel | LK |

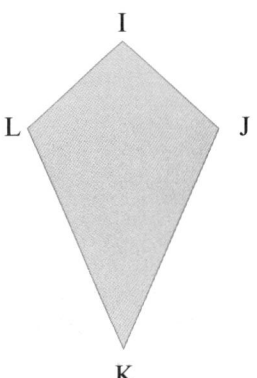

a *IJ* is the same length as .... and *JK* is the same length
as ....

b None of the sides are ....

c Angle *ILK* is .... to angle *IJK* but
angle *LIJ* is .... equal to angle *LKJ*.

5 Look at parallelogram *MNOP*.

Copy and complete these sentences using the options
in the box.

| equal | MP | opposite | MN | MPO |

a .... sides are the same length.

b *NO* is parallel to .... and *PO* is parallel to
....

c Angle *PMN* is .... to angle *NOP* and angle
MNO is equal to angle ....

6 Look at rhombus *QRST*.

Copy and complete these sentences using the options in
the box.

| parallel | TSR | all | QRS |

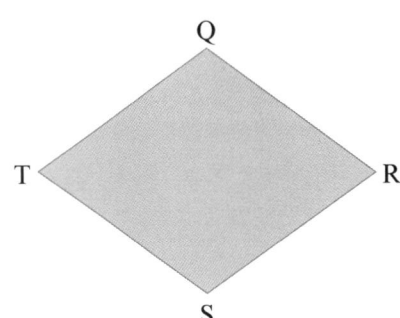

a .... sides are the same length.

b Opposite sides are ....

c Angle *TQR* is equal to angle .... and angle *QTS* is
equal to angle ....

Practice

 7 Write true (**T**) or false (**F**) for each statement about regular polygons.

a   A hexagon has five lines of symmetry.

b   An octagon has order of rotation 8.

c   A pentagon has order of rotation 10.

d   A decagon has 10 lines of symmetry.

e   A polygon with 15 lines of symmetry has 15 sides.

f   A polygon with order of rotation 20 has 19 sides.

 8 Match each **quadrilateral** with its correct side and angle properties.

A square **B** rectangle **C** rhombus **D** parallelogram

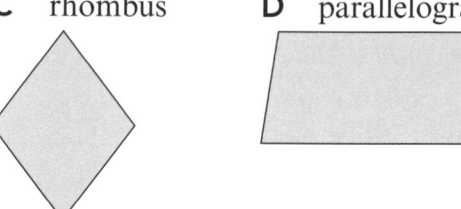

i	All sides the same length
	Two pairs of parallel sides
	Opposite angles are equal

ii	All sides the same length
	Two pairs of parallel sides
	All angles are 90°

iii	Two pairs of sides the same length
	Two pairs of parallel sides
	Opposite angles are equal

iv	Two pairs of sides the same length
	Two pairs of parallel sides
	All angles are 90°

9 Sofia is describing a rectangle to Zara.

My quadrilateral has two pairs of parallel sides and two pairs of sides the same length. What is the name of my quadrilateral?

Has Sofia given Zara enough information for her to work out that the quadrilateral is a rectangle?

Explain your answer.

10 Match each quadrilateral with its correct properties.

A trapezium   B isosceles trapezium   C kite

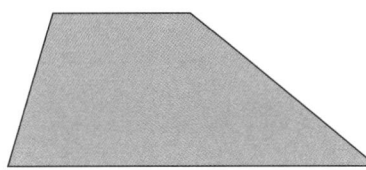 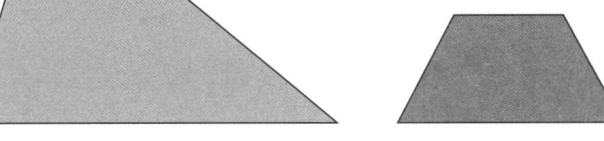 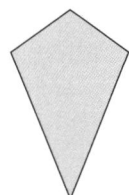

i One pair of sides the same length One pair of parallel sides Two pairs of equal angles	ii Two pairs of sides the same length One pair of equal angles	iii One pair of parallel sides

11 Arun is describing an isosceles trapezium to Marcus.

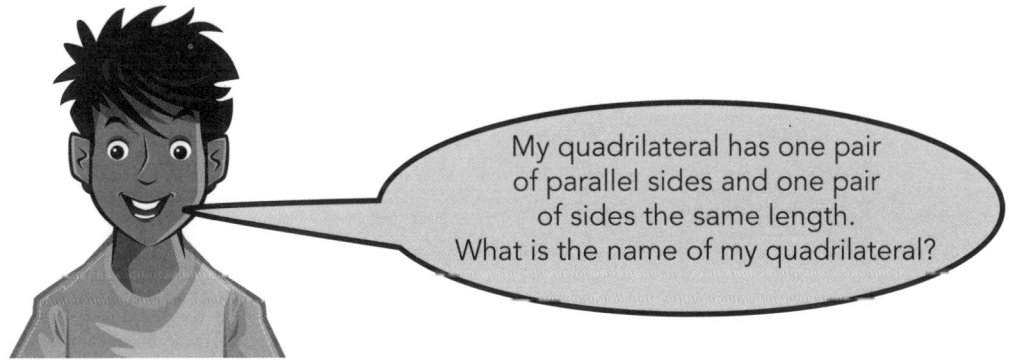

My quadrilateral has one pair of parallel sides and one pair of sides the same length. What is the name of my quadrilateral?

Has Arun given Marcus the correct information?
Explain your answer.

Challenge

 12 Put each quadrilateral through this classification flow chart.

Write the letter where each shape comes out.

a rhombus

b trapezium

c kite

d rectangle

e square

f isosceles trapezium

g parallelogram

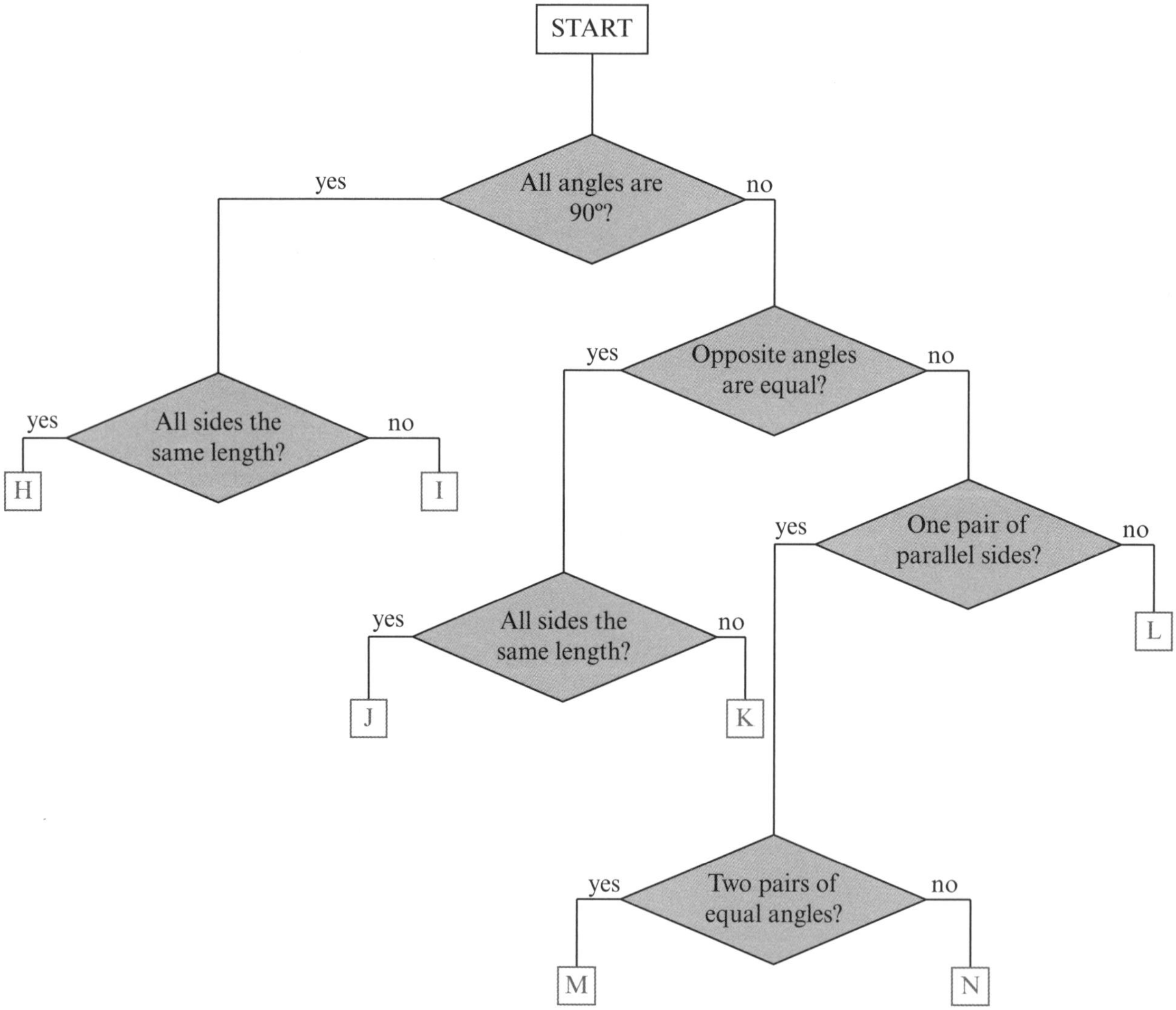

START

yes — All angles are 90°? — no

yes — All sides the same length? — no

H   I

yes — Opposite angles are equal? — no

yes — All sides the same length? — no

J   K

yes — One pair of parallel sides? — no

L

yes — Two pairs of equal angles? — no

M   N

13 This diagram shows the **hierarchy** of quadrilaterals.

In the diagram, a quadrilateral below another is a special case of the one above it.

For example, a square is a special rectangle but a rectangle is not a square.

Use the diagram to decide if each statement is true (**T**) or false (**F**).

a A rhombus is a special parallelogram

b A kite is a special quadrilateral

c A trapezium is a special parallelogram

d A rectangle is a special rhombus

e A kite is a special parallelogram

f A square is a special rhombus.

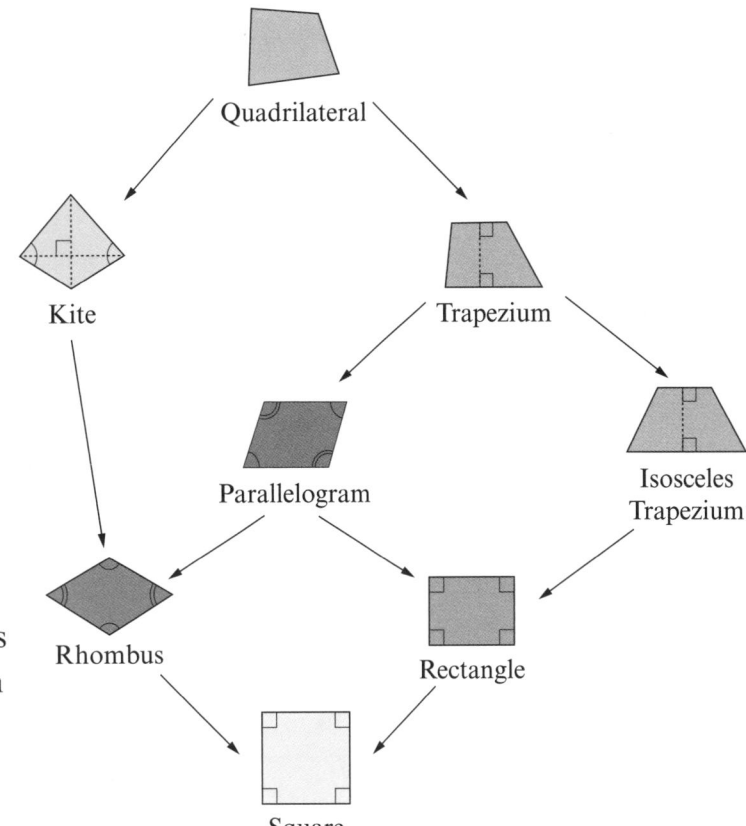

14 Make a copy of the coordinate grid shown.

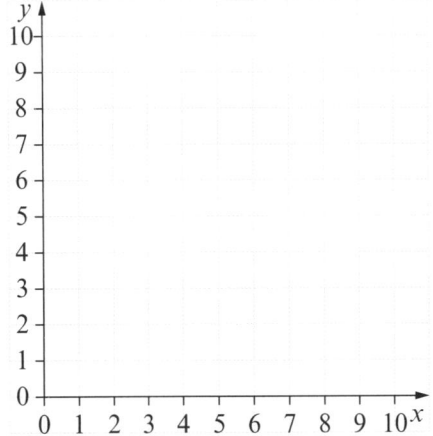

On the grid, plot the following points:

(2, 2) (6, 2) (0, 4) (4, 4) (8, 4) (2, 6) (2, 8) (6, 8) (4, 9)

Which four points can you join to make each of these quadrilaterals?

a rectangle

b square

c parallelogram

d kite

e trapezium

› 8.2 The circumference of a circle

The formula for the **circumference** of a circle is

$C = \pi d$ where: C is the circumference of the circle

d is the **diameter** of the circle.

Exercise 8.2

Focus

1 Copy and complete the workings to find the circumference of each circle.

Use **pi** = 3.14

Round each answer correct to 1 decimal place (1 d.p.).

Tip

Remember:
$C = \pi d$ means
$C = \pi \times d$

a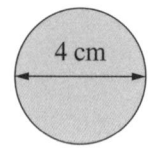
4 cm

$d = 4\,\text{cm}$

$C = \pi d$

$\quad = 3.14 \times 4$

$\quad = \boxed{}\,\text{cm}$

b
5 cm

$d = 5\,\text{cm}$

$C = \pi d$

$\quad = 3.14 \times 5$

$\quad = \boxed{}\,\text{cm}$

2 Copy and complete the workings to find the circumference of each circle.
Use $\pi = 3.142$

Round each answer correct to 2 decimal places (2 d.p.).

a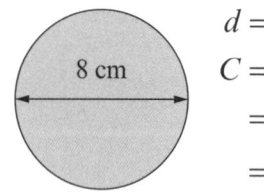
8 cm

$d = 8\,\text{cm}$

$C = \pi d$

$\quad = 3.142 \times 8$

$\quad = \boxed{}\,\text{cm}$

b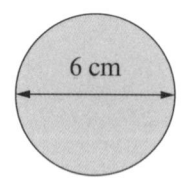
6 cm

$d = 6\,\text{cm}$

$C = \pi d$

$\quad = 3.142 \times 6$

$\quad = \boxed{}\,\text{cm}$

3 Copy and complete the workings to find the circumference of each circle.
Use the π button on your calculator.
Round each answer correct to 2 decimal places (2 d.p.).

a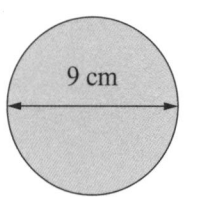
9 cm

$d = 9\,\text{cm}$

$C = \pi d$

$\quad = \pi \times 9$

$\quad = \boxed{}\,\text{cm}$

b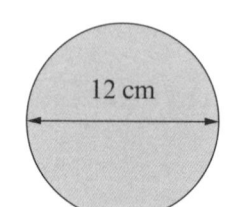
12 cm

$d = 12\,\text{cm}$

$C = \pi d$

$\quad = \pi \times 12$

$\quad = \boxed{}\,\text{cm}$

4   Copy and complete the workings to find the circumference of each circle.
     Use $\pi = 3.14$

a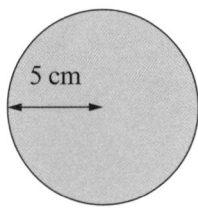

b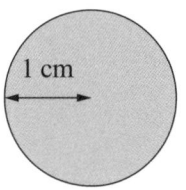

radius, $r = 5\,\text{cm}$

diameter, $d = 2 \times 5 = \boxed{}\,\text{cm}$

$C = \pi d$

$\quad = 3.14 \times 10$

$\quad = \boxed{}\,\text{cm}$

radius, $r = 1\,\text{cm}$

diameter, $d = 2 \times 1 = \boxed{}\,\text{cm}$

$C = \pi d$

$\quad = 3.14 \times 2$

$\quad = \boxed{}\,\text{cm}$

Practice

For the rest of the questions in this exercise, use the π button on your calculator.

5   Work out the circumference of each circle.
     Round each answer correct to 2 decimal places (2 d.p.).
     a   diameter $= 16\,\text{cm}$ b   diameter $= 9.5\,\text{m}$
     c   radius $= 10\,\text{cm}$ d   radius $= 2.8\,\text{m}$

6   Work out the diameter of a circle with
     a   circumference $= 35\,\text{cm}$ b   circumference $= 8.95\,\text{m}$.
     Round each answer correct to 1 decimal place (1 d.p.).

7   Work out the radius of a circle with
     a   circumference $= 23\,\text{cm}$ b   circumference $= 17.8\,\text{m}$.
     Round each answer correct to 2 decimal places (2 d.p.).

8   The circumference of a circular coin is $56\,\text{mm}$.
     Work out the diameter of the coin.
     Give your answer correct to the nearest millimetre.

9   A circular pond has a circumference of $10.45\,\text{m}$.
     Show that the radius of the pond is $166\,\text{cm}$ correct to the nearest centimetre.

> **Tip**
>
> Remember, you can rearrange $C = \pi d$ to give $d = \dfrac{C}{\pi}$

> **Tip**
>
> Remember, you can rearrange $C = 2\pi r$ to give $r = \dfrac{C}{2\pi}$

Challenge

10   Work out the perimeter of this **semicircle**.
     Round your answer correct to 2 decimal places (2 d.p.).

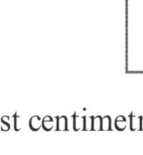
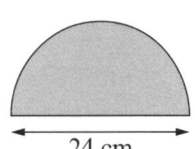

24 cm

11 The diagram shows a semicircle and three-quarters of a circle.

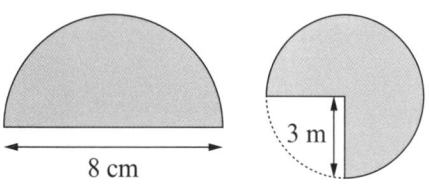

8 cm

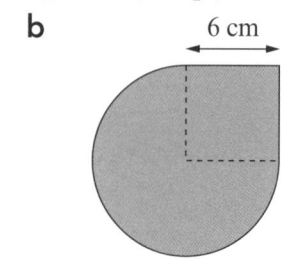

3 m

I think the perimeter of the semicircle is less than the perimeter of the three-quarter circle shape.

Is Marcus correct? Show working to support your answer.

12 Work out the perimeter of each compound shape.

Give your answers correct to two decimal places (2 d.p.).

a

8.4 cm

12.6 cm

b

6 cm

13 The diagram shows an athletics track.

The radius of the inner semicircle at each end is 36.8 m.

The length of the straight section is 84.39 m.

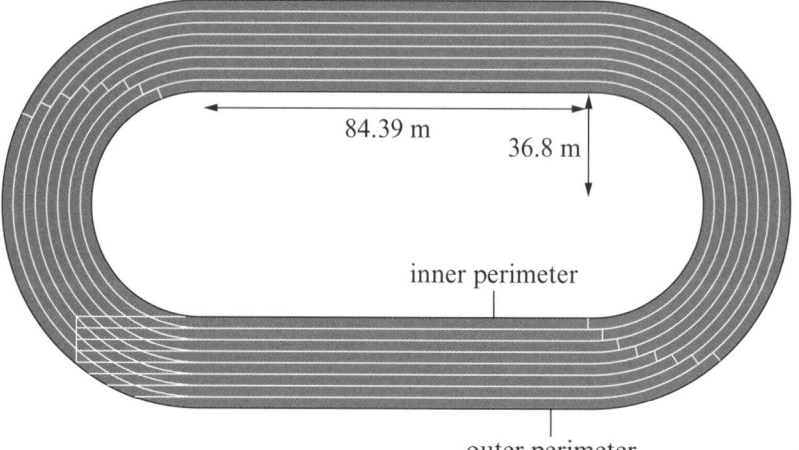

84.39 m

36.8 m

inner perimeter

outer perimeter

a Work out the length of the inner perimeter of the track.

Give your answer correct to the nearest metre.

b The width of each lane is 1.22 m. There are eight lanes.

Work out the radius of the outer semicircle at each end of the track.

c Work out the length of the outer perimeter of the track.

Give your answer correct to the nearest metre.

> 8.3 3D shapes

Exercise 8.3

Focus

Key words

front view, front elevation

side view, side elevation

top view, plan view

1 **a** The diagram shows a pentagonal prism.

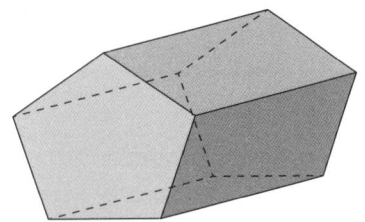

Write the number of faces, vertices and edges for this prism.

b The formula linking the number of faces (F), vertices (V) and edges (E) for a 3D shape with no curved surfaces is

$$E = F + V - 2$$

Substitute your values for F and V (from part **a**) into the formula to check your value for E.

c Use the formula to work out the number of edges of a shape with 8 faces and 12 vertices.

d Use the formula to work out the number of vertices of a shape with 11 faces and 20 edges.

Tip

Start by rearranging the formula $E = F + V - 2$ to get $V = \boxed{}$

2 The diagram shows a cuboid.

The **top view**, **front view** and **side view** of the cuboid are drawn on centimetre squared paper.

The scale used is 1 : 6.

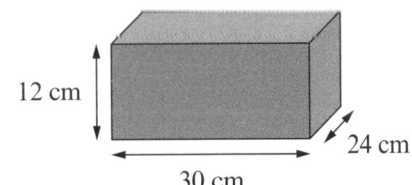

12 cm

30 cm

24 cm

a Copy and complete the workings to find the dimensions of the scale drawing.

$30 \div 6 = 5\,cm$ $\qquad 24 \div 6 = \boxed{}\,cm$ $\qquad 12 \div 6 = \boxed{}\,cm$

b Match each drawing with the correct view.

| A | Top view | | B | Front view | | C | Side view |

i

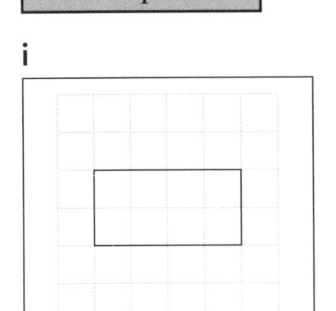

ii

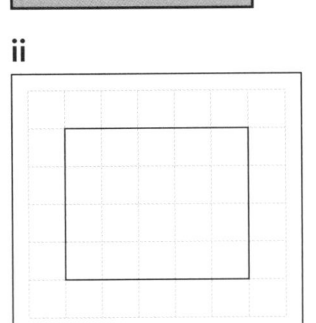

iii

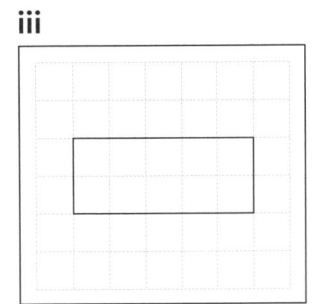

3 Copy and complete the workings and scale drawings for this question.
Draw the top view, front view and side view of each shape.
Use a scale of 1 : 2

a cube

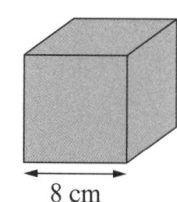

8 cm

Dimensions for the drawing:
$8 \div 2 = \boxed{}$ cm

Top view

> **Tip**
>
> Draw a square of side length 4 cm.

Front view

> **Tip**
>
> Draw a square of side length 4 cm.

Side view

> **Tip**
>
> Draw a square of side length 4 cm.

b cuboid

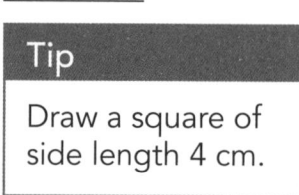

6 cm

12 cm   10 cm

Dimensions for the drawing:
$6 \div 2 = \boxed{}$ cm
$10 \div 2 = \boxed{}$ cm
$12 \div 2 = \boxed{}$ cm

Top view

> **Tip**
>
> Draw a rectangle 6 cm by 5 cm.

Front view

> **Tip**
>
> Draw a rectangle $\boxed{}$ cm by $\boxed{}$ cm.

Side view

> **Tip**
>
> Draw a rectangle $\boxed{}$ cm by $\boxed{}$ cm.

c cylinder

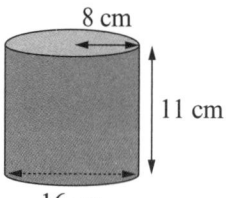

8 cm

11 cm

16 cm

Dimensions for the drawing:
$8 \div 2 = \boxed{}$ cm
$11 \div 2 = \boxed{}$ cm
$16 \div 2 = \boxed{}$ cm

Top view

> **Tip**
>
> Draw a circle radius 4 cm.

Front view

> **Tip**
>
> Draw a rectangle $\boxed{}$ cm by $\boxed{}$ cm.

Side view

> **Tip**
>
> Draw a rectangle $\boxed{}$ cm by $\boxed{}$ cm.

4   The diagram shows a 3D shape.

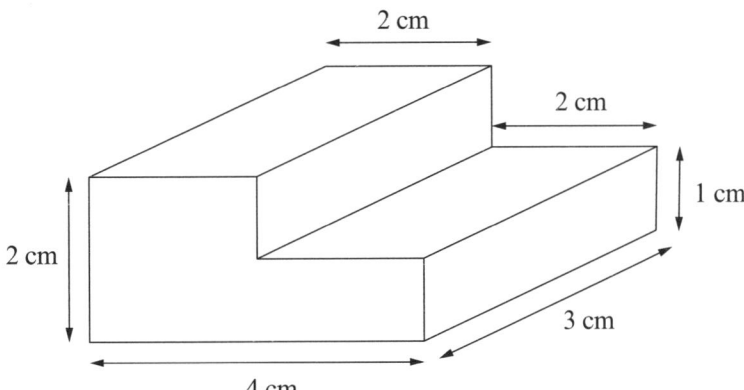

Tip

Remember, the plan view is the same as the top view and the side elevation is the same as the side view.

The plan view, front elevation and side elevations are drawn on centimetre squared paper.

Write if **A**, **B** or **C** is the correct scale drawing for each view.

The scale used is 1 : 1.

a   plan view

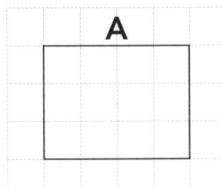   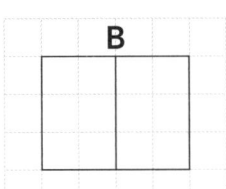   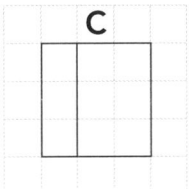

b   front elevation

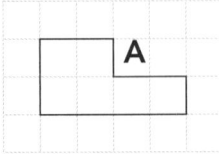   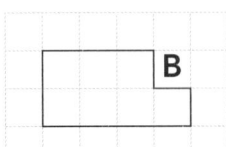   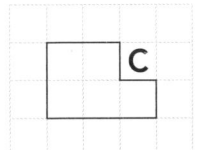

c   side elevation from the left

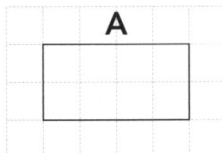   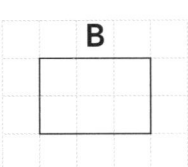   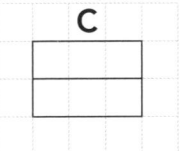

d   side elevation from the right

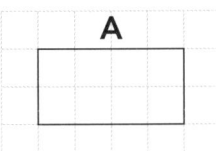   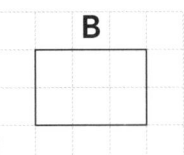   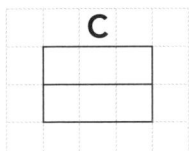

5 The diagram shows the dimensions of a shipping container.

Abbie makes a house from three shipping containers.

The containers are arranged as shown in the diagram.

Draw the plan view, the front elevation and the side elevation of her house.

Use a scale of 1 : 120

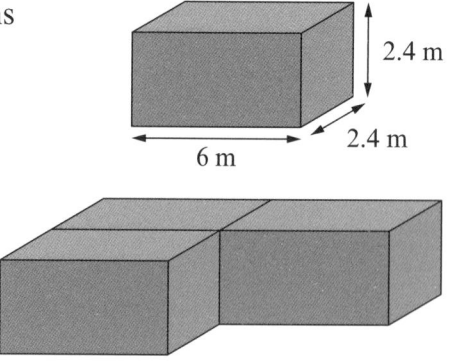

6 Draw the plan view, the front elevation and the side elevation of this 3D shape.

Use a scale of 1 : 4

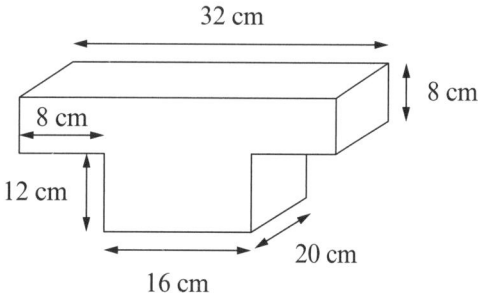

7 Draw the plan view, the front elevation and the side elevation of this right-angled triangular prism.

Use a scale of 1 : 5

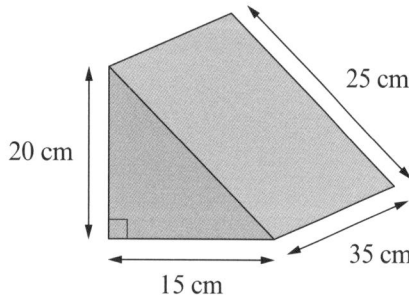

8 Draw the plan view, the front elevation and the side elevation of this isosceles triangular prism.

Use a scale of 1 : 20

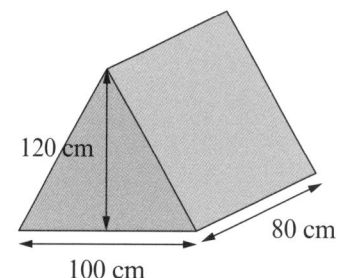

Challenge

9   The diagram shows four shapes drawn on dotty paper.
     The shapes are made from 1 cm cubes.

a

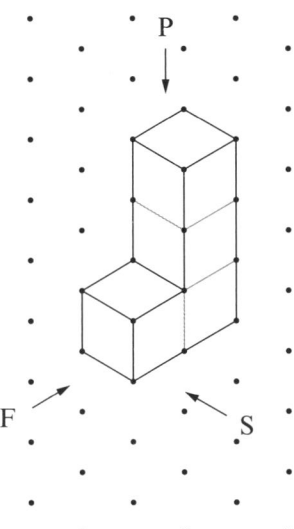

b

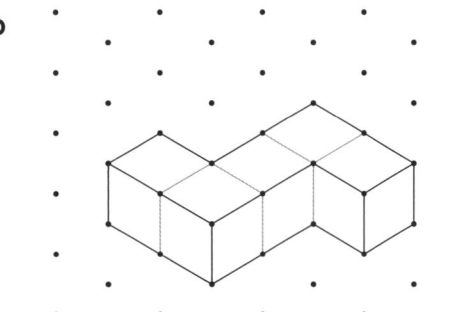

c

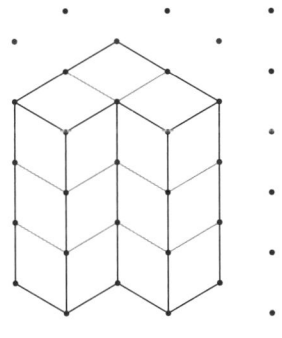

d

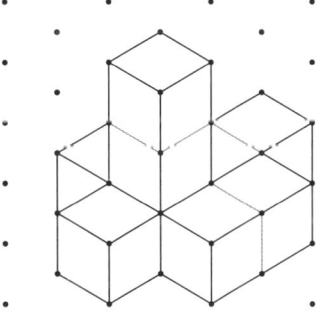

Accurately draw the plan view, the front elevation and the side elevation for each shape.

Use 1 cm squared paper.

The arrows in part **a** show the directions from which you look at each shape to draw the plan view (P), the front elevation (F) and the side elevation (S).

10   This is part of Sara's homework.

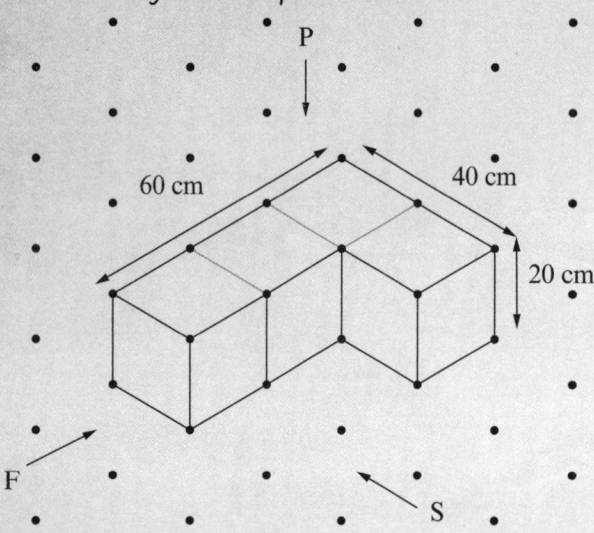

Question

Accurately draw the plan view, front elevation and side elevation of this shape.

60 cm   40 cm   20 cm

Use a scale of 1 : 10. Use 1 cm squared paper.

Answer

The height of the shape is 20 cm, so it is made from 20 cm cubes.

Scale is 1 : 10, so the height of 20 cm needs to be 20 ÷ 10 = 2 cm

The length of 60 cm needs to be 60 ÷ 10 = 6 cm

The width of 40 cm needs to be 40 ÷ 10 = 4 cm

Plan view   Side elevation   Front elevation

Which of Sara's drawings are incorrect?
Explain the mistakes she has made.

11 The diagram shows a shape drawn on dotty paper.

The shape is made from cubes.

The width of the shape is shown in the diagram.

Accurately draw the plan view, front elevation and side elevation for this shape.

Use a scale of 1:3. Use 1 cm squared paper.

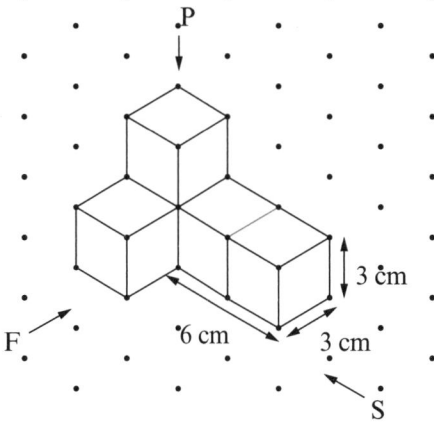

12 The diagram shows a shape drawn on dotty paper.

The shape is made from cubes.

The width of the shape is shown in the diagram.

Accurately draw the plan view, front elevation and side elevation for this shape.

Use a scale of 1:2. Use 1 cm squared paper.

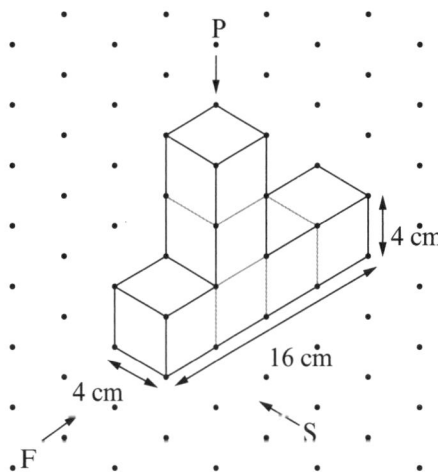

9 ▶ Sequences and functions

> 9.1 Generating sequences

Exercise 9.1

Focus

1   Copy and complete the workings to find the term-to-term rule and the next two terms of each sequence.

a $8, 8\frac{1}{2}, 9, 9\frac{1}{2}, \ldots$ $8+\frac{1}{2}=8\frac{1}{2},$ $8\frac{1}{2}+\boxed{}=9,$ $9+\boxed{}=9\frac{1}{2}$

The term-to-term rule is: add $\boxed{}$

The next two terms are:

$9\frac{1}{2}+\boxed{}=\boxed{}$

$\boxed{}+\boxed{}=\boxed{}$

b $8, 8.3, 8.6, 8.9, \ldots$ $8+0.3=8.3,$ $8.3+\boxed{}=8.6,$ $8.6+\boxed{}=8.9$

The term-to-term rule is: add $\boxed{}$

The next two terms are:

$8.9+\boxed{}=\boxed{}$

$\boxed{}+\boxed{}=\boxed{}$

c $5\frac{1}{3}, 5, 4\frac{2}{3}, 4\frac{1}{3}, \ldots$ $5\frac{1}{3}-\frac{1}{3}=5,$ $5-\boxed{}=4\frac{2}{3},$ $4\frac{2}{3}-\boxed{}=4\frac{1}{3}$

The term-to-term rule is: subtract $\boxed{}$

The next two terms are:

$4\frac{1}{3}-\boxed{}=\boxed{}$

$\boxed{}-\boxed{}=\boxed{}$

d $9.4, 9, 8.6, 8.2, \ldots$ $9.4-0.4=9,$ $9-\boxed{}=8.6,$ $8.6-\boxed{}=8.2$

The term-to-term rule is: subtract $\boxed{}$

The next two terms are:

$8.2-\boxed{}=\boxed{}$

$\boxed{}-\boxed{}=\boxed{}$

2 Match each sequence card with the correct term-to-term rule card.
The first one is done for you: **A** and **iii**

A $5, 7\frac{1}{2}, 10, 12\frac{1}{2}, ...$	**i** subtract $1\frac{1}{2}$
B $10, 8\frac{1}{2}, 7, 5\frac{1}{2}, ...$	**ii** add $\frac{2}{3}$
C $8, 8\frac{2}{3}, 9\frac{1}{3}, 10, ...$	**iii** add $2\frac{1}{2}$
D $5, 4\frac{1}{3}, 3\frac{2}{3}, 3, ...$	**iv** subtract $\frac{2}{3}$

3 For each sequence, write

 i the term-to-term rule **ii** the next two terms.

 a $1\frac{1}{4}, 1\frac{1}{2}, 1\frac{3}{4}, 2, ...$ **b** $9, 10\frac{1}{2}, 12, 13\frac{1}{2}, ...$

 c $3.2, 3.4, 3.6, 3.8, ...$ **d** $10, 9\frac{1}{2}, 9, 8\frac{1}{2}, ...$

 e $15, 14\frac{3}{5}, 14\frac{1}{5}, 13\frac{4}{5}, ...$ **f** $17, 16.75, 16.5, 16.25, ...$

4 Write the first three terms of each sequence. The first one has been done for you.

	First term	Term-to-term rule	First three terms
a	2	Add 0.8	2, 2.8, 3.6
b	3	Add $3\frac{1}{2}$	
c	10	Subtract 1.2	
d	30	Subtract $2\frac{1}{5}$	
e	0.3	Multiply by 2	
f	18	Divide by 2	

5 In this sequence, some of the terms are missing.

$2, 3\frac{1}{3}, \square, 6, \square, 8\frac{2}{3}, \square, \square$

 a Write the term-to-term rule.
 b Use the term-to-term rule to work out the missing terms.

> **Tip**
>
> Use the first two terms to work out the term-to-term rule.

Practice

6 Copy these finite sequences and fill in the missing terms.

a $6, 7\frac{1}{5}, \square, 9\frac{3}{5}, \square, 12, \square$

b $2, 5\frac{1}{4}, 8\frac{1}{2}, \square, \square, 18\frac{1}{4}, \square$

c $20\frac{3}{4}, 20\frac{1}{2}, \square, \square, 19\frac{3}{4}, \square, 19\frac{1}{4}$

d $40, 39\frac{4}{7}, \square, 38\frac{5}{7}, \square, 37\frac{6}{7}, \square$

e $7, \square, \square, 11.2, 12.6, \square, \square$

f $\square, \square, 19, 18.3, \square, 16.9$

7 a In the sequence $1.3, 1.8, 2.3, 2.8, \ldots$ what is the first term greater than 15?

b Is 100 a term in the sequence $10\frac{1}{5}, 20\frac{2}{5}, 30\frac{3}{5}, \ldots$? Explain your answer.

c Is $4\frac{1}{2}$ a term in the sequence $40, 37\frac{1}{3}, 34\frac{2}{3}, 32, \ldots$? Explain your answer.

8 Write the first three terms in each of these sequences.
The first one has been started for you.

a first term is 2   term-to-term rule is multiply by 3 then subtract 1

> *first term = 2*
>
> *second term = 2 × 3 − 1 = 6 − 1 = 5*
>
> *third term = 5 × 3 − 1 = $\square$ − 1 = $\square$*

b first term is 10   term-to-term rule is subtract 4 then multiply by 2

c first term is 6   term-to-term rule is divide by 2 then add 7

 9 The first three terms of a sequence are $4, 10, 28, \ldots$

a Which card, **A**, **B** or **C**, shows the correct term-to-term rule?

A	multiply by 3 then subtract 2

B	divide by 2 then add 8

C	subtract 2 then multiply by 5

b Which is the first term in this sequence greater than 700?

10 Work out the first three terms in each sequence.

a first term is 5   term-to-term rule is multiply by 2 then subtract 8

b first term is 12   term-to-term rule is subtract $4\frac{1}{2}$ then multiply by 2

c first term is −8   term-to-term rule is add 4 then divide by 2

Challenge

11 The first term of a sequence is 22. The term-to-term rule is divide by 2 then subtract 3.

Show that the first term in this sequence which is a negative number is $-2\frac{1}{2}$.

12 The first term of a sequence is 6. The term-to-term rule is divide by 2 then add 1.

   a   Work out the first ten terms of the sequence. You can use a calculator to help you.

   b   What do you notice about the terms in your sequence?

   c   What number goes at the end of this sentence?

       'The terms in this sequence are all greater than ☐.'

       Explain why this happens.

13 This is part of Sian's homework.

> <u>Question</u>
> The 10th term of a sequence is $24\frac{3}{8}$. The term-to-term rule is add $2\frac{5}{8}$.
> What is the 5th term of the sequence?
>
> <u>Answer</u>
> 5th term = 10th term ÷ 2 = $24\frac{3}{8}$ ÷ 2 = $12\frac{3}{16}$

   a   Explain why Sian's method is wrong.

   b   Work out the correct answer. Show all your working.

14 The 5th term of a sequence is 489.

The term-to-term rule is subtract 2 then multiply by 3.

What is the 3rd term of the sequence?

Show all your working.

15 The answers to the calculations on these cards are the first three terms of a sequence.

| 20% of 42 | $\frac{3}{5} \times 21$ | 0.56×30 |

a What is the term-to-term rule for the sequence?

b What is the 10th term in the sequence?

This card is the calculation for the 10th term in the sequence.

| $4 \times \boxed{} + 7.8$ |

c What is the missing number on the card? Show all your working.

> 9.2 Finding rules for sequences

Exercise 9.2

Focus

Key words

position number

position-to-term rule

sequence of patterns

1 This **sequence of patterns** is made from grey triangles.

Pattern 1   Pattern 2   Pattern 3

a Write the sequence of the numbers of grey triangles.

b Write the term-to-term rule.

c Draw the next pattern in the sequence.

d Copy and complete the table to find the **position-to-term rule**.

position number	1	2	3	4
term	3	5		
2 × position number	2	4		
2 × position number + ☐				

Position-to-term rule is: term = 2 × **position number** + ☐

2 This pattern is made from squares.

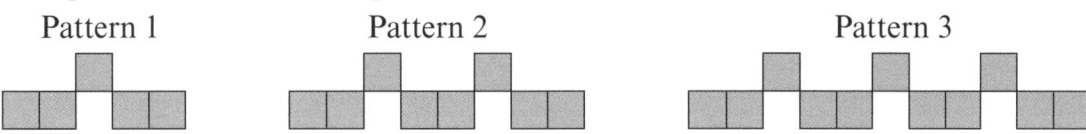

Pattern 1   Pattern 2   Pattern 3

a   Write the sequence of the numbers of squares.

b   Write the term-to-term rule.

c   Draw the next pattern in the sequence.

d   Copy and complete the table to find the position-to-term rule.

position number	1	2	3	4
term	5	8		
3 × position number	3	6		
3 × position number + ☐				

Position-to-term rule is: term = 3 × position number + ☐

3 This pattern is made from dots.

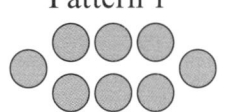  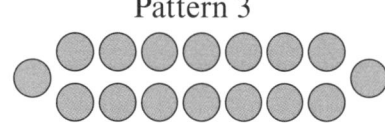

Pattern 1   Pattern 2   Pattern 3

a   Write the sequence of the numbers of dots.

b   Write the term-to-term rule.

c   Draw the next pattern in the sequence.

d   Copy and complete the table to find the position-to-term rule.

position number	1	2	3	4
term	8	12		
4 × position number	4	8		
4 × position number + ☐				

Position-to-term rule is: term = 4 × position number + ☐

4 This pattern is made from triangles.

Pattern 1   Pattern 2   Pattern 3

a   Write the sequence of the numbers of triangles.

b   Write the term-to-term rule.

c   Draw the next pattern in the sequence.

d   Copy and complete the table to find the position-to-term rule.

position number	1	2	3	4
term	7	10		
3 × position number	3	6		
3 × position number +				

Position-to-term rule is: term = 3 × position number +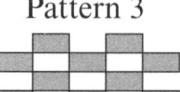

Practice

5   This pattern is made from rectangles.

Pattern 1   Pattern 2   Pattern 3

            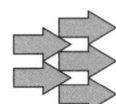   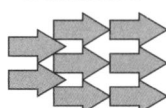

    a   Write the sequence of the numbers of rectangles.

    b   Write the term-to-term rule.

    c   Draw the next pattern in the sequence.

    d   Draw and complete a table like the one in Question 4, to find the position-to-term rule.

6   This pattern is made from grey arrows.

Pattern 1   Pattern 2   Pattern 3

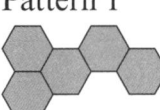   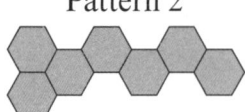   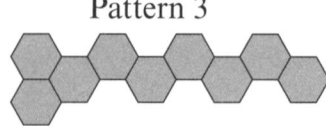

    a   Write the sequence of the numbers of grey arrows.

    b   Write the term-to-term rule.

    c   Draw the next pattern in the sequence.

    d   Draw and complete a table to find the position-to-term rule.

 7   This pattern is made from hexagons.

Pattern 1   Pattern 2   Pattern 3

Sami thinks the position-to-term rule for the sequence of the numbers of hexagons is:

term = 5 × position number + 2

Is Sami correct? Explain the method you used to work out your answer.

8   Work out the position-to-term rule for each sequence.

    a   7, 12, 17, 22, …   b   10, 25, 40, 55, …

9 This is part of Kai's homework.

> *Question*
> Work out the position-to-term rule for this sequence of octagons.
>
> Pattern 1   Pattern 2   Pattern 3
>
> *Answer*
> The sequence starts with 3 and increases by 5 every time, so the
> position-to-term rule is: term = 5 × position number + 3

a Explain the mistake Kai has made. **b** Work out the correct answer.

Challenge

10 This pattern is made from rhombuses.

Pattern 1 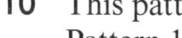 Pattern 2  Pattern 3

How many rhombuses will there be in Pattern 25?

Show how you worked out your answer.

11 A sequence has position-to-term rule: term = 3 × position number + 1

  a Work out the first three terms in this sequence.

  b Draw a pattern using shapes to show the first three terms in this sequence.
  Use a shape of your choice.

12 Betty is working out the position-to-term rule for a sequence of numbers.

She has drawn a table, but she has spilt juice on her work.

position number	1	2	3	4
term		8		
× position number				
× position number − 6				

a   What is the position-to-term rule for her sequence? Explain how you worked out your answer.

b   Work out the 10th term of the sequence.

13   Anil is using the area of rectangles to make a sequence of numbers.
The diagram shows the first three rectangles.

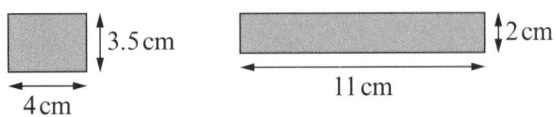
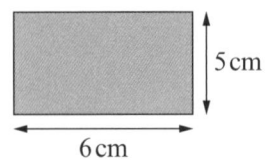

The 8th rectangle in the sequence has a width of 2.5 cm.

What is the length of this rectangle?

Show how you worked out your answer.

> **Tip**
>
> Start by working out the area of each of the first three rectangles. Then find the position-to-term rule.

> 9.3 Using the *n*th term

Exercise 9.3

> **Key word**
>
> *n*th term

Focus

1   Copy and complete the workings to find the first four terms of each sequence.

a   **nth term** is $4n$ 1st term $= 4 \times 1 = 4$ 2nd term $= 4 \times 2 = \boxed{}$

3rd term $= 4 \times 3 = \boxed{}$ 4th term $= 4 \times 4 = \boxed{}$

b   *n*th term is $n + 12$ 1st term $= 1 + 12 = 13$ 2nd term $= 2 + 12 = \boxed{}$

3rd term $= 3 + 12 = \boxed{}$ 4th term $= 4 + 12 = \boxed{}$

c   *n*th term is $2n - 1$ 1st term $= 2 \times 1 - 1 = 1$ 2nd term $= 2 \times 2 - 1 = \boxed{}$

3rd term $= 2 \times 3 - 1 = \boxed{}$ 4th term $= 2 \times 4 - 1 = \boxed{}$

d   *n*th term is $3n + 2$ 1st term $= 3 \times 1 + 2 = 5$ 2nd term $= 3 \times 2 + 2 = \boxed{}$

3rd term $= 3 \times 3 + 2 = \boxed{}$ 4th term $= 3 \times 4 + 2 = \boxed{}$

2   Work out the first three terms and the 10th term of the sequences with the given *n*th term.

a $8n$ b $5n - 3$ c $n + 3$ d $n - 7$

e $2n + 8$ f $3n - 2$ g $6n + 1$ h $5n - 4$

3   Each card shows one term from a different sequence.

A 8th term in the sequence, *n*th term is $2n + 14$	B 5th term in the sequence, *n*th term is $7n - 4$

Which card has the smaller value, **A** or **B**? Show your working.

4 A sequence has the *n*th term $\frac{1}{2}n + 3$.

Show that the first four terms of the sequence are $3\frac{1}{2}$, 4, $4\frac{1}{2}$ and 5.

5 Work out the first three terms and the 8th term of the sequences with the given *n*th term.

a $\frac{1}{2}n + 3\frac{1}{2}$ b $4n - \frac{1}{2}$ c $6n + 1.75$ d $2.5n - 0.4$

Practice

6 **a** Work out the first four terms of the sequences with the given *n*th term.

| A $\quad 4n + 7$ | B $\quad 15 - n$ | C $\quad \frac{1}{4}n + 10$ | D $\quad 20 - \frac{1}{3}n$ |

b In which of the sequences in part **a** are the terms increasing?

c In which of the sequences in part **a** are the terms decreasing?

d Look at the following sequences but **do not** work out the terms.

| A $\quad 16 - \frac{1}{8}n$ | B $\quad 12n - 4$ | C $\quad 34 - 3n$ | D $\quad \frac{2}{5}n + 8$ |

Are the terms in each sequence increasing or decreasing?
Explain your decisions.

7 Look at this number sequence.

20, 23, 26, 29, 32, ...

Explain why you can tell – simply by looking at the numbers in the sequence – that the *n*th term expression for this sequence cannot be $23 - 3n$.

8 **a** The *n*th term expression for a sequence is $4n + 1$. Is the number 61 a term in this sequence?

b The *n*th term expression for a sequence is $3n - 5$. Is the number 48 a term in this sequence?

9 Copy and complete the workings to find the *n*th term expression for the sequence 8, 11, 14, 17, ...

position number (*n*)	1	2	3	4
term	8	11	14	17
$3 \times n$	3	6		
$3 \times n + \square$	8	11	14	17

*n*th term is $3n + \square$

> **Tip**
>
> What do you need to add to 3 to get 8? What do you need to add to 6 to get 11?

10 Work out an expression for the nth term of each sequence.
Draw a table like the one in Question **9** to help you.

a 3, 5, 7, 9, ... **b** 10, 13, 16, 19, ...

c 1, 5, 9, 13, ... **d** 4, 9, 14, 19, ...

11 This pattern is made from hexagons.

Pattern 1   Pattern 2   Pattern 3   Pattern 4

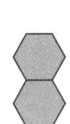 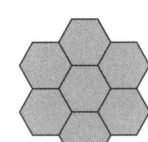 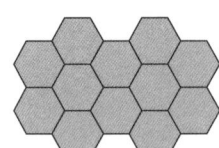 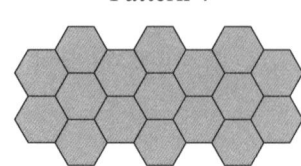

a Write the sequence of the numbers of hexagons.

b Work out an expression for the nth term for the sequence.
Draw a table like the one in Question **9** to help you.

c Use your nth term expression to find the number of hexagons
in the 30th pattern in the sequence.

Challenge

12 Work out an expression for the nth term of each sequence.

a $-15, -10, -5, 0, ...$ **b** $1\frac{3}{5}, 3\frac{3}{5}, 5\frac{3}{5}, 7\frac{3}{5}, ...$

c 3.3, 8.3, 13.3, 18.3, ...

 13 Sofia is looking at the number sequence $-14, -8, -2, 4, ...$
Read what she says.

The 50th term of this sequence is 280

Is Sofia correct? Show all your working.

14 Work out an expression for the nth term of each sequence.

a 7, 6, 5, 4, ... **b** 7, 4, 1, -2, ...

c 7, 0, -7, -14, ...

15 Use the nth term expression to work out the 20th term of each
sequence in Question **14**.

16 The cards show two different sequences.

| **A** | $-12\frac{1}{2}, -10, -7\frac{1}{2}, -5, \ldots$ |

| **B** | $75.75, 71.5, 67.25, 63, \ldots$ |

You can see that the first four terms in sequence **A** are smaller than the first four terms in sequence **B**.

What is the term number of the first term in sequence **A** that is larger than the equivalent term in sequence **B**?

Show all your working.

Tip

For example, is it the 20th term, the 50th term or a different term, when A > B?

> 9.4 Representing simple functions

Exercise 9.4

Focus

Key words

function
function machine
inverse function
inverse function equation
mapping diagram
two-step function

1 For each of these **function machines**, copy and complete

    i the table of values   **ii** the **mapping diagram**

    iii the equation.

a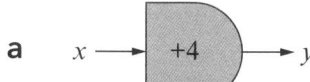

   i

x	0	2	3	$5\frac{1}{2}$
y	4			

   ii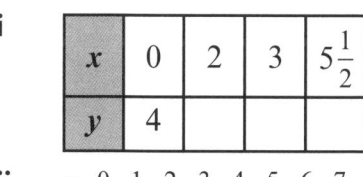

   iii $x + 4 = y$, so $y = \ldots\ldots$

Tip

When $x = 0$, $y = 0 + 4 = 4$

When $x = 2$, $y = 2 + 4 = \square$

When $x = 3$, $y = 3 + 4 = \square$

When $x = 5\frac{1}{2}$, $y = 5\frac{1}{2} + 4 = \square$

b $x \longrightarrow$ ×3 $\longrightarrow y$

i

x	$1\frac{1}{2}$	3	4	6
y	$4\frac{1}{2}$			

> **Tip**
>
> When $x = 1\frac{1}{2}$, $y = 1\frac{1}{2} \times 3 = 4\frac{1}{2}$
> When $x = 3$, $y = 3 \times 3 = \square$
> When $x = 4$, $y = 4 \times 3 = \square$
> When $x = 6$, $y = 6 \times 3 = \square$

ii

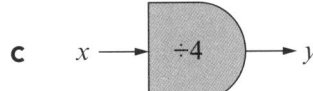

x 0 1 2 3 4 5 6 7 8 9 10 11 12 13 14 15 16 17 18 19 20

y 0 1 2 3 4 5 6 7 8 9 10 11 12 13 14 15 16 17 18 19 20

iii $x \times 3 = y$, so $y = \ldots\ldots$

c $x \longrightarrow$ ÷4 $\longrightarrow y$

i

x	4	6	8	14
y		$1\frac{1}{2}$		

> **Tip**
>
> When $x = 4$, $y = 4 \div 4 = \square$
> When $x = 6$, $y = 6 \div 4 = 1\frac{1}{2}$
> When $x = 8$, $y = 8 \div 4 = \square$
> When $x = 14$, $y = 14 \div 4 = \square$

ii

x 0 1 2 3 4 5 6 7 8 9 10 11 12 13 14 15

y 0 1 2 3 4 5 6 7 8 9 10 11 12 13 14 15

iii $\frac{x}{4} = y$, so $y = \ldots\ldots$

2 For each function machine, copy and complete

    i the table of values   **ii** the equation.

a $x \longrightarrow$ ×2 $\longrightarrow$ −1 $\longrightarrow y$

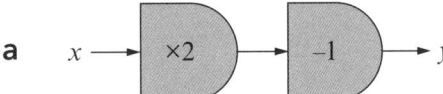

> **Tip**
>
> When $x = 2$,
> $y = 2 \times 2 - 1 = 4 - 1 = 3$
> When $x = 3$,
> $y = 3 \times 2 - 1 = 6 - 1 = \square$

i

x	2	3	4	$4\frac{1}{2}$
y	3			

ii $x \times 2 - 1 = y$ is written as $y = 2x - \square$

b 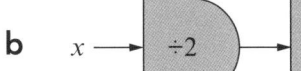 $x \longrightarrow \div2 \longrightarrow +1 \longrightarrow y$

  i

x	3	6	8	11
y	$2\frac{1}{2}$			

  ii $\dfrac{x}{2} + 1 = y$ is written as $y = \dfrac{x}{2} + \boxed{}$

c 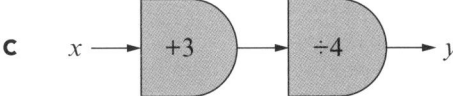 $x \longrightarrow +3 \longrightarrow \div4 \longrightarrow y$

  i

x	7	9	13	23
y	$2\frac{1}{2}$			

  ii $\dfrac{x+3}{4} = y$ is written as $y = \ldots\ldots\ldots$

d 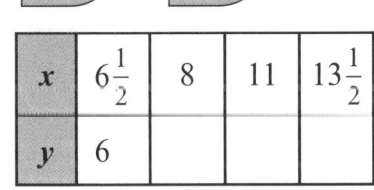 $x \longrightarrow -5 \longrightarrow \times4 \longrightarrow y$

  i

x	$6\frac{1}{2}$	8	11	$13\frac{1}{2}$
y	6			

  ii $(x-5) \times 4 = y$ is written as $y = 4(\ldots\ldots\ldots)$

3 Copy and complete the table for each function machine.

  a $x \longrightarrow +12 \longrightarrow y$

x	2	$5\frac{1}{2}$		
y			20	28

  b $x \longrightarrow \times5 \longrightarrow y$

x	1	3		
y			20	35

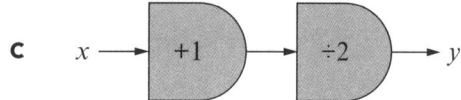

c

x	5	12		
y			9	$15\frac{1}{2}$

> **Tip**
>
> When $x = 5$,
> $y = (5 + 1) \div 2 = \square \div 2 = \square$
> Reverse the function machine:
> When $y = 9$,
> $y = 9 \times 2 - 1 = \square - 1 = \square$

Practice

4   a   Copy and complete the tables for these function machines.

i

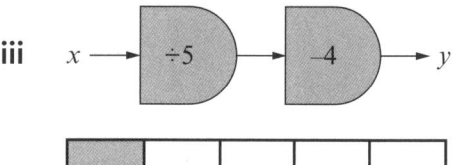

x	10	$15\frac{1}{4}$		
y			9	$11\frac{1}{3}$

ii

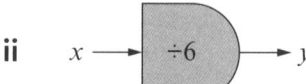

x	12		39	
y		5		12

iii

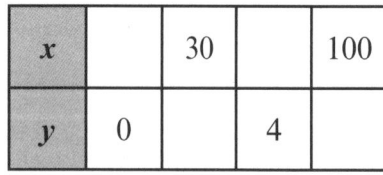

x		30		100
y	0		4	

iv

x		$2\frac{1}{2}$		$7\frac{1}{2}$
y	20		24	

b   Write each **function** in part **a** as an equation.

5   Copy and complete these **inverse function** machines and equations.

a

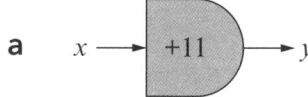

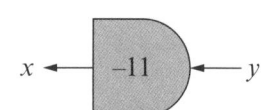

equation: $\qquad y = x + 11$

inverse function equation: $x = \ldots\ldots\ldots\ldots$

b

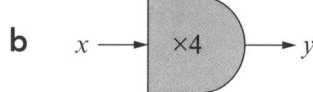

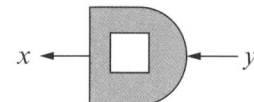

equation: $\qquad y = 4x$

inverse function equation: $x = \ldots\ldots\ldots\ldots$

c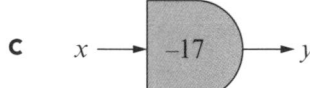

equation: $y = x - 17$
inverse function equation: $x = \ldots\ldots\ldots$

d

equation: $y = \ldots\ldots\ldots$
inverse function equation: $x = \ldots\ldots\ldots$

e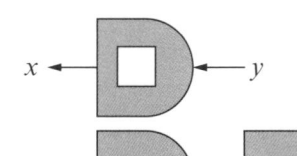

equation: $y = 12(x - 1)$
inverse function equation: $x = \ldots\ldots\ldots$

f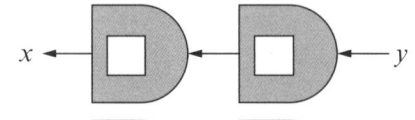

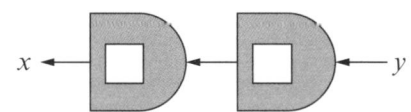

equation: $y = \ldots\ldots\ldots$
inverse function equation: $x = \ldots\ldots\ldots$

6 Match each function equation with the correct **inverse function equation**.
The first one is done for you: **A** and **ii**

A $y = x - 4$	**i** $x = 3y + 9$
B $y = \dfrac{x}{12}$	**ii** $x = y + 4$
C $y = \dfrac{x - 9}{3}$	**iii** $x = 5(y - 10)$
D $y = 6x + 1$	**iv** $x = \dfrac{y}{6} + 2$
E $y = \dfrac{x}{5} + 10$	**v** $x = 12y$
F $y = 6(x - 2)$	**vi** $x = \dfrac{y - 1}{6}$

7   a   For this function, write

    i   the equation
    ii   the inverse function equation.

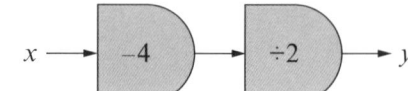

    b   Copy and complete this table of values. Use your answers to part **a**.

x	−6	−3		
y			8	$13\frac{1}{2}$

8   a   For this function, write

    i   the equation
    ii   the inverse function equation.

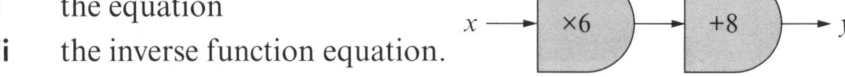

    b   Copy and complete this table of values. Use your answers to part **a**.

x	−5		$2\frac{1}{2}$	
y		−7		47

Challenge

9   a   Copy and complete the function machine for each table of values.

    i $x \longrightarrow \square \longrightarrow y$

x	−5	−3	2.5	4.4
y	−9	−7	−1.5	0.4

    ii $x \longrightarrow \square \longrightarrow y$

x	−24	−6	4.4	12.8
y	−6	−1.5	1.1	3.2

    b   Write each function in part **a** as an equation.

10 Arun and Sofia are looking at this function machine and table of values.

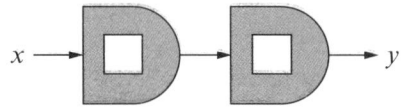

x	-2	4	7
y	$-3\frac{1}{2}$	$11\frac{1}{2}$	19

I think the equation for the function is $y = 3x + 2\frac{1}{2}$

I think the equation for the function is $y = 2\frac{1}{2}x + 1\frac{1}{2}$

Is either of them correct? Show all your working.

11 Work out the equation for this function machine and table of values.

x	1	3	5
y	1	11	21

Explain how you worked out your answer.

12 Zara is putting numbers into a **two-step function** machine. Read what Zara says.

When $x = 2$, $y = -4$.
As my x-values increase by 2, my y-values increase by 16.

Work out the equation for Zara's function. Show all your working.

10 ▶ Percentages

❯ 10.1 Percentage increases and decreases

Exercise 10.1

Key words

percentage decrease

percentage increase

Focus

1   a   Find 30% of 120 kg
    b   Increase 120 kg by 30%
    c   Increase 120 kg by 60%
2   a   Find 70% of $40
    b   Decrease $40 by 70%
    c   Increase $40 by 70%
3   Increase 200 km by
    a   10%   b   25%   c   75%
4   Decrease 15 hours by
    a   50%   b   20%   c   80%
5   Increase 280 by
    a   15%   b   85%   c   135%
6   Decrease 6400 by
    a   12%   b   62%   c   92%

Practice

7   a   What percentage of 400 is 250?
    b   What percentage of 250 is 400?
8   A car costs $24 700 and a motorcycle costs $9500
    a   What percentage of the cost of the car is the cost of the motorcycle?
    b   What percentage of the cost of the motorcycle is the cost of the car?

9   In a sale, the price of a phone is decreased by 60%.

The original price was $230. Calculate the sale price.

10 Copy and complete this table to show the results of percentage changes.

The first row is done for you.

Original value	New value	Absolute change	Percentage change
600	700	100	16.7% increase
75	40		
36	100		
43	12		
250			30% decrease
90			160% increase

11 a   Calculate the missing numbers in this chart.

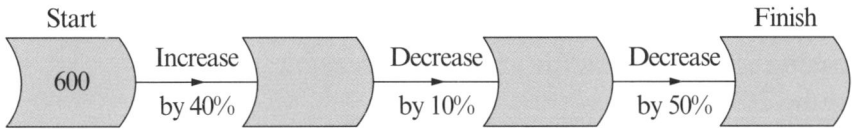

b   Work out the overall percentage change from the start to the finish.

12 The price of a television is $480. The price is reduced by $50.

Then it is reduced by another $50.

a   Calculate the percentage reduction each time. Round your answers to 1 decimal place.

b   Find the absolute change after the two reductions.

c   Calculate the overall **percentage decrease** in price.

Challenge

13 a   The price of a jacket increases from $245 to $275.

Work out

i   the increase in price

ii   the **percentage increase**.

b   The price of a hat increases from $42 to $72.

Work out

i   the increase in price

ii   the percentage increase.

c   The price of a shirt increases by $30. This is a 50% increase.

What was the original price of the shirt?

14 One week there are 2324 visitors to an exhibition. The next week there are 5018 visitors.

    a Find the absolute increase in visitors.

    b Calculate the percentage increase in the number of visitors.

    c If the number of visitors increases by the same percentage in the following week, how many visitors will there be?

15 Look at this table.

Year	Population (billion)
1970	3.70
1990	5.33
2010	6.96

It shows the population of the world in billions.

Has the world population increased at the same rate from 1970 to 2010? Justify your answer.

 16 **a** Show that increasing $80 by 50% is the same as increasing it by 25% and then by 20%.

    b Is decreasing $80 by 50% the same as decreasing it by 25% and then by 20%? Justify your answer.

> 10.2 Using a multiplier

Exercise 10.2

Focus

Key word

multiplier

Use a **multiplier** method to answer these questions.

1 Find the multiplier for

    a an increase of 5%   **b** an increase of 95%

    c an increase of 132%   **d** an increase of 200%.

2 Find the multiplier for a decrease of

    a 14%   **b** 67%   **c** 97%

3 Increase each of these amounts by 60%.

    a $60   **b** 95 kg   **c** 280 cm   **d** 750 mg

4 **a** Increase 200 by 75%   **b** Increase 200 by 62.5%

    c Decrease 200 by 12.5%

5 What is the percentage change when you multiply by
    a   1.6   b   1.08   c   4
    d   0.6   e   0.99   f   0.07?

6   a   Increase 240 by 60%
    b   Decrease 384 by 37.5%
    c   What do you notice about your answers to **a** and **b**?

Practice

7   a   What percentage of 4 hours is 6.5 hours?
    b   The length of a train journey increases from 4 hours to 6.5 hours.
        What is the percentage increase?

8   a   What percentage of $680 is $490?
    b   A price is reduced from $680 to $490. What is the percentage decrease?

9   The money in a bank account increases from $400 to $1000.
   Copy and complete these sentences.
    a $1000 is ......% of $400.
    b   The money has increased by ......%.

10 There are 320 people in a room.
   Show that an increase of 10% followed by an increase of 50% is the same as an increase of 65%.

Challenge

11 Work out the four missing numbers in this chart.

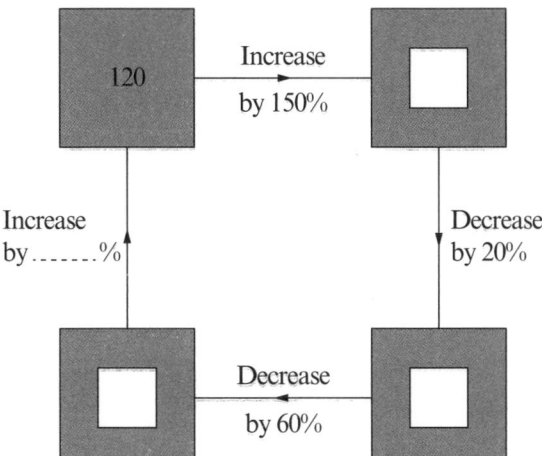

12 This table shows the population of Indonesia.

Year	Population (million)
1960	88
1970	115
1980	147
1990	181
2000	212
2010	242

    a   Work out the percentage increase from 1960 to 2010.

    b   Which decade had the largest percentage increase in population? What was the percentage?

    c   Which decade had the smallest percentage increase in population? What was the percentage?

    d   Use the table to estimate the population in 2020. Justify your answer.

13 a Here is a sequence of numbers increasing by 30 each time.

$$120 \rightarrow 150 \rightarrow 180 \rightarrow 210$$

Calculate the percentage increase for each step. Round your answers to 1 decimal place.

    b   Here is a sequence of numbers decreasing by 50 each time.

$$600 \rightarrow 550 \rightarrow 500 \rightarrow 450$$

Calculate the percentage decrease for each step.

    c   In this sequence the percentage increase for each step is the same.

$$300 \rightarrow 540 \rightarrow \ldots\ldots \rightarrow \ldots\ldots$$

Calculate the two missing numbers.

 14 A new car costs $40 000.

The value falls by 20% per year. Show that after four years the value is approximately 60% less than the original value.

11 ▶ Graphs

› 11.1 Functions

Exercise 11.1

Focus

1   The cost of hiring a ladder is in two parts.
    There is a delivery charge of $10, plus a charge per day of $5.
    a   Work out the cost of hiring a ladder for
        i   3 days   ii   6 days.
    b   The cost of hiring a ladder for n days is $$h$.
        Write a function for h in terms of n.

2   Cinema tickets cost $8 each and there is a single booking fee of $4.
    a   Work out the total cost of booking 5 tickets.
    b   The total cost of booking t tickets is $$y$.
        Write a function for y in terms of t.

3   The cost of renting an apartment is in two parts.
    There is an agent's fee of $65, plus a monthly rent of $750.
    a   Find the total cost of renting for
        i   3 months   ii   6 months.
    b   The cost for m months is $$r$.
        Write a function for r.

4   A car has 37 litres of petrol in its tank at the start of a journey.
    It uses petrol at a rate of 6 litres per hour.
    a   Work out how many litres are in the tank after
        i   2 hours   ii   3 hours.
    b   There are L litres in the tank after t hours. Write a formula for L.

Practice

5   A gardener plants a tree and measures the height every year.
    The height is h metres after t years and $h = 2t + 3$.
    a   Find the height after 6 years.
    b   By how much does the height increase each year?
    c   What was the height of the tree when it was planted?

6   Here is a function: $s = 24 - 2t$
    a   Work out the value of s when
    i $t = 0$ **ii** $t = 3$ **iii** $t = 5$
    b   What value of t makes $s = 0$?

7   A man is 5 years more than twice a woman's age.
    a   Work out the man's age if the woman is 20.
    b   Work out the man's age if the woman is 32.
    c   The woman is w years old and the man is m years old.
            Write a function to show the relationship between their ages.

8   A boy is b years old and a girl is g years old $g = 3b - 6$.
    a   Work out the girl's age if the boy is 5 years old.
    b   Describe in words the relationship between the ages of the girl
            and the boy.

Challenge

9   **a**   Work out the perimeter of this shape when $x = 6$.

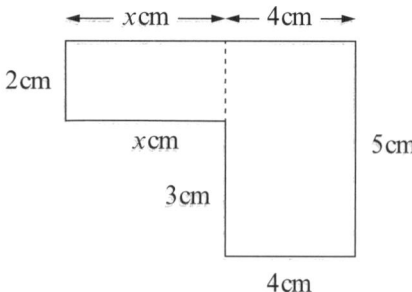

    b   The perimeter is p cm. Write a function for p in terms of x.
    c   The area is a cm². Write a function for a.

10 If $x = 2$ then $y = 8$.

Which of these functions could be correct?

| A | $y = 4x$ |
| B | $y = 2x + 4$ |

| C | $y = 6x - 4$ |
| D | $y = 12 - 2x$ |

| E | $y = 9x - 10$ |

11 Here is a function: $y = 30x + 15$

Give the details of a situation this function could describe.

Explain what the numbers 30 and 15 represent.

12 Here is a function: $y = 5n + 10$

It shows the cost, in dollars, of hiring a bike for n days.

    a Show that the cost for 14 days is less than twice the cost for 7 days.

    b Zara pays to hire the bike for a certain number of days but she returns the bike one day early. She gets a refund for the day she did not use. How much is the refund?

> 11.2 Plotting graphs

Exercise 11.2

Focus

Key word
plot

1 A function is $y = 2x - 2$.

    a Copy and complete this table of values.

x	−2	−1	0	1	2	3	4	5
$y = 2x - 2$	−6							8

    b Use the table to **plot** a graph of $y = 2x - 2$.

2 Here is a function: $y = 3x + 4$

    a Copy and complete this table of values.

x	−3	−2	−1	0	1	2	3
$y = 3x + 4$	−5			4			

    b Use the table to draw a graph of $y = 3x + 4$.

3 Here is a function: $y = 5 - x$

    a Copy and complete this table.

x	−2	−1	0	1	2	3	4	5	6
$y = 5 - x$	7			4				0	

    b Use the table to draw a graph of $y = 5 - x$.

4 Here is a function: $y = 4x - 1$

    a If $x = 3$ work out the value of y.

    b Copy and complete this table.

x	−3	−2	−1	0	1	2	3
$y = 4x - 1$							

    c Use the table to draw a graph of $y = 4x - 1$.

Practice

5 Here is a function: $y = 6 - 2x$

    a If $x = -2$ show that $y = 10$.

    b Copy and complete this table.

x	−2	−1	0	1	2	3	4
$y = 6 - 2x$							

    c Use the table to draw a graph of $y = 6 - 2x$.

    d If the line is extended, which of these points will be on the line?

        A (−4, 14)   **B** (6, −4)   **C** (−8, 20)

        D (10, −14)   **E** (−10, 26)

6 $y = 15x + 10$

    a Copy and complete this table.

x	−2	−1	0	1	2	3	4
$y = 15x + 10$							

    b Draw a graph of $y = 15x + 10$.

    c Where does the line cross the y-axis?

7 **a** Copy and complete this table of values for $60 - x$.

x	−20	−10	0	10	20	30	40
$60 - x$	80						20

    b Use your table to draw a graph of $y = 60 - x$.

    c Where does the line cross the y-axis?

    d If the line is extended, where does it cross the x-axis?

8   a   Copy and complete this table of values for $5x + 20$.

x	−2	−1	0	1	2	3	4
$5x+20$		15				35	

b   Draw a graph of $y = 5x + 20$.

c   Copy and complete this table of values for $30 - 5x$.

x	−2	−1	0	1	2	3	4
$30-5x$	40						10

d   On the same axes as for part **b**, draw a graph of $y = 30 - 5x$.

e   Where do the two lines cross?

9   Here is the equation of a line: $y = 25x - 10$

Copy and complete the coordinates of these points on the line.

a $(5, \boxed{})$ **b** $(8, \boxed{})$ **c** $(-2, \boxed{})$

d $(\boxed{}, 15)$ **e** $(\boxed{}, 90)$

Challenge

10   The width of this rectangle is x cm.

The length is 3 cm more than the width.

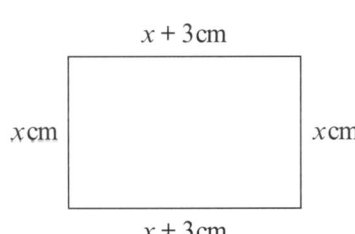

a   The perimeter is p cm. Write a function for p.

b   Copy and complete this table of values.

x	1	2	3	4	5	6	7
p					26		

c   Use the table to draw a graph. Put p on the vertical axis.

d   The perimeter of the rectangle is 20 cm. Use your graph to find the width of the rectangle.

11   An electrician visits a customer's home. The total cost is in two parts: a fixed charge of $50 and an hourly rate of $30.

a   The total charge for t hours is y dollars. Write a formula for y.

b   Copy and complete this table of values.

t	1	2	3	4	5
y					

c   Use your table to draw a graph. Put t on the horizontal axis.

d   The electrician charges $185 for a job. Use the graph to work out how long it took.

12 The temperature ($T°C$) after m minutes is given by the function
$T = 70 - 6m$.

   a Construct a table for values of m, from 1 to 6, and T.

   b Use the table to draw a graph of $T = 70 - 6m$. Put m on the horizontal axis.

   c How does the graph show that the temperature is decreasing at a constant rate?

   d Use your graph to find the time when the temperature is 55 °C.

13 The cost ($\$y$) of hiring a drill for x days is given by the function
$y = 4x + 10$.

   a Draw a graph to show the cost of hiring the drill for up to 7 days.

   b Explain what the 10 in the function tells you.

   c Explain what the 4 in the function tells you.

> 11.3 Gradient and intercept

Exercise 11.3

Focus

Key words

equation of a line
gradient
x-intercept
y-intercept

1 **a** Copy and complete this table of values.

x	−4	−3	−2	−1	0	1	2	3	4
$x+2$	−2							5	

   b Plot a graph of $y = x + 2$.

   c On the same axes, plot a graph of $y = x$.

   d Find the **gradient** of each line.

2 **a** Copy and complete this table of values.

x	−4	−3	−2	−1	0	1	2	3	4
$2x-1$	−9					1			

   b Plot a graph of $y = 2x - 1$.

   c On the same axes, plot a graph of $y = 2x$.

   d Find the gradient of each line.

   e Find the **y-intercept** of each line.

3 **a** Copy and complete this table of values.

x	−4	−3	−2	−1	0	1	2	3	4
5x		−15					10		
5x + 10		−5					20		

b On the same axes, plot graphs of $y = 5x$ and $y = 5x + 10$.

c Find the gradient of each line.

d Find the y-intercept of each line.

4 **a** Copy and complete this table.

x	−3	−2	−1	0	1	2	3
x + 3	0						6

b Copy and complete this table.

x	−3	−2	−1	0	1	2	3
2x + 3	−3						9

c On the same axes, plot the lines $y = x + 3$ and $y = 2x + 3$.

d Find the gradient of each line.

e Find the y-intercept of each line.

Practice

5 Here are the equations of three lines.

$$y = x \qquad y = 2x \qquad y = 3x$$

a On the same axes, plot a graph of each line.

b Write the gradient of each line.

6 **a** Copy and complete this table.

x	−2	−1	0	1	2	3	4
−x + 7	9						3

b Copy and complete this table.

x	−2	−1	0	1	2	3	4
−x + 2				1			

c On the same axes, plot graphs of $y = -x + 7$ and $y = -x + 2$.

d Write the gradient of each line.

e Write the y-intercept of each line.

f Write the **x-intercept** of each line.

7 Here is the **equation of a line**: $y = 10 - 5x$

    a What is the gradient of the line?

    b Where does the line cross the y-axis?

    c Where does the line cross the x-axis?

    d Write the equation of a parallel line that passes through the origin.

8 **a** Copy and complete this table.

x	-2	-1	0	1	2	3
$10x + 20$		10				50

    b Plot a graph of $y = 10x + 20$.

    c On the same axes, plot a graph of $y = 5x + 20$.

    d Write the gradient and the y-intercept of each line.

Challenge

9 Four lines are plotted on this diagram.

They all cross the y-axis at $(0, 6)$.

The gradients of the lines are 1, -1, 2 and -2.

    a Write the equation of each line.

    b Write the coordinates of the x-intercept of each line.

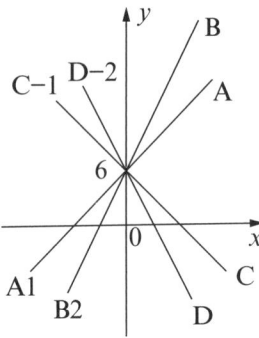

10 The water in a tank is leaking out.

The number of litres (y) left in the tank after x hours is given by the function $y = 18 - 3x$.

    a Copy and complete this table.

x	0	1	2	3	4	5	6
$18 - 3x$				9			

    b Plot a graph to show the quantity of water in the tank over time.

    c What happens after 6 hours?

    d What does the y-intercept tell you?

    e What is the gradient? What does it tell you?

11 Here are three parallel lines.

    a The equation of one of the lines is $y = 10x + 20$.

       Which line is this?

    b Find the equations of the other two lines.

    c Write the equation of a parallel line that passes through $(0, -10)$.

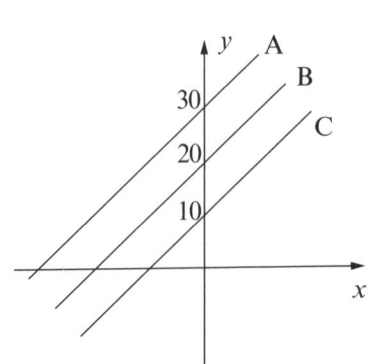

12 The cost of a holiday depends on the number of nights.
The cost for n nights is $\$c$ where $c = 100n + 50$.
   a Construct a table to show the cost for different values of n.
   b Draw a graph to show the cost.
   c Explain what the gradient of the line represents.

> 11.4 Interpreting graphs

Exercise 11.4

Focus

1 Sofia and Zara are walking along the same path.
   a How far does Zara walk every 10 minutes?
   b Sofia starts after Zara. How long after?
   c How far does Sofia walk every 10 minutes?
   d The lines cross. What does the point where they cross show you?

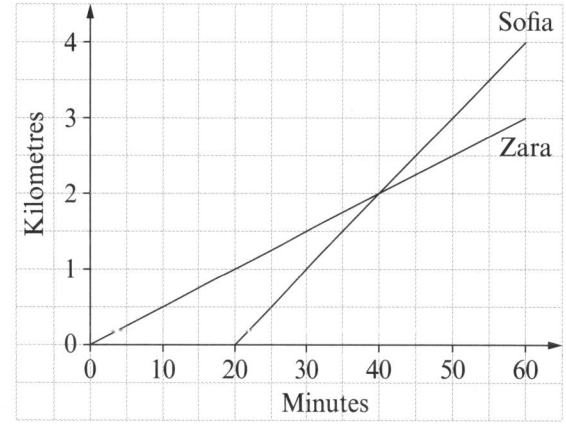

2 Two buckets are being filled with water.
   a How much water is in each bucket initially?
   b Find the number of litres in each bucket after 1 minute.
   c How many litres are added to Bucket 1 each minute?
   d How many litres are added to Bucket 2 each minute?
   e When do the two buckets contain the same amount of water?

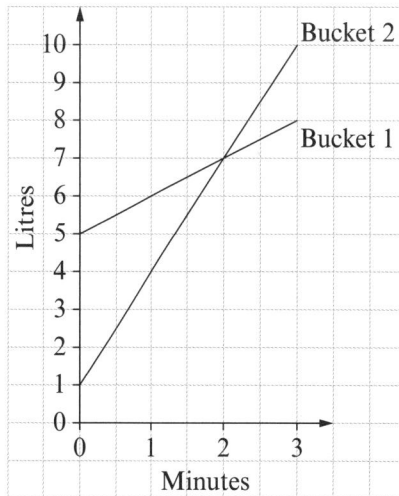

3 Zara and Sofia live together.

Zara leaves home at 09:00 and cycles to the shops. When she gets there she waits for Sofia.

a How long did Zara take to get to the shops?

b How far are the shops from Zara's house?

Sofia leaves home after Zara and cycles to the shops.

c What time did Sofia leave home?

d Who cycled faster, Zara or Sofia? Give a reason for your answer.

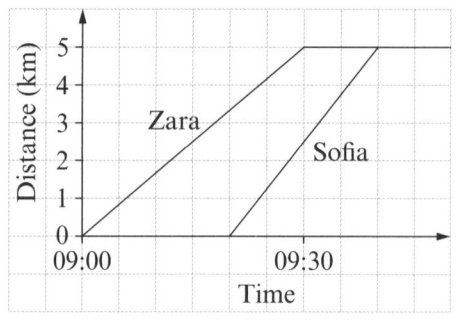

4 A car and a lorry use petrol. The graph shows the amount of petrol left in each vehicle.

a How much petrol is in the lorry initially?

b How much petrol does the lorry use each hour?

c How much petrol is in the car initially?

d Copy and complete this table for the car.

Hours	0	1	2	3	4
Litres					

e How much petrol does the car use each hour?

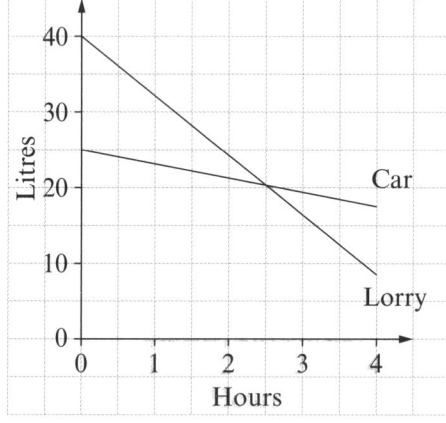

Practice

5 This graph shows the charges for two plumbers. Each plumber has a fixed charge and an hourly charge.

a Which plumber is cheaper for a job that lasts 1.5 hours?

b Find the fixed charge for each plumber.

c Copy and complete this table for Plumber A.

Hours	0	1	2	3	4	5
Cost						

d Work out the hourly charge for Plumber A.

e Work out the hourly charge for Plumber B.

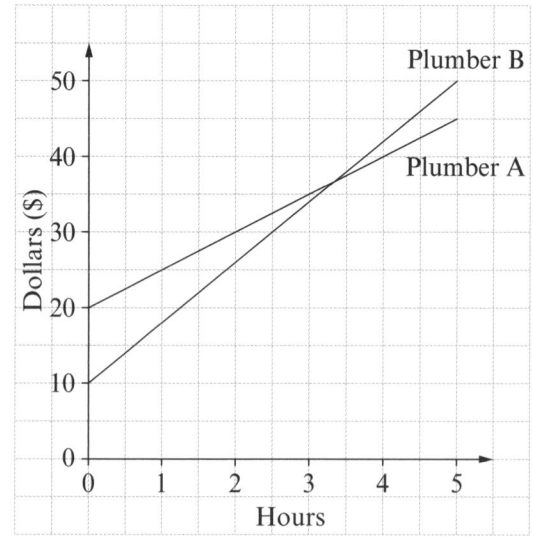

6 Arun and Marcus are 400 metres apart.
They run towards each other.

This graph shows their distances from Arun's
starting point.

a How long does Arun take to run 200 m?

b How far does Arun run every 10 seconds?

c How far does Marcus run every
10 seconds?

d What does the point where the lines cross
show you?

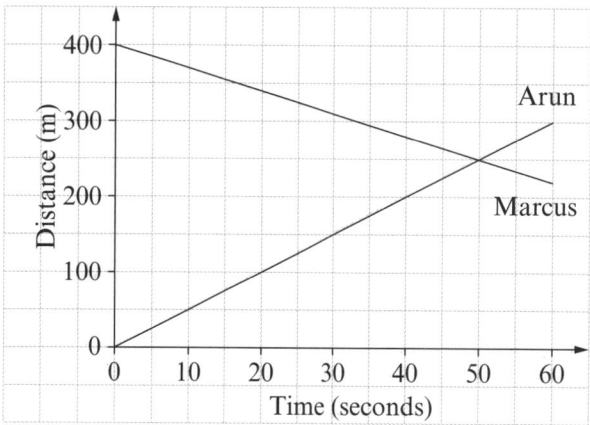

7 The cost of hiring a coach depends on the
number of people.

This graph gives the costs for two different
companies, A and B.

a Find the cost of a coach for 30 people with
company A.

b When is company A cheaper than
company B?

c Copy and complete this table of values for
company A.

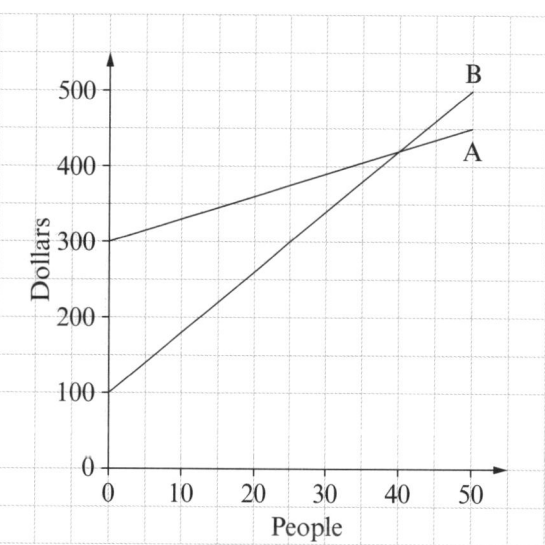

People	0	10	20	30	40	50
Cost ($)	300					

For each company, there is a fixed charge and a
cost per person.

d For company A, work out

   i the fixed charge   **ii** the charge per person.

e For company B, work out

   i the fixed charge   **ii** the charge per person.

Challenge

8 The heights of two plants are measured each week. The results are shown on this graph.

   a Work out the initial height of each plant.

   b How does the graph show that each plant grows an equal amount each week?

   c How much does each plant grow each week?

   d After x weeks, the height of a plant is y cm.

   The equation of the line for plant X is $y = 5x + 10$.

   Work out a similar equation for plant Y.

   e Assume the plants continue to grow at the same rate.

   When will they be the same height?

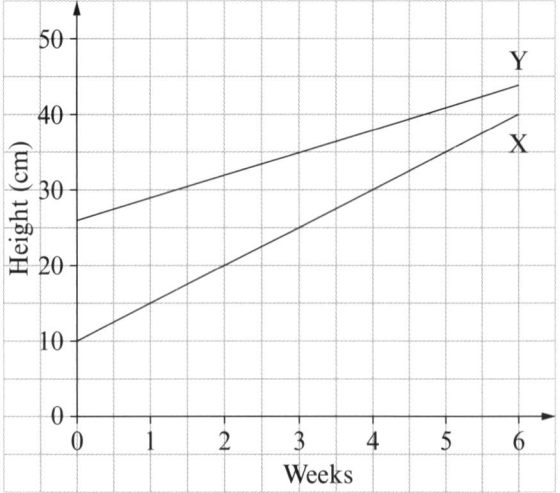

9 Two liquids are heated to 78 °C.

   a Work out how much the temperature of liquid A increases each minute.

   b The temperature of liquid B increases in three stages.

   Work out the rate of increase per minute at each stage.

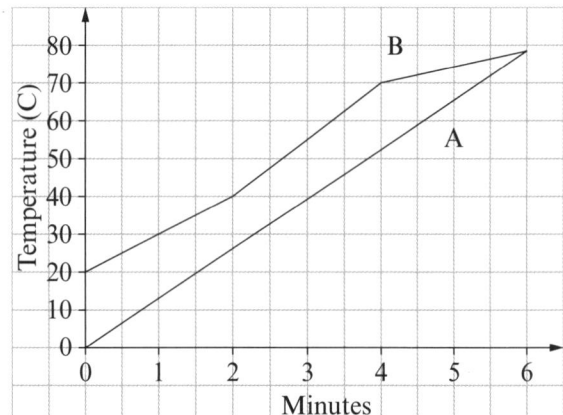

10 A company offers two types of cement mixer for hire. The graph shows the costs of hiring these cement mixers.

   a For each type of cement mixer, A and B, find the charge for 4 days' hire.

   Suppose the charge for x days is $\$y$.

   b Show that, for mixer A, the equation of the line is $y = 20x + 180$.

   c Find a similar equation for mixer B.

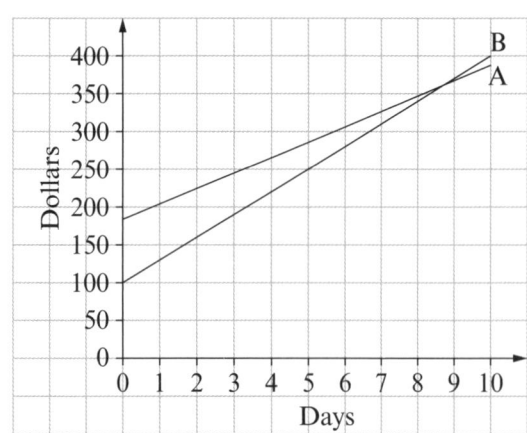

12 ▶ Ratio and proportion

> 12.1 Simplifying ratios

Exercise 12.1

Key words

ratio
simplify

Focus

1   **Simplify** each **ratio**. Some of them have been started for you.

a $\div 3$ $\overset{3\ :\ 9}{\boxed{} : \boxed{}}$ $\div 3$

b $\div 2$ $\overset{2\ :\ 18}{\boxed{} : \boxed{}}$ $\div 2$

c $5 : 40$

d $3 : 12$

e $6 : 18$

f $\div 2$ $\overset{10\ :\ 2}{\boxed{} : \boxed{}}$ $\div 2$

g $\div 3$ $\overset{30\ :\ 3}{\boxed{} : \boxed{}}$ $\div 3$

h $27 : 3$

i $700 : 10$

j $16 : 4$

2   Simplify each ratio. Some of them have been started for you.

a $\div 2$ $\overset{6\ :\ 8}{\boxed{} : \boxed{}}$ $\div 2$

b $\div 4$ $\overset{8\ :\ 12}{\boxed{} : \boxed{}}$ $\div 4$

c $12 : 15$

d $15 : 25$

e $25 : 35$

f $\div 8$ $\overset{32\ :\ 24}{\boxed{} : \boxed{}}$ $\div 8$

g $\div 12$ $\overset{36\ :\ 24}{\boxed{} : \boxed{}}$ $\div 12$

h $27 : 24$

i $36 : 27$

j $40 : 24$

3 Simplify each ratio. Divide all the numbers in the ratio by the highest common factor (written in the bracket). The first one is done for you.

    a   2:10:12   (divide by 2)   Answer is 1:5:6

    b   8:12:16   (divide by 4)   Answer is ....

    c   12:9:15   (divide by 3)   Answer is ....

4 Simplify each ratio.

    a   25:30:10   **b**   32:8:64   **c**   36:9:15

 5 This is part of Karen's homework.

> _Question_
>
> Simplify the ratio 6:20:10
>
> _Answers_
>
> 6:20 simplifies to 3:10
>
> 20:10 simplifies to 2:1
>
> So the ratio is 3:10:2:1

    a   Explain the mistake Karen has made.

    b   Work out the correct answer.

Practice

6 Simplify each ratio.

    a   250 m : 1 km   **b**   2 m : 15 cm

    c $1.26 : 60 cents   **d**   2.4 kg : 600 g

    e   1 minute : 42 seconds   **f**   1.75 t : 500 kg

7 Arun uses 600 g of walnuts and 1 kg of dates in a fruit loaf.

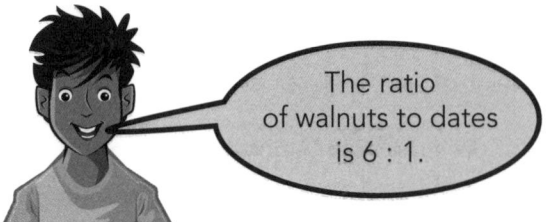

The ratio of walnuts to dates is 6 : 1.

Is Arun correct? Explain your answer.

8 Simplify each ratio.

    a   400 m : 0.8 km : 60 m   **b**   4 g : 2200 mg : 0.8 g

    c $\frac{1}{2}$ hour : 1 minute : 20 seconds   **d**   45 cents : $0.15 : $2

    e   6 m : 0.09 km : 300 cm   **f**   48 cm : 88 mm : 0.4 m

> **Tip**
>
> Remember, both quantities must be in the same units before you simplify.

9 Zara and Marcus are baking a huge cake.

They mix 450 g of butter with 550 g of sugar and 1.1 kg of flour.

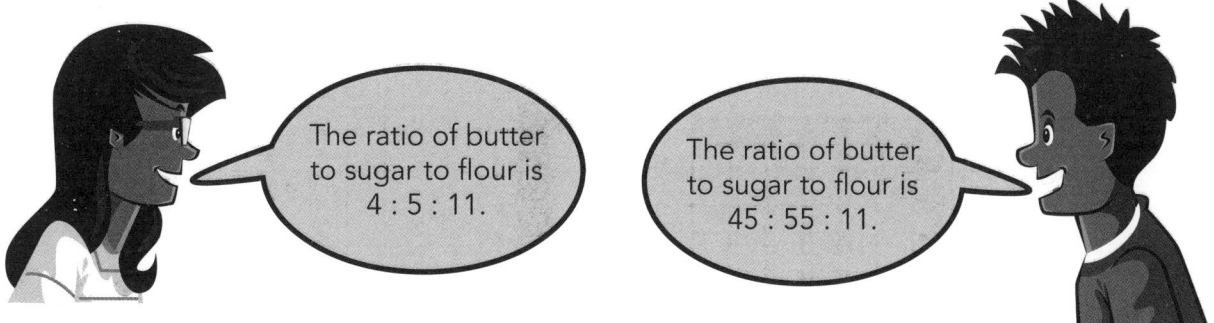

The ratio of butter to sugar to flour is 4 : 5 : 11.

The ratio of butter to sugar to flour is 45 : 55 : 11.

Is either of them correct? Explain your answer.

10 Work out.

a Two cups hold 450 ml and five mugs hold 1.25 litres.

Which holds more liquid, one cup or one mug?

b Three bags of red rice have a mass of 960 g and four bags of brown rice have a mass of 1.22 kg.

Which has a greater mass, one bag of red rice or one bag of brown rice?

c Jules can text 16 words in 48 seconds. Sion can text 10 words in 35 seconds.

Who can text more quickly, Jules or Sion?

Challenge

11 Simplify each ratio.

a 0.4 : 2   b 2.5 : 5   c 0.8 : 3.2

d 0.5 : 2.5   e 3.6 : 1.8   f 2.1 : 1.5

g 2.5 : 6   h 2.1 : 1.4   i 0.05 : 0.3 : 1

> **Tip**
>
> Remember to multiply by 10 or 100 first so all the numbers are whole numbers not decimals.

12 Abbie is trying to find the quickest way to drive to her new job.

She tries three different routes and writes down how long each one takes.

a Abbie thinks the ratio of her times for routes 1, 2 and 3 is 5 : 6 : 7. Without doing any calculations, explain how you know that Abbie is wrong.

Route 1	55 mins
Route 2	$1\frac{1}{2}$ hours
Route 3	1 hour 10 mins

b Abbie's mum uses this method to work out the ratio of Abbie's times.

> _Route 1_ : _Route 2_ : _Route 3_
>
> 55 mins : $1\frac{1}{2}$ hours : 1 hour 10 mins
>
> 0.55 : 1.5 : 1.1
>
> Multiply by 100 55 : 15 : 11
>
> Divide by 5 11 : 3 : 2

Explain the mistakes that Abbie's mum has made.

c Work out the correct ratio of Abbie's times.

13 Any ratio can be written in the form $1:n$ or $n:1$, like this:

In the form $1:n$, $\div 4$ ⌐ 4 : 10 ⌐ $\div 4$
               1 : 2.5

In the form $n:1$, $\div 10$ ⌐ 4 : 10 ⌐ $\div 10$
               0.4 : 1

Write these ratios

    i in the form $1:n$ **ii** in the form $n:1$.

a 2:4   **b** 3:12   **c** 5:25   **d** 25:200

14 a On a piece of paper, draw three squares with side lengths 3 cm, 4 cm and 5 cm.

Measure the length of the diagonal of each square, correct to the nearest millimetre.

Copy and complete the table below. You can use a calculator to work out the value for n in the last column of the table. Write your values for n correct to 1 d.p.

Length of side	Length of diagonal	Ratio of lengths side : diagonal	Ratio of lengths side : diagonal in the form 1 : n
3 cm			
4 cm			
5 cm			

b What do you notice about the ratios in the form $1:n$?

c What do you think the length of the diagonal will be for a square with side length 8 cm?

Explain how you worked out your answer.

d Predict the side length for a square with diagonal length 14 cm.

Explain how you worked out your answer.

> 12.2 Sharing in a ratio

Exercise 12.2

Key words

profit

share

Focus

1   Copy and complete the workings to **share** $72 between Ali, Bob and Carl in the ratio $4:1:3$.

Total number of parts: $4 + 1 + 3 = \boxed{}$

Value of one part: $\$72 \div \boxed{} = \boxed{}$

Ali gets: $4 \times \boxed{} = \boxed{}$

Bob gets: $1 \times \boxed{} = \boxed{}$

Carl gets: $3 \times \boxed{} = \boxed{}$

2   Share these amounts among Ali, Bob and Carl in the given ratios. Use the same method as in Question **1**.

a $90 in the ratio $1:3:5$

b $240 in the ratio $3:4:5$

c $1000 in the ratio $3:5:2$

d $350 in the ratio $5:2:7$

3   Gita, Harry and Indira share their electricity bill in the ratio $2:4:5$.

a   How much does each of them pay when their electricity bill is

  i $110   ii $165   iii $352?

b   Show how to check your answers to part **a**.

4   A gardening club is made up of men, women and children in the ratio $5:4:11$.

Altogether, the club has 240 members.

a   How many members of the gardening club are

  i   men   ii   women   iii   children?

b   Show how to check your answers to part **a**.

5   The angles in a triangle are in the ratio $2:3:4$.

What are the sizes of the angles in the triangle?

Tip

The angles in a triangle add up to 180°.

Practice

6   A box of shapes contains triangles, squares and rectangles in the ratio $5:1:2$.

The box contains 56 shapes altogether.

a   How many shapes in the box are

   i   triangles

   ii   squares

   iii   rectangles?

14 of the shapes are taken out.

There are now 42 shapes left in the box.

The ratio of the numbers of triangles, squares and rectangles in the box is now $4:1:2$.

b   Now, how many shapes in the box are

   i   triangles

   ii   squares

   iii   rectangles?

> **Tip**
>
> Remember, there are now 42 shapes in the box.

7   Zara, Sofia, Arun and Marcus run their own business.

They share the money they earn from each project in the ratio of the number of hours they work on the project.

This is the time-sheet for one of their projects.

How much does each of them earn from this project?

Project earnings:		$750	
Time spent working on the project:			
Zara	5 hours	Sofia	12 hours
Arun	4 hours	Marcus	9 hours

 8   Four children are given a painting.

They sell it and share the money in the ratio of their ages.

The children are 6, 8, 11 and 13 years old.

The painting sells for $4750.

Show that the oldest child receives $1625.

9   Every year, Patrick shares 280 oranges between his
    children in the ratio of their ages.

    This year, the children are 3, 7 and 10 years old.

    How many **more** oranges will the youngest child receive in five
    years' time, than she received this year?

10 Tatiana, Lucia and Gianna buy a house for $120 000.

    Tatiana pays $10 000, Lucia pays $70 000 and Gianna pays the rest.

    Four years later, they sell the house for $210 000.

    They share the money in the same ratio in which they bought
    the house.

    Gianna thinks she will make $30 000 **profit** on the sale of the house.

    Is Gianna correct? Show all your working.

Challenge

11 Xiu, Zane and Mike buy a boat.

    The information shows how much each of them pays for
    the boat.

    Three years later, they sell the boat for $3300.

    They share the money from the sale of the boat in the same
    ratio in which they bought the boat.

    a How much does each of them receive from the sale of
         the boat?

    b How much money did Mike lose from the sale of the boat?

    c Who made the smallest loss from the sale of the boat? How
         much did he lose?

5th August 2019	
Xiu paid:	$1400
Zane paid:	$1050
Mike paid:	$1750
Total cost of boat:	$4200

12 There are 24 coins in Zara's purse.

    The ratio of 50 cent to 25 cent to 10 cent coins is $2:3:7$.

    Show that she has $4.90 in her purse in total.

13 Heidi makes her favourite colour paint by mixing blue, yellow and
    green in the ratio $0.8:1.1:0.1$.

    Copy and complete the table to show how much of each colour she
    needs to make the quantities shown.

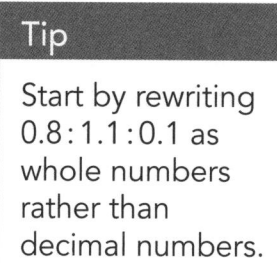

Tip

Start by rewriting
$0.8:1.1:0.1$ as
whole numbers
rather than
decimal numbers.

Size of tin	Blue	Yellow	Green
1 litre			
1.5 litres			
2.5 litres			

14   Salim draws a quadrilateral. The angles are in the ratio $1:4:5:2$.
Salim thinks the largest angle is 110° more than the smallest angle.
Is Salim correct? Explain your answer.

> 12.3 Ratio and direct proportion

Exercise 12.3

Focus

Look at the example below.

Harry and Misha make grey paint by mixing white and black paint.

Harry mixes white with black in the ratio $2:8$

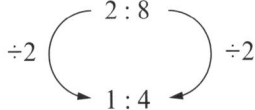 

Misha mixes white with black in the ratio $3:9$

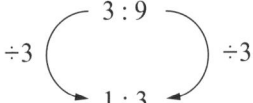 

Harry has the darker paint because he has four black for every white,
while Misha has only three black for every white.

1   Arshan and Oditi make pink paint by mixing white paint and
red paint. Arshan mixes white and red in the ratio $3:6$. Oditi mixes
white and red in the ratio $4:12$. Copy and complete the workings
to find out who has the darker paint.

Arshan   Oditi

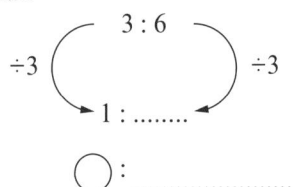   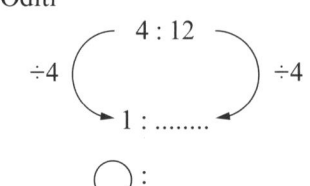

Who makes the darker paint?

Tip

Think of Harry
mixing four tins of
black paint with
one tin of white
paint, while Misha
mixes three tins
of black paint
with one tin of
white paint.

Tip

Draw and colour
the circles you
need for the red
paint, to help you
compare.

2   Jake and Razi make light blue paint by mixing white paint and blue paint.

Jake mixes white and blue in the ratio 4:20. Razi mixes white and blue in the ratio 5:15.

Copy and complete the workings to find out who has the darker paint.

Jake 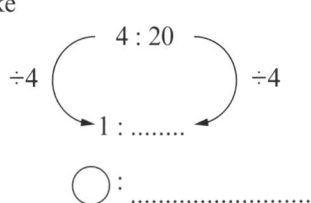   Razi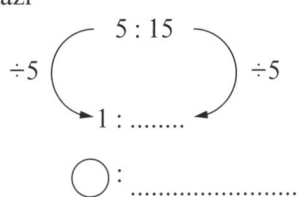

Tip
Draw and colour the circles you need for the blue paint, to help you compare.

Who makes the darker paint?

3   Copy and complete the workings to change each ratio into a fraction.

a   A bag of nuts has brazil nuts and almonds in the ratio 2:3.
What fraction of the nuts are   i   brazil nuts   ii   almonds?
Total number of parts $= 2 + 3 = \boxed{}$

i   Fraction that are brazil nuts $= \dfrac{2}{\boxed{}}$ ii   Fraction that are almonds $= \dfrac{3}{\boxed{}}$

b   A box of balls has tennis balls and footballs in the ratio 5:4.
What fraction of the balls are   i   tennis balls   ii   footballs?
Total number of parts $= 5 + 4 = \boxed{}$

i   Fraction that are tennis balls $= \dfrac{5}{\boxed{}}$ ii   Fraction that are footballs $= \dfrac{4}{\boxed{}}$

c   A basket of vegetables has onions and potatoes in the ratio 1:9.
What fraction of the vegetables are   i   onions   ii   potatoes?
Total number of parts $= 1 + 9 = \boxed{}$

i   Fraction that are onions $= \dfrac{1}{\boxed{}}$ ii   Fraction that are potatoes $= \dfrac{9}{\boxed{}}$

4   Jay mixes two **shades** of orange paint.
He uses the following ratios of orange:white.

Orange sunset 3:2	Orange flame 5:3

a   Copy and complete the workings to find the fraction of each paint that is orange.

Orange sunset: total number of parts $= 3 + 2 = \boxed{}$ fraction orange $= \dfrac{\boxed{}}{5}$

Orange flame: total number of parts $= 5 + 3 = \boxed{}$ fraction orange $= \dfrac{\boxed{}}{8}$

b Copy and complete the workings to write the fractions with a common denominator.

Orange sunset: fraction orange $= \dfrac{\square}{5} = \dfrac{\square \times 8}{5 \times 8} = \dfrac{\square}{40}$

Orange flame: fraction orange $= \dfrac{\square}{8} = \dfrac{\square \times 5}{8 \times 5} = \dfrac{\square}{40}$

c Which paint has the greater fraction that is orange, orange sunset or orange flame?

d Which paint is darker, orange sunset or orange flame? Explain your answer.

5 Copy and complete the workings to answer this question.

A school cricket club has 45 members. The ratio of boys to girls is $5:4$.

a What fraction of the club members are boys?

Total number of parts $= 5 + 4 = \square$ Fraction boys $= \dfrac{\square}{\square}$

b How many boys are in the club?

Boys in the club $=$ fraction boys $\times 45 = \dfrac{\square}{\square} \times 45 = \square$

6 Ken mixes two different fruit drinks.

He uses the following ratios of grape juice : pear juice.

Fruit drink **A** $= 2:7$ Fruit drink **B** $= 5:13$

a Copy and complete the workings to find the fraction of each drink that is pear juice.

Fruit drink **A**:   total number of parts $= 2 + 7 = \square$ fraction pear juice $= \dfrac{\square}{\square}$

Fruit drink **B**:   total number of parts $= 5 + 13 = \square$ fraction pear juice $= \dfrac{\square}{\square}$

b Copy and complete the workings to write the fractions with a common denominator.

Fruit drink **A**:   fraction pear juice $= \dfrac{\square}{9} = \dfrac{\square \times 2}{9 \times 2} = \dfrac{\square}{18}$

Fruit drink **B**:   fraction pear juice $= \dfrac{\square}{\square}$

c Which drink has the greater fraction that is pear juice, A or B?

d Which drink will taste more of pear, A or B? Explain your answer.

Practice

7 A bag of dried fruit contains banana chips and apricots in the ratio $7:3$.

The bag contains 40 pieces of dried fruit.

   a What fraction of the pieces of dried fruit are apricots?

   b How many apricots are there in the bag?

8 The ratio of boys to girls in a swimming club is $3:5$.

Which of these cards shows the number of children that could be in the swimming club?

 **A** 29    **B** 35    **C** 68   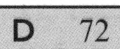 **D** 72    **E** 82

Justify your choice.

9 The ratio of men to women in a cafe is $7:6$.

The number of adults in the cafe is greater than 30 but less than 40.

How many adults are in the cafe?

10 Work out.

   a A bag contains blue and white counters. $\frac{3}{4}$ of the counters are blue.

     What is the ratio of blue to white counters?

   b A box contains CDs and DVDs. $\frac{5}{9}$ of the items are DVDs.

     What is the ratio of CDs to DVDs?

   c $\frac{7}{10}$ of the learners in a Madarin class are women. The rest are men.

     What is the ratio of women to men in the Mandarin class?

11 Ru Shi mixes two shades of yellow paint.

She uses the following ratios of yellow : white.

> Banana yellow $5:3$ Mellow yellow $7:5$

   a What fraction of each shade of yellow paint is white?

   b Which shade of yellow paint is lighter?

     Show all your working. Justify your choice.

> **Tip**
>
> The paint which is lighter has a greater **proportion** of white.

12 Gavin mixes a fruit drink. He uses orange juice and pineapple juice in the ratio $2:7$.

Matt mixes a fruit drink. He uses orange juice and pineapple juice in the ratio $3:10$.

   a What fraction of each fruit drink is pineapple juice?

   b Whose fruit drink, Gavin's or Matt's, has the higher proportion of pineapple juice?

     Show all your working. Justify your choice.

Challenge

13 Li and Su collect magazines and puzzle books.

Li has 30 magazines and 12 puzzle books.

Su has 45 magazines and 18 puzzle books.

Who has the greater proportion of magazines? Justify your choice.

14 Two clothes shops sell coats and jumpers.

'Clothes 4 U' has 24 coats and 60 jumpers for sale.

'Clothes 2 Keep' has 40 coats and 95 jumpers for sale.

Which shop has the greater proportion of coats? Justify your choice.

15 A builder makes concrete for a floor. He uses cement, sand and gravel in the ratio $1:2:4$.

    a   What fraction of the concrete is sand?

The builder makes 2.1 tonnes of concrete.

    b   How many kilograms of sand does he use?

16 The ratio of women to men in a badminton club is $?:5$.

There are more men than women.

The number of adults in the badminton club is 28.

How many women are in the badminton club?

Tip
Start by trying different values for ? in the ratio.

13 Probability

> 13.1 Calculating probabilities

Exercise 13.1

Focus

1   A spinner has sectors in different colours.

The probability it is green is 0.15 and the probability it is brown is 0.4.

Find the probability that it is

a   not green   b   not brown.

2   A train can arrive early, on time or late.

The probability the train arrives early is 5% and the probability it arrives late is 15%.

Work out the probability that it is

a   not early   b   not late   c   not on time.

3   A dice is biased.

The probability of throwing 3 is $\frac{1}{4}$ and the probability of throwing 6 is $\frac{1}{8}$.

Work out the probability of

a   not throwing 3

b   not throwing 6.

4   Arun throws a coin repeatedly until he throws a head.

This table shows the probability for different numbers of throws.

Throws	1	2	3	4	5	6	7 or more
Probability	$\frac{1}{2}$	$\frac{1}{4}$	$\frac{1}{8}$	$\frac{1}{16}$	$\frac{1}{32}$	$\frac{1}{64}$	$\frac{1}{64}$

Find the probability that Arun takes

a   more than 1 throw   b   more than 2 throws.

Practice

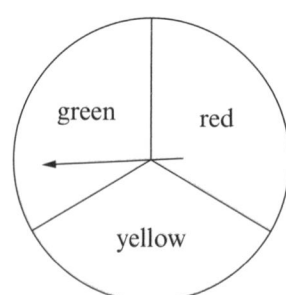

5   A spinner has 3 equally likely colours, red (R), yellow (Y) and green (G).

The spinner is spun twice.

a   Copy and complete this table of outcomes.

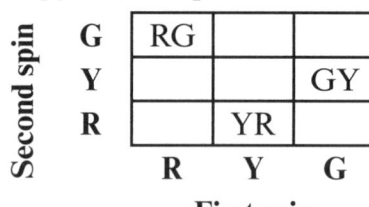

Second spin		First spin	
G	RG		
Y			GY
R		YR	
	R	**Y**	**G**

Find the probability of

b   green on both spins   **c**   a red and a yellow

d   not getting red   **e**   getting red at least once.

6   A spinner has 7 equally likely sectors numbered 1, 2, 3, 4, 5, 6 and 7.

The spinner is spun and a coin is thrown.

a   Draw a table to show the possible outcomes.

Work out the probability of

b   a head and a 5

c   a tail and an even number

d   a head but not a 5.

7   Here are three numbered cards.

Sofia puts the cards in a line at random
to make a 3-digit number.

a   List all the possible outcomes.

b   Find the probability that the number is

    i   an odd number   **ii**   a multiple of 5

    iii   less than 700.

8   Here are two sets of cards.

Set A   **Set B**

| 1 | 2 | 3 | | 1 | 2 | 4 | 3 |

One card is taken at random from each set and they are added
together.

a   Copy and complete this table to show the possible totals.

	1	2	3	4
3				7
2				
1		3		

b Work out the probability that the total is

    i   3   **ii**   5

    iii   less than 5   **iv**   an odd number.

9 Two fair six-sided dice are thrown and the numbers are multiplied together.

    a Draw a table to show the possible outcomes.

    b What is the most likely product? What is the probability of this product?

    c Find the probability of getting more than 15.

    d Find the probability of getting an odd number.

Challenge

10 Two fair six-sided dice are thrown and the difference between the numbers is found.

Find all the possible differences and find the probability of each one.

> **Tip**
>
> For example, if 3 and 5 are thrown, the difference is 2.

11 Here are four number cards. | 3 | | 4 | | 5 | | 6 |

Two cards are chosen at random to make a 2-digit number.

    a List all the 2-digit numbers you can make with these cards.

    b Find the probability that the number has a 4 as one of the digits.

Three cards are chosen at random to make a 3-digit number.

    c List all the 3-digit numbers you can make with these cards.

    d Find the probability that the number is not a multiple of 5.

    e How many 4-digit numbers can you make with these cards? Give a reason for your answer.

    f A 4-digit number is made at random. What is the probability that it is not 6534?

12 A spinner has 3 equal sectors coloured red (R), green (G) and blue (B).

The spinner is spun twice.

    a Copy and complete this tree diagram to show the possible outcomes.

    b Find the probability of

        i   red on both spins

        ii   green on both spins

        iii not getting green on both spins

        iv getting green on at least one spin.

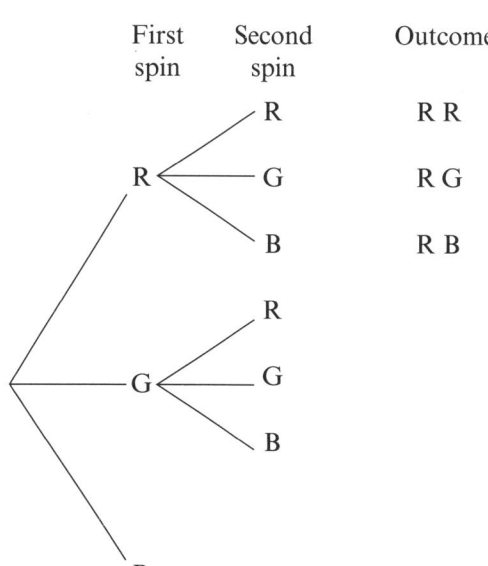

First spin   Second spin   Outcome

13 Here are two words on cards.

S	Q	U	A	R	E

T	R	I	A	N	G	L	E

One card is taken at random from each word.

Find the probability that both cards show the same letter.

Show how you found the answer.

> 13.2 Experimental and theoretical probabilities

Exercise 13.2

Focus

Key words

experimental probability

theoretical probability

1   Arun makes a six-sided cardboard dice. He colours three faces orange, two faces pink and one face white.

He throws his dice 80 times.

Here are the results.

Colour	orange	pink	white
Frequency	34	28	18

a   Calculate the experimental frequency for each colour.

b   Work out the theoretical frequency for each colour.

2   A dice is thrown 80 times. Here are the results.

6	4	5	2	3	3	3	5	1	2
3	1	4	3	5	3	6	5	2	1
4	4	5	4	4	4	6	1	5	6
4	4	1	6	3	3	5	6	6	6
6	5	1	1	1	3	2	1	4	4
3	4	5	5	6	3	4	5	4	3
4	4	2	6	6	1	5	1	4	4
1	6	4	1	5	5	5	2	1	1

a Use the first two rows to find an **experimental probability** of getting a 1.

b Use the first four rows to find an experimental probability of getting a 1.

c Use all eight rows to find an experimental probability of getting a 1.

d Which of your experimental probabilities is closest to the **theoretical probability**?

e Repeat parts **a** to **d** but this time find the probabilities of getting an even number.

3 A spinner has four equal parts coloured yellow, blue, green and red.

Here are the results of 60 spins.

B	Y	R	G	R	G	G	Y	Y	R	B	Y
G	B	Y	G	G	G	G	Y	G	R	B	R
Y	G	Y	Y	R	B	B	G	G	R	R	G
Y	G	G	Y	R	R	B	G	G	Y	B	G
B	G	B	G	R	G	B	B	B	B	G	R

a Find the experimental probability of each colour.

b Compare the experimental probabilities with the theoretical probabilities.

Practice

4 A spinner has five equal sectors numbered 1, 2, 3, 4, 5.

Here are the results of 400 spins.

Score	1	2	3	4	5
Frequency	90	83	86	66	75

a Find the experimental probabilities of

i 2 **ii** an odd number **iii** 4 or 5

b Find the theoretical probabilities of

i 2 **ii** an odd number **iii** 4 or 5

c Do you think the spinner is fair? Give a reason for your answer.

5 When you throw three coins you can get 0, 1, 2 or 3 heads.

Here are the results of a computer simulation of 500 throws of three coins.

Number of heads	0	1	2	3
Frequency	59	180	192	69

a Find the experimental probabilities of 0, 1, 2 and 3 heads.

b Work out the theoretical probabilities of 0, 1, 2 and 3 heads.

c How close are the experimental probabilities to the theoretical ones?

Here are the results of another 500 simulations.

Number of heads	0	1	2	3
Frequency	69	196	172	63

d   Combine the two sets of results to find experimental probabilities based on 1000 throws.

e   Are the experimental probabilities in part **d** closer to the theoretical probabilities than those in part **a**?

Challenge

6   A dice has 10 faces. Each face is one of three colours, green, gold or black.

Here are the results of 400 throws.

Colour	green	gold	black
Frequency	121	231	48

a   Find the experimental probability for each colour.

b   Make a conjecture about the number of faces of each colour. Give a reason for your answer.

Here are the results of another 600 throws.

Colour	green	gold	black
Frequency	172	372	56

c   Calculate new experimental probabilities based on all the results.

d   Do you want to change your conjecture in part **b**? Give a reason for your answer.

7   a   Can you throw a coin fairly? Do an experiment to find out.

Decide how many times you will throw the coin.

Use your results to calculate experimental frequencies and compare them with the theoretical frequencies.

State your conclusion about your throwing. Give a reason.

b   How can you modify your experiment to see if you can throw two coins fairly?

14 ▸ Position and transformation

⟩ 14.1 Bearings

Exercise 14.1

Focus

1   Match each diagram to the **bearing** you need to walk on to get from *A* to *B*.
    The first one is done for you: **A** and **iii**

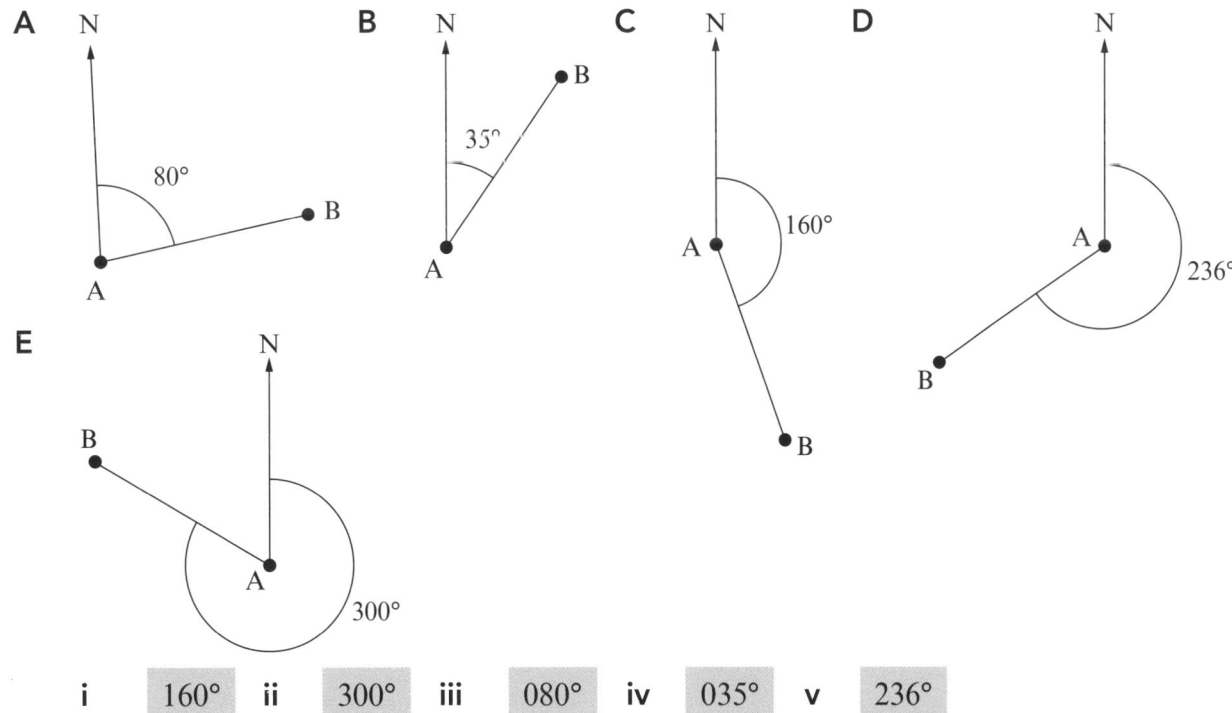

i   160°   ii   300°   iii   080°   iv   035°   v   236°

2 For each diagram, write the bearing you need to walk on to get from *C* to *D*.

The first one is done for you.

a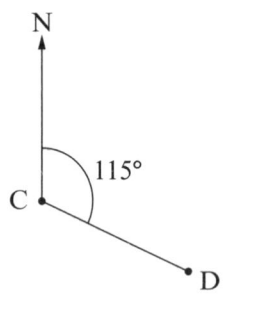

Bearing 115°

b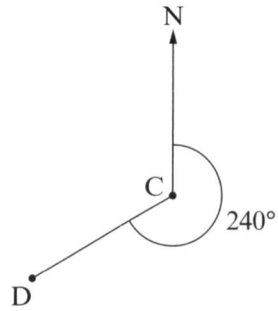

c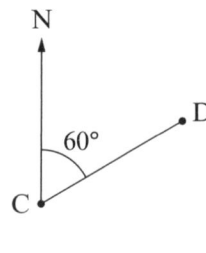

d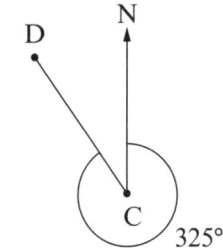

e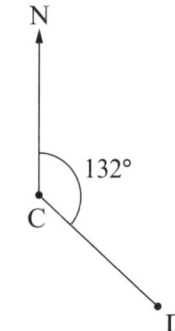

3 Use a protractor to measure each of the angles shown.

Write the bearing you need to walk on to get from *X* to *Y*.

a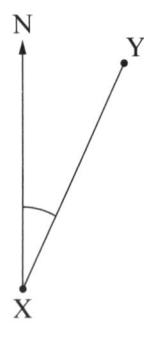

b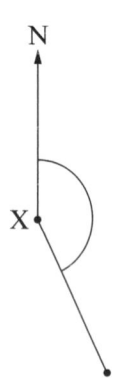

c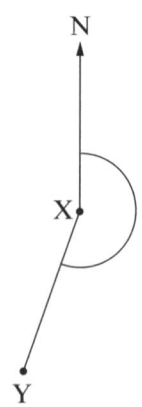

4 Draw a diagram, similar to those in Question **3**, to show each bearing of *Y* from *X*.

    a 065°   **b** 105°   **c** 230°   **d** 350°

Practice

5 This is part of Ivan's homework.

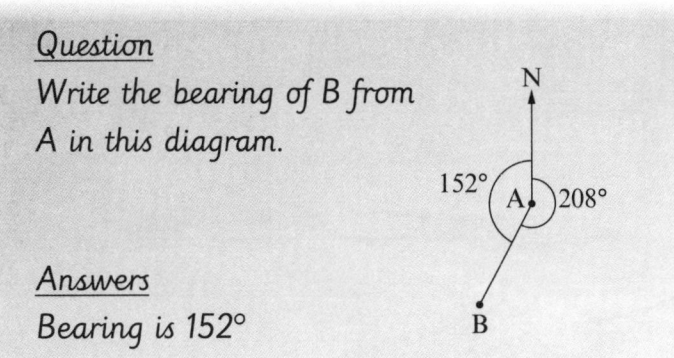

Question
Write the bearing of B from
A in this diagram.

Answers
Bearing is 152°

Is Ivan correct? Explain your answer.

6 The diagram shows the positions of a park and a library.

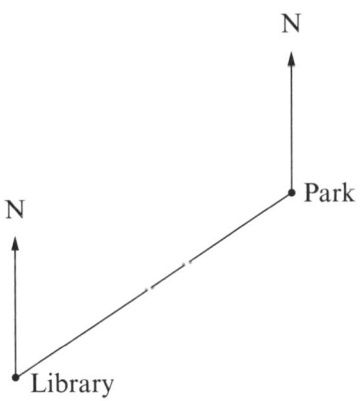

> **Tip**
>
> To find the bearing of the park **from the library**, you need to measure the angle at the **library**.
>
> To find the bearing of the library **from the park**, you need to measure the angle at the **park**.

  a Write the bearing of the park from the library.
  b Write the bearing of the library from the park.

7 Bethan enters a running competition.

The diagram shows the position of the start and finish and the four checkpoints Bethan must find.

Measure and write the bearing Bethan takes to run from

  a the start to checkpoint 1
  b checkpoint 1 to checkpoint 2
  c checkpoint 2 to checkpoint 3
  d checkpoint 3 to checkpoint 4
  e checkpoint 4 to the finish.

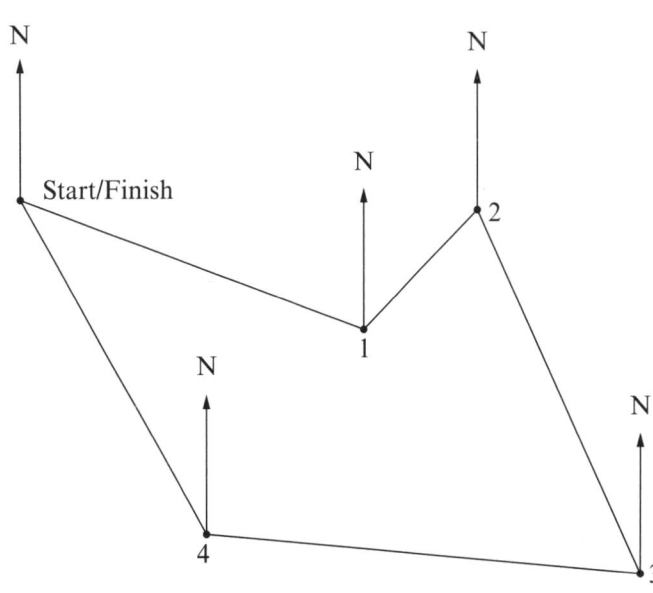

8 **a** For each diagram, measure and write

   i the bearing of *Y* from *X*

   ii the bearing of *X* from *Y*.

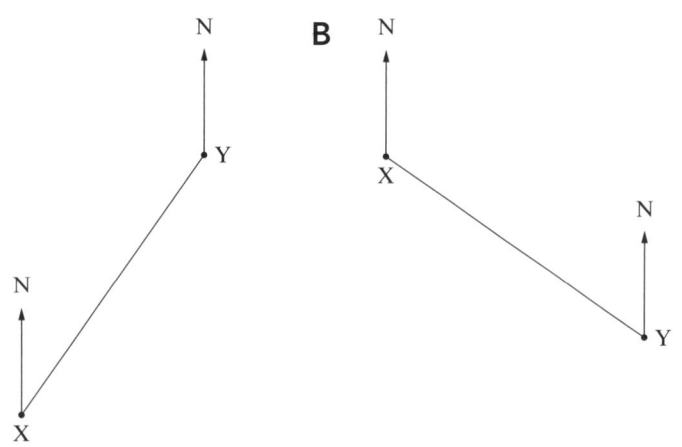

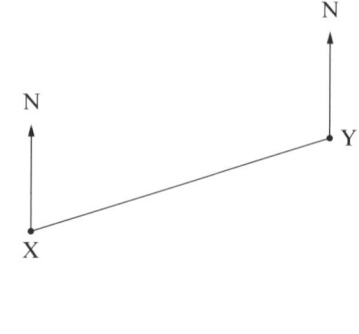

A

B

C

b What do you notice about each pair of answers in part **a**?

c For each diagram

   i write the bearing of *Y* from *X*

   ii work out the bearing of *X* from *Y*.

D

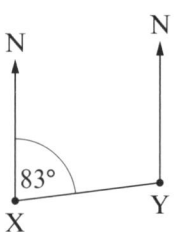

E

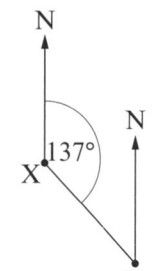

F

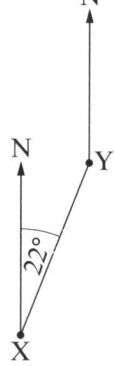

9 a For each diagram, measure and write
      i   the bearing of *X* from *Y*
      ii   the bearing of *Y* from *X*.

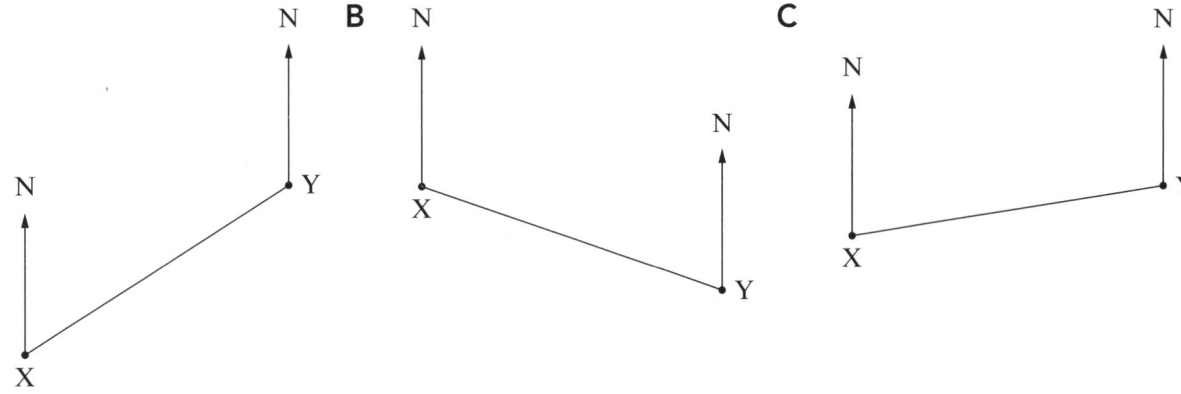

   b What do you notice about each pair of answers in part **a**?
   c For each diagram
      i   write the bearing of *X* from *Y*
      ii   work out the bearing of *Y* from *X*.

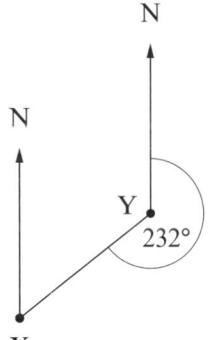 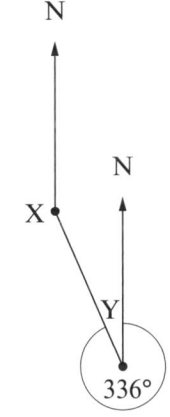 

Challenge

10 The diagram shows three points: *A*, *B* and *C*.
    The diagram is **not** drawn accurately.
    a Write the bearing of *B* from *A*.
    b Work out the bearing of *A* from *B*.
    c Show that the bearing of *C* from *B* is 110°.

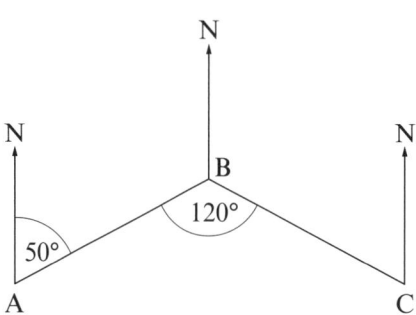

d Read what Marcus says.

I think the bearing of B from C is 300°.

Is Marcus correct? Explain your answer.

e Do you think it is possible to work out the bearing of C from A?

Explain your answer.

11 The diagram shows a regular hexagon, *ABCDEF*.

All the internal angles are 120°.

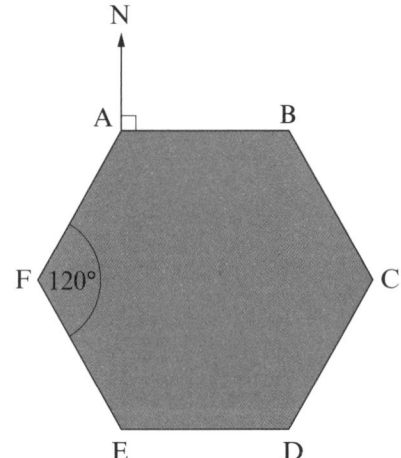

a Write the bearing to get from *A* to *B*.

b Work out the bearing to get from

  i *B* to *C*   **ii** *C* to *D*   **iii** *D* to *E*

  iv *E* to *F*   **v** *F* to *A*.

c Show that the bearing to get from *A* to *D* is 150°.

d Read what Zara says.

I think the bearing of B from E is 030°.

Is Zara correct? Explain your answer.

> 14.2 The midpoint of a line segment

Exercise 14.2

Focus

1 The diagram shows three **line segments**, *AB*, *CD* and *EF*.
Use the diagram to copy and complete these coordinates.

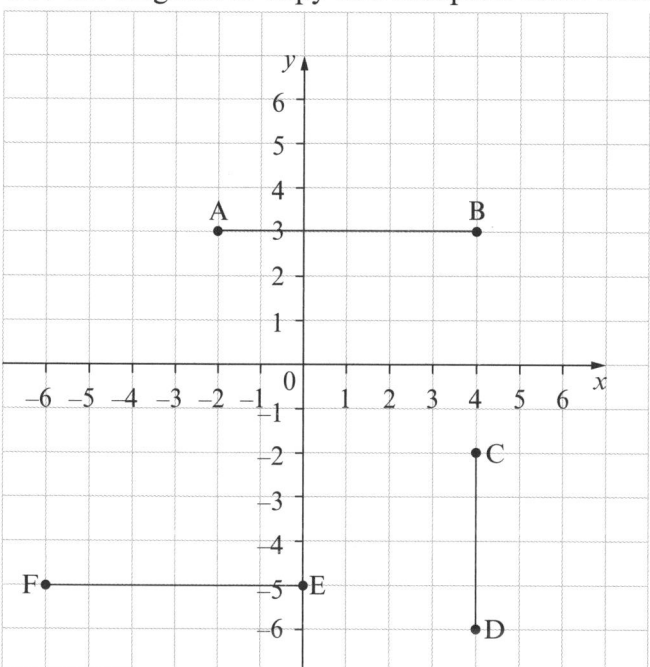

a *A* is (☐ , ☐)   *B* is (☐ , ☐)
The **midpoint** of *AB* is (☐ , ☐)

b *C* is (☐ , ☐)   *D* is (☐ , ☐)
The midpoint of *CD* is (☐ , ☐)

c *E* is (☐ , ☐)   *F* is (☐ , ☐)
The midpoint of *EF* is (☐ , ☐)

2 Work out the midpoint of the line segment joining each pair of points.
Write whether **A**, **B** or **C** is the correct answer.

a (2, 3) and (2, 7)   **A** (2, 4)   **B** (2, 5)   **C** (2, 10)

b (8, 12) and (8, 20)   **A** (8, 8)   **B** (8, 15)   **C** (8, 16)

c (4, 1) and (6, 1)   **A** (5, 1)   **B** (2, 1)   **C** (10, 1)

d (2, 15) and (10, 15) **A** (12, 15) **B** (8, 15)   **C** (6, 15)

> **Tip**
>
> You can plot the points on a coordinate grid to help you.

3 Make a copy of this coordinate grid.
Read what Sofia says.

I think the midpoint of (1, 3) and (6, 3) is at (3, 3).

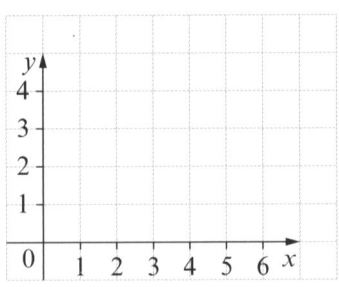

Is Sofia correct? Use the coordinate grid to help you explain your answer.

4 The diagram shows four line segments, *PQ*, *RS*, *TU* and *VW*.

Use the diagram to copy and complete these coordinates.

a *P* is ($\square$, $\square$)   *Q* is ($\square$, $\square$)
The midpoint of *PQ* is ($\square$, $\square$)

b *R* is ($\square$, $\square$)   *S* is ($\square$, $\square$)
The midpoint of *RS* is ($\square$, $\square$)

c *T* is ($\square$, $\square$)   *U* is ($\square$, $\square$)
The midpoint of *TU* is ($\square$, $\square$)

d *V* is ($\square$, $\square$)   *W* is ($\square$, $\square$)
The midpoint of *VW* is ($\square$, $\square$)

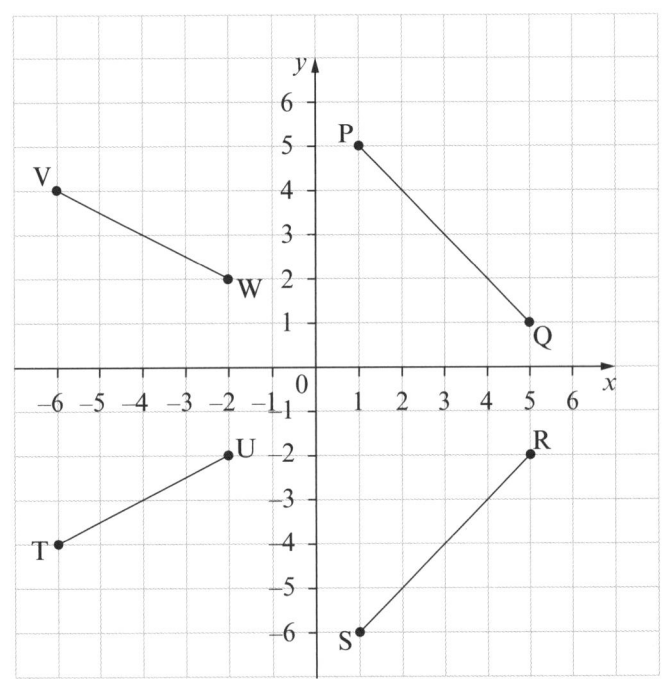

5 Copy and complete the workings to calculate the midpoint of the line segment joining each pair of coordinates.

a (1, 4) and (7, 6) $\left(\dfrac{1+7}{2}, \dfrac{4+6}{2}\right) = \left(\dfrac{8}{2}, \dfrac{10}{2}\right) = (\square, \square)$

b (18, 0) and (8, 8) $\left(\dfrac{18+8}{2}, \dfrac{0+8}{2}\right) = \left(\dfrac{\square}{2}, \dfrac{\square}{2}\right) = (\square, \square)$

c (7, 3) and (5, 10) $\left(\dfrac{\square+\square}{2}, \dfrac{\square+\square}{2}\right) = \left(\dfrac{\square}{2}, \dfrac{\square}{2}\right) = \left(\square, \square\dfrac{\square}{\square}\right)$

d (1, 4) and (4, 15) $\left(\dfrac{\square+\square}{2}, \dfrac{\square+\square}{2}\right) = \left(\dfrac{\square}{2}, \dfrac{\square}{2}\right) = \left(\square\dfrac{\square}{\square}, \square\dfrac{\square}{\square}\right)$

Practice

6 **a** *A* is the point (−8, 0), *B* is the point (6, 0) and *C* is the point (4, 10).
Work out the midpoint of the line segments

i *AB*   **ii** *AC*   **iii** *BC*.

b Draw a coordinate grid. Plot the points *A*, *B* and *C*.
Check your answers to part **a** by finding the midpoints on
your diagram.

7 Find the midpoint of the line segment joining each pair of points.

a (4, 2) and (10, 12)   **b** (5, −3) and (−3, −7)   **c** (−6, 8) and (8, −6).

8 Sasha works out the midpoint of the line joining the points
(−3, 8) and (5, −2).
This is what she writes.

x-coordinate: $\dfrac{-3 + -2}{2} = \dfrac{-5}{2} = -2\dfrac{1}{2}$

y-coordinate: $\dfrac{8 + 5}{2} = \dfrac{13}{2} = 6\dfrac{1}{2}$

Midpoint is at $\left(-2\dfrac{1}{2},\ 6\dfrac{1}{2}\right)$

Is Sasha correct? Explain your answer.

9 *ABCD* is a rectangle.

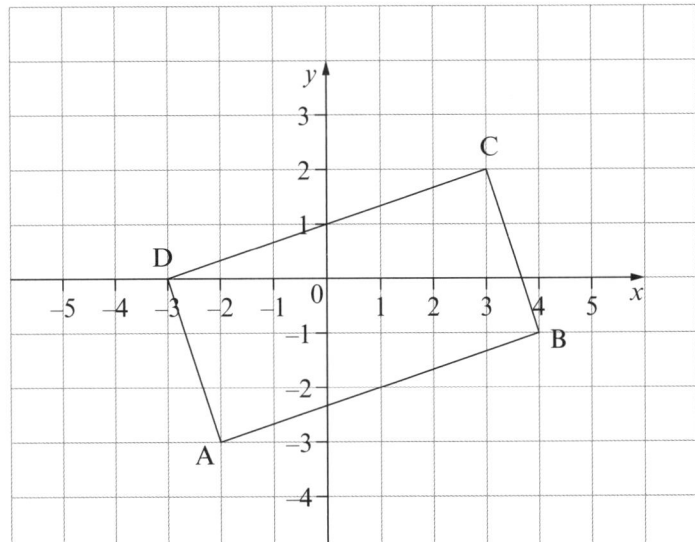

a Find the midpoint of the line segment *AC*.

b Show that the midpoint of the line segment *BD* is the same
as the midpoint of the line segment *AC*.

Challenge

10 *A* is the point (2.4, 6.2), *B* is the point (3.6, 2.4) and *C* is the point (−3.8, −1.4). Find
  a   the midpoint of *AB*   b   the midpoint of *AC*.

11 *ABCD* is a square. The coordinates of *A* are (−2, −6). The coordinates of *C* are (−3, −1). Where is the centre of the square? Explain how you worked out your answer.

12 *P* is the point (0, 9) and the midpoint of *PQ* is (5, 7). Find the coordinates of *Q*.

13 *A* is the point (16, 0) and *B* is the point (0, 8).
  C is the midpoint of *AB*. *D* is the midpoint of *BC*.
  E is the midpoint of *CD*.
  Show that the coordinates of *E* are (6, 5).

14 The midpoint of the line segment *GH* is at (3, 2).
  Work out three possible pairs of coordinates for *G* and *H*.
  Show all your working.

> 14.3 Translating 2D shapes

Exercise 14.3

Focus

> **Key words**
>
> column vector
> image
> object
> translate

1 Match each **column vector** to the correct description.
  The first one is done for you: **A** and **iv**

  A $\begin{pmatrix} 2 \\ 3 \end{pmatrix}$ i   Move the shape 2 units left and 3 units down

  B $\begin{pmatrix} 2 \\ -3 \end{pmatrix}$ ii   Move the shape 3 units right and 2 units up

  C $\begin{pmatrix} -2 \\ -3 \end{pmatrix}$ iii   Move the shape 2 units left and 3 units up

  D $\begin{pmatrix} -3 \\ 2 \end{pmatrix}$ iv   Move the shape 2 units right and 3 units up

  E $\begin{pmatrix} -2 \\ 3 \end{pmatrix}$ v   Move the shape 3 units left and 2 units up

  F $\begin{pmatrix} 3 \\ 2 \end{pmatrix}$ vi   Move the shape 2 units right and 3 units down

2   Write the missing numbers and words to complete each statement.

a   The column vector $\begin{pmatrix} 4 \\ 5 \end{pmatrix}$ means move the shape ☐ units right and 5 units ☐.

b   The column vector $\begin{pmatrix} -1 \\ 6 \end{pmatrix}$ means move the shape 1 unit ☐ and ☐ units up.

c   The column vector $\begin{pmatrix} 2 \\ -4 \end{pmatrix}$ means move the shape 2 units ☐ and 4 units ☐.

3   Copy each diagram and **translate** the rectangle using the given column vector.

a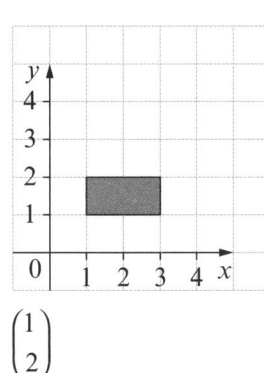

$\begin{pmatrix} 1 \\ 2 \end{pmatrix}$

b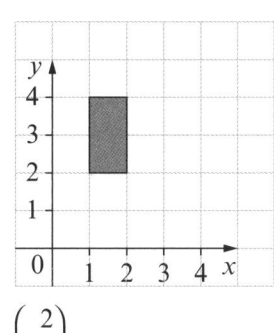

$\begin{pmatrix} 2 \\ -1 \end{pmatrix}$

c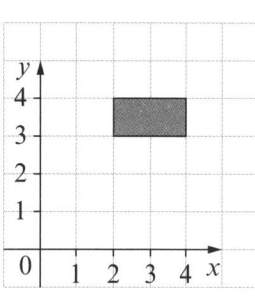

$\begin{pmatrix} -1 \\ -2 \end{pmatrix}$

4   The diagram shows **object** A on a coordinate grid.

Copy the grid, then draw the **image** of shape A after each translation.

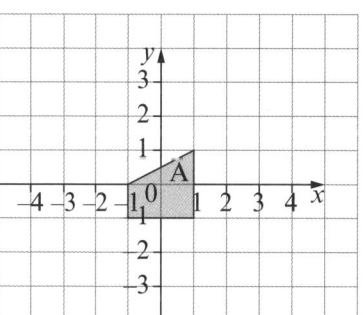

a $\begin{pmatrix} 2 \\ 1 \end{pmatrix}$ **b** $\begin{pmatrix} 1 \\ -1 \end{pmatrix}$ **c** $\begin{pmatrix} -3 \\ 2 \end{pmatrix}$ **d** $\begin{pmatrix} -2 \\ -1 \end{pmatrix}$

5   This is part of Adah's homework.

> *Question*
>
> Translate shape B using the column vector $\begin{pmatrix} 2 \\ 3 \end{pmatrix}$.
> Label the image B'.
>
> *Answer*
>
>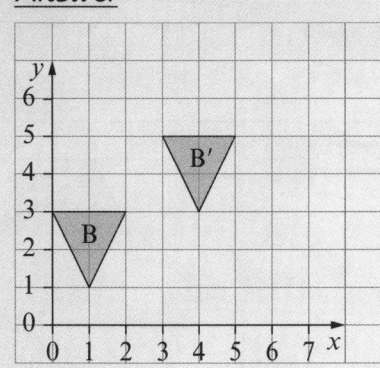

Is Adah's answer correct? Explain your answer.

Practice

6 The diagram shows shape *C* on a coordinate grid.

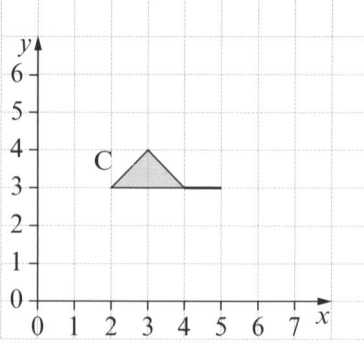

    a Copy the grid. Then translate shape *C* using the vector $\begin{pmatrix} 1 \\ -2 \end{pmatrix}$. Label the image *C′*.

    b Show that you can use the vector $\begin{pmatrix} -1 \\ 2 \end{pmatrix}$ to translate *C′* back to *C*.

    c Explain how you can work out the column vector you must use to translate a shape back to its original position.

7 Write the column vector to translate a shape back to its original position after each translation.

    a $\begin{pmatrix} 3 \\ 4 \end{pmatrix}$ **b** $\begin{pmatrix} 7 \\ -8 \end{pmatrix}$ **c** $\begin{pmatrix} -1 \\ -9 \end{pmatrix}$ **d** $\begin{pmatrix} m \\ n \end{pmatrix}$

8 The diagram shows shapes *A*, *B*, *C* and *D* on a coordinate grid.

Write the column vector that translates

    a shape *A* to shape *B*

    b shape *B* to shape *C*

    c shape *C* to shape *A*

    d shape *C* to shape *D*.

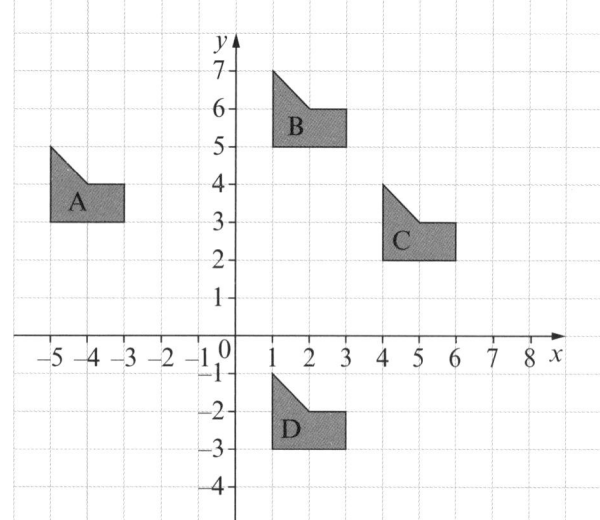

Challenge

9 The diagram shows trapezium *GHIJ*.

Carla is going to translate *GHIJ* using the column vector $\begin{pmatrix} -6 \\ 5 \end{pmatrix}$.

Carla works out the coordinates of *G′H′I′J′* first. This is what Carla writes.

> Coordinates of G′ are: $(1, -3) + \begin{pmatrix} -6 \\ 5 \end{pmatrix}$
> $= (1 + -6, -3 + 5)$
> $= (-5, 2)$

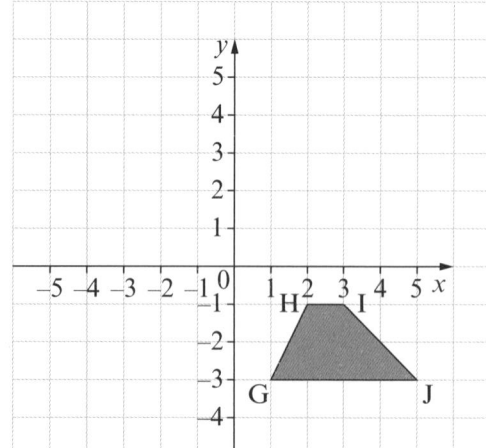

    a Use Carla's method to calculate the coordinates of *H′*, *I′* and *J′*.

    b Make a copy of the diagram. Translate *GHIJ* using the column vector $\begin{pmatrix} -6 \\ 5 \end{pmatrix}$.

    c Use your diagram in part **b** to check your answers to part **a**.

10 A parallelogram *PQRS* has vertices at the points *P* (−1, 1), *Q* (0, 3), *R* (3, 3) and *S* (2, 1).

Aki is going to translate *PQRS* using the column vector $\begin{pmatrix} 6 \\ -4 \end{pmatrix}$.

Aki works out that the coordinates of *P′* are (5, −5).

a Is Aki correct? Explain your answer.

b Calculate the coordinates of *Q′*, *R′* and *S′*.

c Check your answers by drawing a diagram and translating parallelogram *PQRS*.

11 A square *RSTU* has vertices at *R* (2, 2), *S* (2, −2), *T* (−2, −2) and *U* (−2, 2).

The square is translated and the image is labelled *R′S′T′U′*.

The coordinates of *R′* are (5, 3).

a Write the column vector that translates *RSTU* to *R′S′T′U′*.

b Work out the coordinates of *S′*, *T′* and *U′*.

c Check your answers by drawing a diagram and translating square *RSTU*.

12 The diagram shows shape *A*.

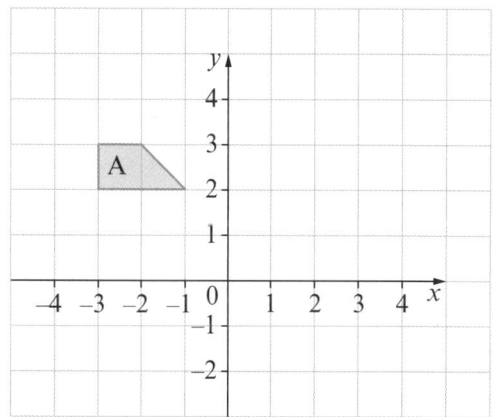

a Translate shape *A* using the vector $\begin{pmatrix} 2 \\ -4 \end{pmatrix}$. Label the image *B*.

b Translate shape *B* using the vector $\begin{pmatrix} 2 \\ 3 \end{pmatrix}$.

Label the image *C*.

c What is the vector that translates shape *A* directly to shape *C*?

What do you notice about your answer and the vectors in parts **a** and **b**?

d Write the missing numbers in each statement.

i Translating a shape $\begin{pmatrix} 1 \\ 3 \end{pmatrix}$ and then $\begin{pmatrix} 5 \\ 2 \end{pmatrix}$ is the same as the single vector $\begin{pmatrix} \square \\ \square \end{pmatrix}$

ii Translating a shape $\begin{pmatrix} -2 \\ 6 \end{pmatrix}$ and then $\begin{pmatrix} -3 \\ -4 \end{pmatrix}$ is the same as the single vector $\begin{pmatrix} \square \\ \square \end{pmatrix}$

e Use algebra to complete this rule.

Translating a shape $\begin{pmatrix} a \\ b \end{pmatrix}$ and then $\begin{pmatrix} c \\ d \end{pmatrix}$ is the same as the single vector $\begin{pmatrix} \square \\ \square \end{pmatrix}$

> 14.4 Reflecting shapes

Exercise 14.4

Focus

1   Match each **equation** with the correct lettered **mirror line** shown on the grid.

The first one is done for you: **A** is $y = 5$

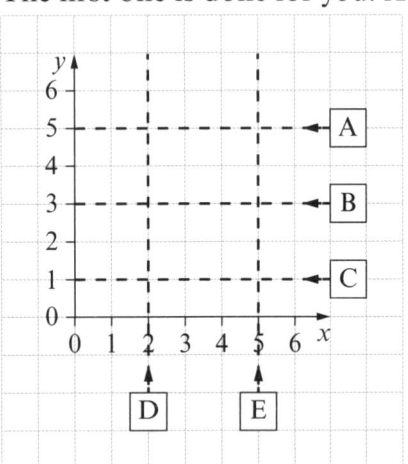

$y = 1$ $x = 5$ $y = 5$

$y = 3$ $x = 2$

Tip

Remember, vertical lines start $x = \ldots$ and horizontal lines start $y = \ldots$

2   Copy and complete each reflection in the mirror line shown.

a
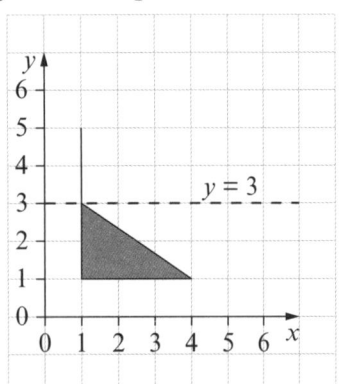

b
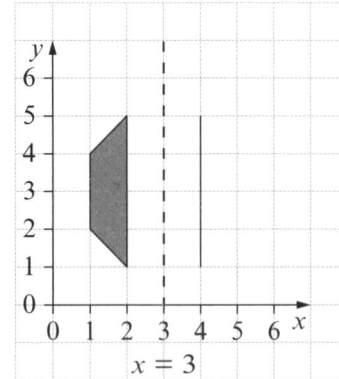

Tip

Remember to **reflect** each shape one corner at a time, then join the points with straight lines.

3   Copy each diagram and reflect the shape in the mirror line with
    the given equation.

a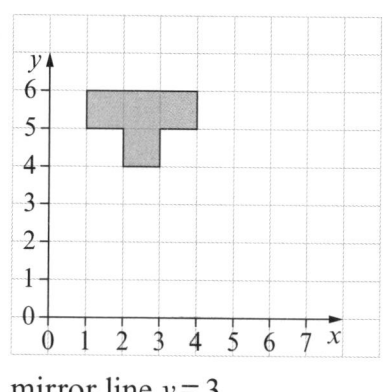

mirror line $y = 3$

b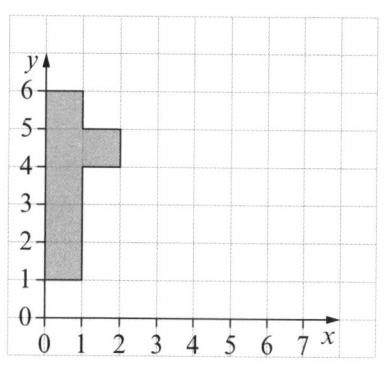

mirror line $x = 3$

c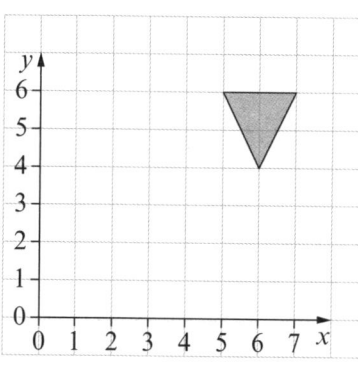

mirror line $x = 4$

4   Copy each diagram and reflect the shape in the mirror line with the
    given equation.

a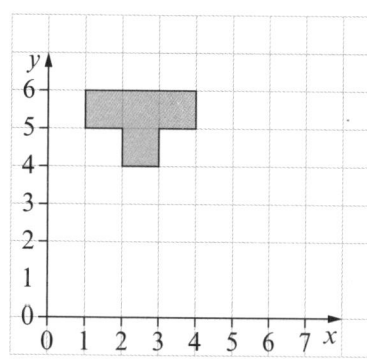

mirror line $x = 4$

b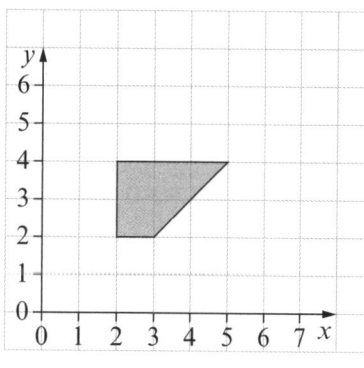

mirror line $y = 4$

c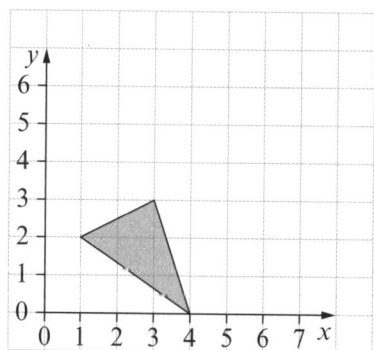

mirror line $y = 3$

5   This is part of Silvie's homework.

Question
Reflect shape A in the line $x = -2$. Label the shape A'.

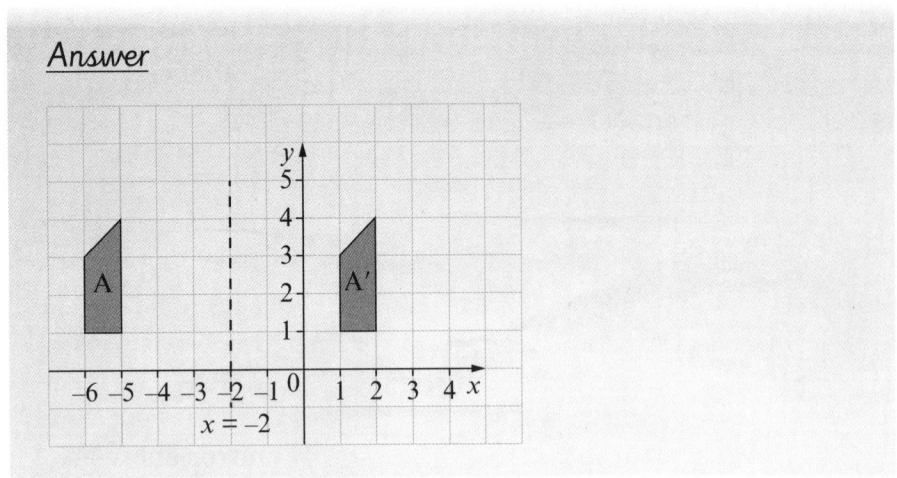

Answer

a   Explain the mistake Silvie has made.

b   Copy the diagram of shape *A* and draw the correct reflection.

Practice

6   The diagram shows shape *B* on a coordinate grid.

Draw the image of shape *B* after it has been reflected in each line.

a $x = -1$

b $y = -2$

c $x = 1.5$

d $y = -0.5$

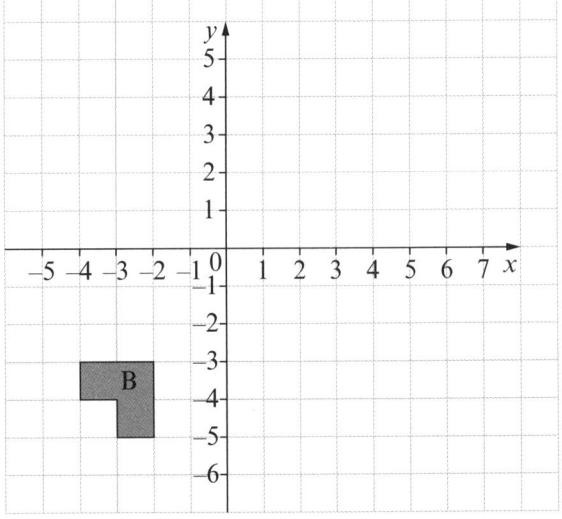

7   Make two copies of this diagram.

a   On the first diagram, reflect the triangle in the line $x = 4$.

b   On the second diagram, reflect the triangle in the line $y = 3$.

c   Explain the method you use to reflect a shape when the mirror line goes through the shape.

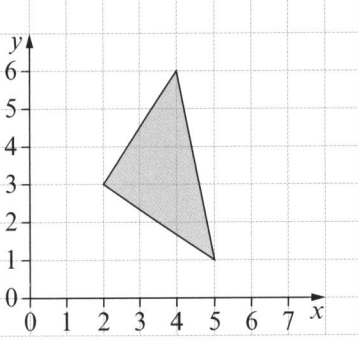

8   The diagram shows three shapes, *A*, *B* and *C*.
    It also shows the line $y = x$.
    Make a copy of the diagram.
    Reflect *A*, *B* and *C* in the line $y = x$.
    Label their images *A'*, *B'* and *C'*.

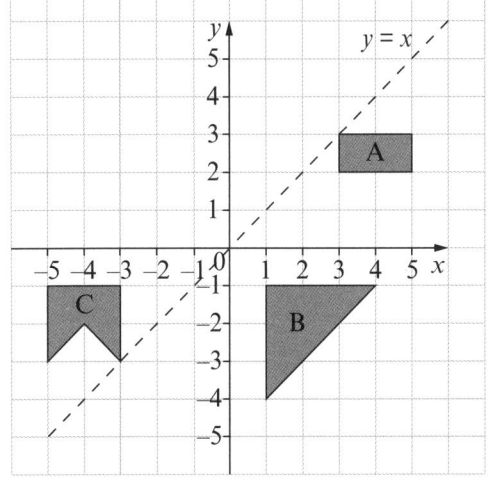

9   Look back at shapes *A* and *A'* in Question **8**.
    a   The table shows the coordinates of the vertices of
        the object (*A*) and its image (*A'*).
        Copy and complete the table.

Object (A)	(3, 3)	(3, 2)	(5, 2)	(5, 3)
Image (A')	(3, 3)	(☐, ☐)	(☐, ☐)	(☐, ☐)

    b   What do you notice about the coordinates of *A* and its
        image *A'*?
    c   Write a rule you can use to work out the coordinates of the
        image of a shape when it is reflected in the line $y = x$.

10 The diagram shows shape *ABCD* on a coordinate grid.
    It also shows the line $y = x$.
    a   Write the coordinates of the points *A*, *B*, *C* and *D*.
    When shape *ABCD* is reflected in the line $y = x$, the image is
    A'B'C'D'.
    b   Use your rule from Question **9** to write the coordinates of
        the points *A'*, *B'*, *C'* and *D'*.
    c   Copy the diagram. Reflect shape *ABCD* in the line $y = x$.
    d   Check the coordinates of the points *A'*, *B'*, *C'* and *D'* you
        worked out in part **b** are correct.

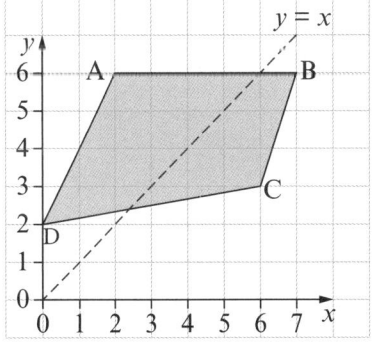

Challenge

11 The diagram shows triangle *EFG* on a coordinate grid.
    It also shows the line $y = -x$.
    a   Make a copy of the diagram. Reflect *EFG* in the line
        $y = -x$ and label the image *E'F'G'*.
    b   The table shows the coordinates of the vertices of the
        object and its image.

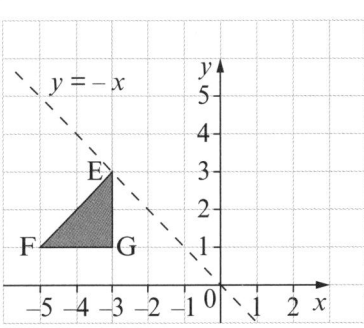

Copy and complete the table.

Object	E (−3, 3)	F (−5, 1)	G (☐, ☐)
Image	E′ (☐, ☐)	F′ (☐, ☐)	G′ (☐, ☐)

c What do you notice about the coordinates of *EFG* and its image *E′F′G′*?

d Write a rule you can use to work out the coordinates of the image of a shape when it is reflected in the line $y = -x$.

12 The diagram shows shape *PQRS* on a coordinate grid.
It also shows the line $y = -x$.

a Write the coordinates of the points *P*, *Q*, *R* and *S*.

When shape *PQRS* is reflected in the line $y = -x$, the image is *P′Q′R′S′*.

b Use your rule from Question **11** to write the coordinates of the points *P′*, *Q′*, *R′* and *S′*.

c Copy the diagram. Reflect shape *PQRS* in the line $y = -x$.

d Check the coordinates of the points *P′*, *Q′*, *R′* and *S′* you worked out in part **b** are correct.

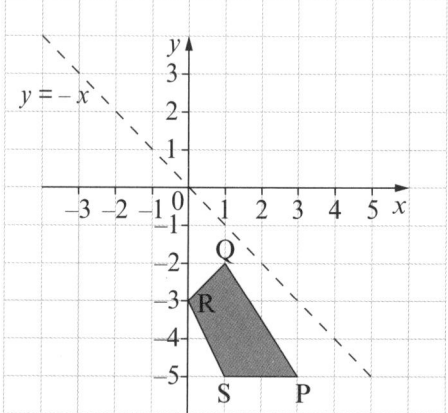

13 The diagram shows shapes *A*, *B*, *C*, *D*, *E* and *F*.

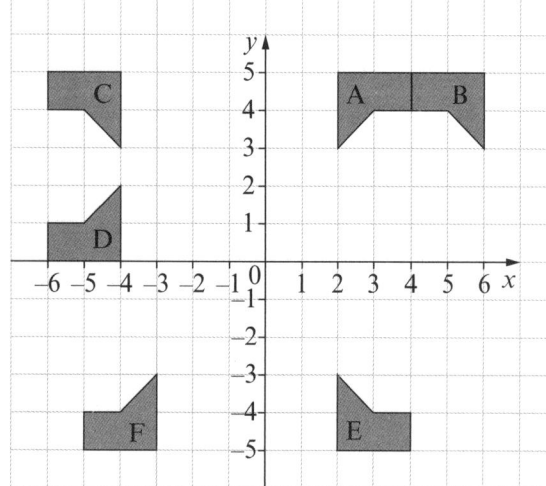

Choose the equation of the correct mirror line for each reflection.

a *A* and *B*   **i** $x = 2$ **ii** $y = 4$ **iii** $x = 4$

b *A* and *C*   **i** $x = -1$ **ii** $y = -1$ **iii** $x = 0$

c *C* and *D*   **i** $y = 2.5$ **ii** $y = 2$ **iii** $x = 2.5$

d *A* and *E*   **i** $x = 2$ **ii** $y = 1$ **iii** $y = 0$

e *E* and *F*   **i** $x = 0$ **ii** $x = -0.5$ **iii** $x = -1$

14 Arun starts with this diagram.

He reflects shape A in the line $y = -x$ and labels the shape B.

He translates shape B using the column vector $\begin{pmatrix} 4 \\ -1 \end{pmatrix}$ and labels the shape C.

He reflects shape C in the line $y = x$ and labels the shape D.

He reflects shape D in the line $y = -1.5$ and labels the shape E.

He translates shape E using the column vector $\begin{pmatrix} -5 \\ 2 \end{pmatrix}$ and labels the shape F.

He reflects shape F in the line $x = -3$ and labels the shape G.

Read what Arun says.

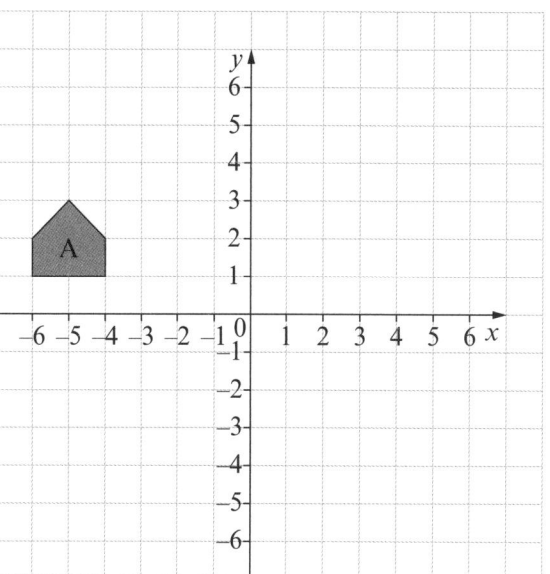

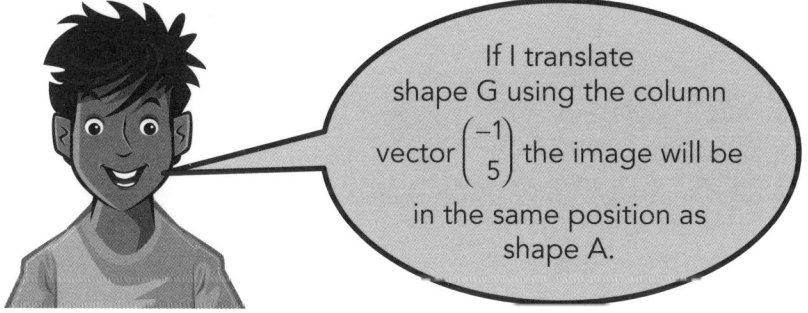

If I translate shape G using the column vector $\begin{pmatrix} -1 \\ 5 \end{pmatrix}$ the image will be in the same position as shape A.

Is Arun correct? Explain your answer. Show all your working.

› 14.5 Rotating shapes

Exercise 14.5

Focus

1   Copy each diagram and rotate the shapes 90° **clockwise** about the **centre of rotation** given.

a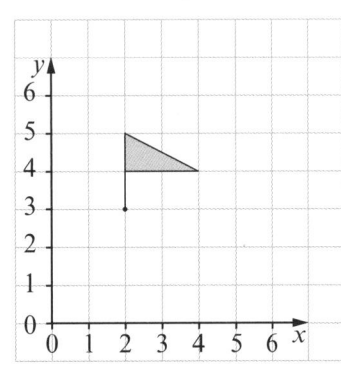

centre (2, 3)

b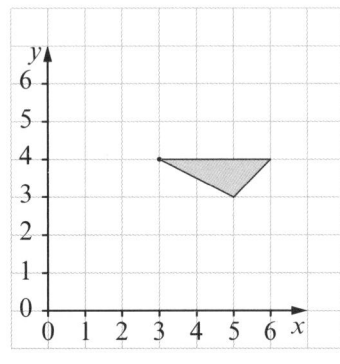

centre (3, 4)

Tip

Use tracing paper to trace the shape, then put your pencil point on the centre of rotation and turn the paper 90° clockwise.

2   Copy each diagram and rotate the shapes 180° about the centre of rotation given.

a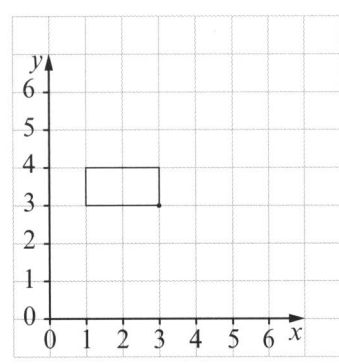

centre (3, 3)

b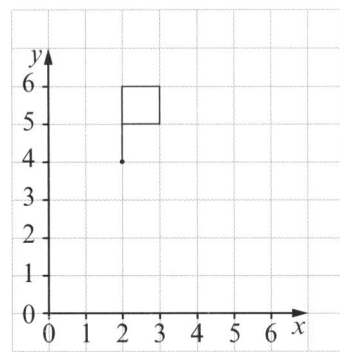

centre (2, 4)

Tip

Use tracing paper to help. For 180° you can turn clockwise or anticlockwise.

3 Rotate each shape 90° **anticlockwise** about the centre of rotation given.

a
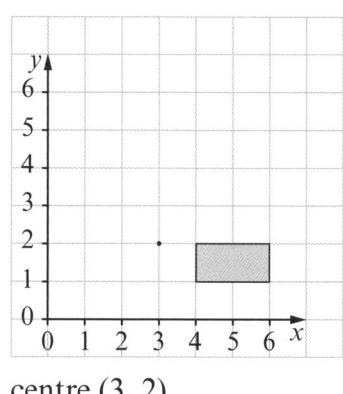
centre (3, 2)

b
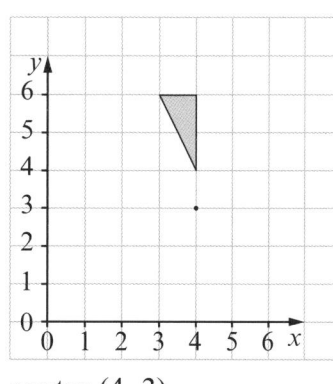
centre (4, 3)

4 Copy each diagram. On your copy, use the information given to rotate the shape.

a
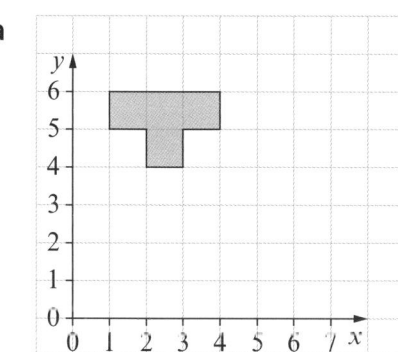
180°
centre (4, 5)

b
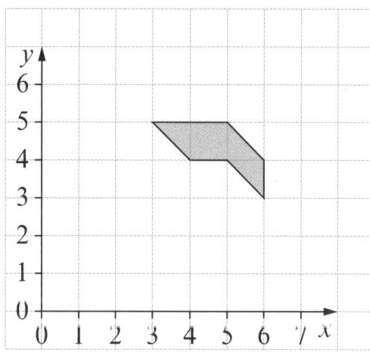
90° anticlockwise
centre (6, 3)

c
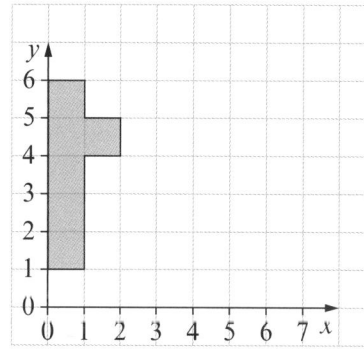
90° clockwise
centre (2, 1)

Practice

5 The diagram shows shape *C* on a coordinate grid. Copy the diagram. Draw the image of shape *C* after a rotation of

  a   90° clockwise about the point (5, 3)

  b   90° anticlockwise about the point (2, 3)

  c   180° about the point (3, 2)

  d   180° about the point (4, 5).

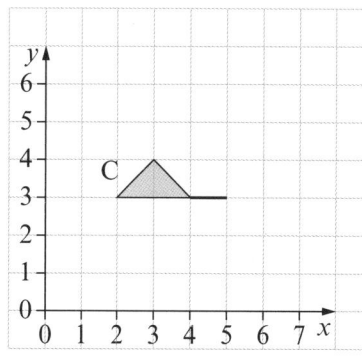

6   This is part of Simon's classwork.

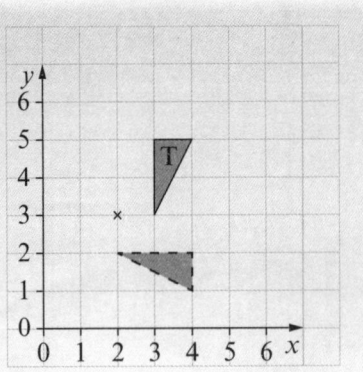

Question
Rotate triangle T 90° clockwise about centre (3, 2).

Answer
I have used a dotted line to show the image.

a   What is wrong with Simon's solution?

b   Copy the object onto squared paper and draw the correct image.

7   Copy and complete the description of the rotation that takes shape A to shape B in each diagram.

a

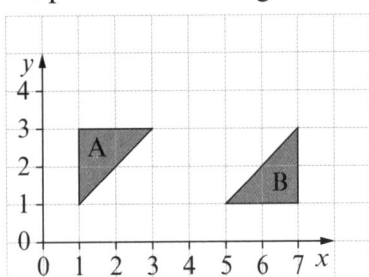

b

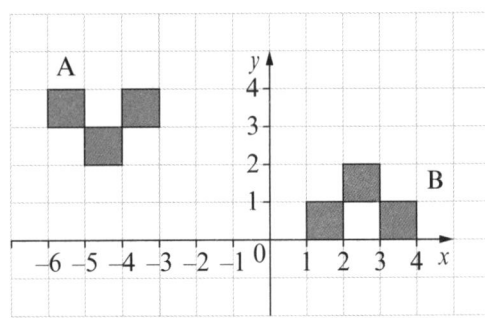

rotation 180°, centre (☐, ☐)   rotation ☐°, centre (☐, ☐)

8   The diagram shows seven triangles.

Match each rotation with the correct description.

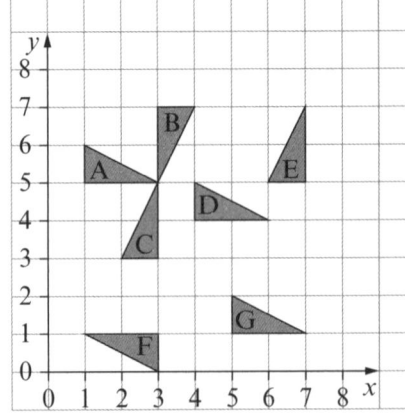

a   A to B   i   90° anticlockwise, centre (4, 3)

b   B to C   ii   180°, centre (5, 6)

c   B to E   iii   180°, centre (3, 5)

d   D to C   iv   90° clockwise, centre (7, 1)

e   F to E   v   180°, centre (4, 1)

f   F to G   vi   90° clockwise, centre (3, 5)

Challenge

9 The diagram shows shapes *A*, *B*, *C*, *D*, *E* and *F* on a coordinate grid.

Describe the rotation that transforms

a shape *A* to shape *B*

b shape *B* to shape *C*

c shape *C* to shape *D*

d shape *D* to shape *E*

e shape *E* to shape *F*.

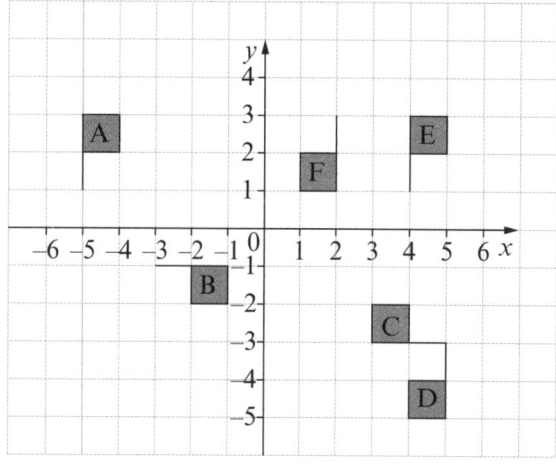

10 The diagram shows shape *A* on a coordinate grid.

Make a copy of the diagram.

a On the diagram, draw a rotation of shape *A* 90° clockwise about centre (3, 3).

Label the image *B*.

b On the diagram, draw a rotation of shape *B* 180° about centre (3, 4).

Label the image *C*.

c On the diagram, draw a rotation of shape *C* 90° anticlockwise about centre (6, 4).

Label the image *D*.

d Describe the rotation that takes shape *A* directly to shape *D*.

e Describe the reflection that takes shape *A* directly to shape *D*.

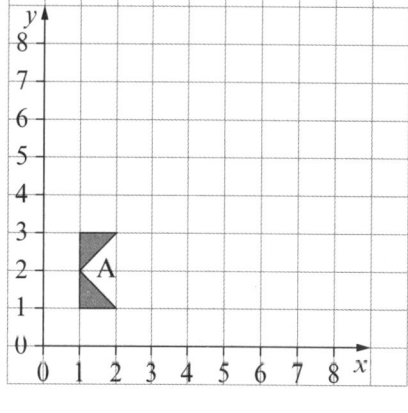

11 The diagram shows triangle *A* on a coordinate grid.

Make a copy of the diagram.

a On the diagram, draw a rotation of triangle *A* 180° about centre (3, 3).

Label the image *B*.

b Describe two different **transformations** that will take triangle *B* back to triangle *A*.

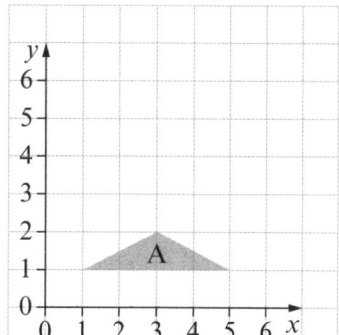

> **Tip**
>
> A transformation can be a rotation, a reflection or a translation.

12 The diagram shows shape *C* on a coordinate grid.
Make a copy of the diagram.

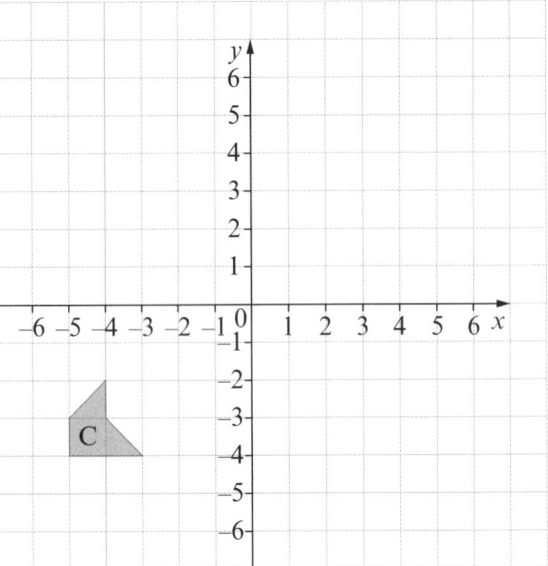

   a Draw the image of shape *C* after reflection
in the line $x = -1$. Label the image *D*.

   b Draw the image of shape *D* after a
translation using column vector $\begin{pmatrix} 2 \\ 1 \end{pmatrix}$. Label
the image *E*.

   c Draw the image of shape *E* after rotation
180° about centre (0, 1). Label the image *F*.

   d Describe the single transformation that will
take shape *F* to shape *C*.

   e Describe the single transformation that will
take shape *D* to shape *F*.

> 14.6 Enlarging shapes

Exercise 14.6

Focus

> **Key words**
>
> centre of enlargement
> enlargement
> scale factor

1 Copy and complete each **enlargement**.

Use a **scale factor** of 2 and the **centre of enlargement** marked *C*.

Follow these steps.

   Step 1 Count the number of squares from the centre of
enlargement to the nearest corner of rectangle A.
Multiply this number by 2 to find the new distance from
the centre of enlargement. Plot this point.

   Step 2 Count the length and width of rectangle A, in squares.
Multiply both dimensions by 2 to find the new length and
width. Draw the enlarged rectangle A' from the corner
you have already plotted.

a

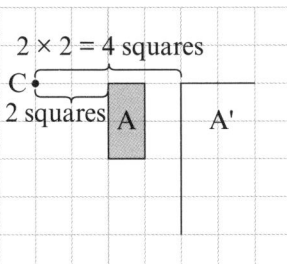

b

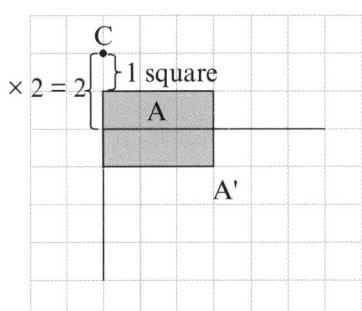

c

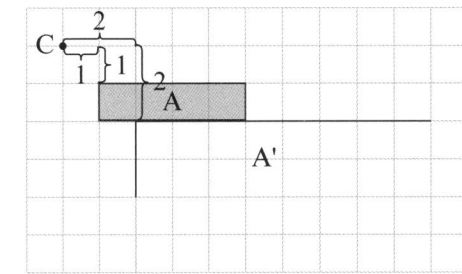

2 Copy and complete each enlargement using a scale factor of 3 and the centre of enlargement marked C.

a

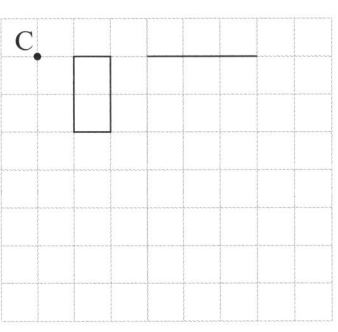

b

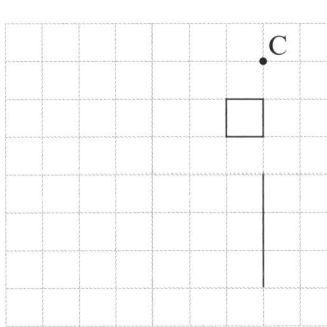

c

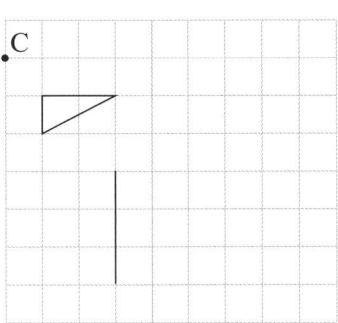

d

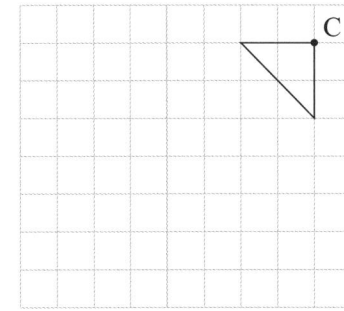

3 Copy each shape onto squared paper.

Enlarge each shape using the given scale factor and the centre of enlargement marked on the diagram.

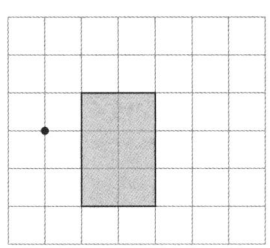 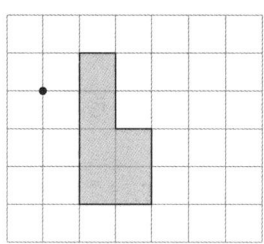 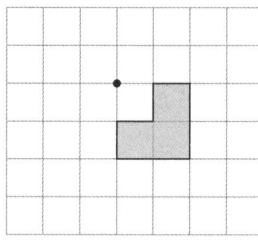

scale factor 2   scale factor 3   scale factor 4

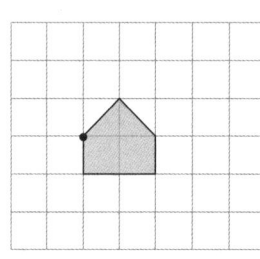 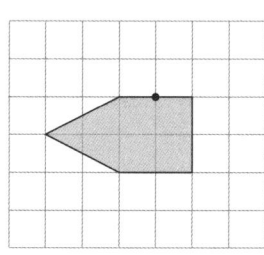

scale factor 2   scale factor 3   scale factor 2

Practice

4 This is part of Amnon's homework.

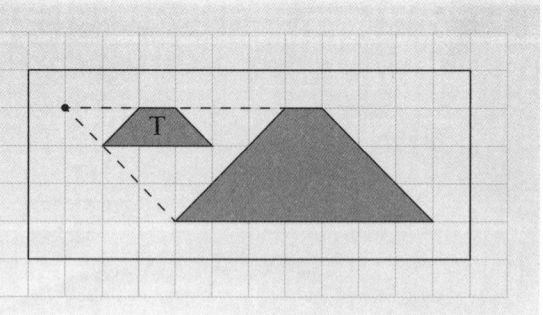

Question and Answer
Enlarge trapezium T using a scale factor of 3 and the centre of enlargement shown.

a Explain the mistake Amnon has made.

b Make a copy of trapezium *T* on squared paper. Draw the correct enlargement.

5 The vertices of this triangle are at (2, 1), (2, 4) and (4, 2).

    a Make a copy of the diagram on squared paper.

       Mark with a dot the centre of enlargement at (1, 2).

       Enlarge the triangle using scale factor 2 from the centre of enlargement.

    b Write the coordinates of the vertices of the image.

    c Is there an invariant point on the object and image?
Explain your answer.

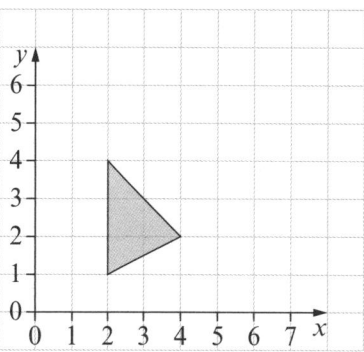

6 The vertices of this parallelogram are at (1, 5), (3, 3), (5, 3) and (3, 5).

    a Make a copy of the diagram on squared paper.

       Mark with a dot the centre of enlargement at (2, 5).

       Enlarge the parallelogram using scale factor 2 from the centre of enlargement.

    b Write the coordinates of the vertices of the image.

    c Is there an invariant point on the object and image?
Explain your answer.

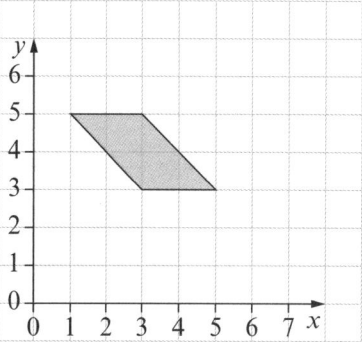

Challenge

7 The diagram shows four objects, *A*, *B*, *C* and *D* and their images after enlargement.

For each object, describe the enlargement.

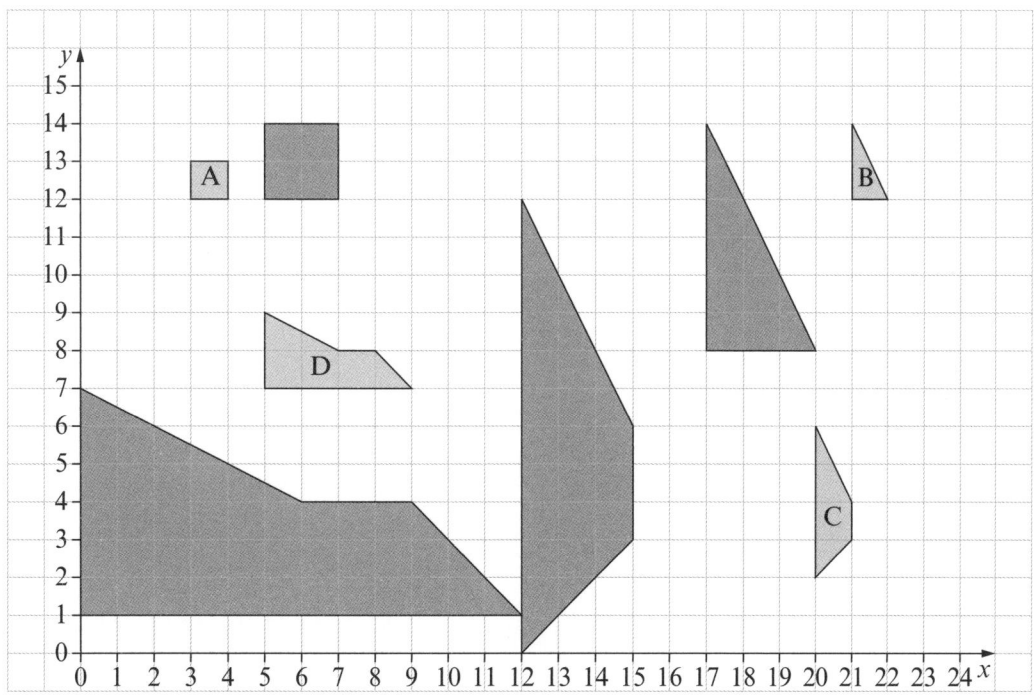

8 The diagram shows pentagon *ABCDE* and its image *A′B′C′D′E′*.

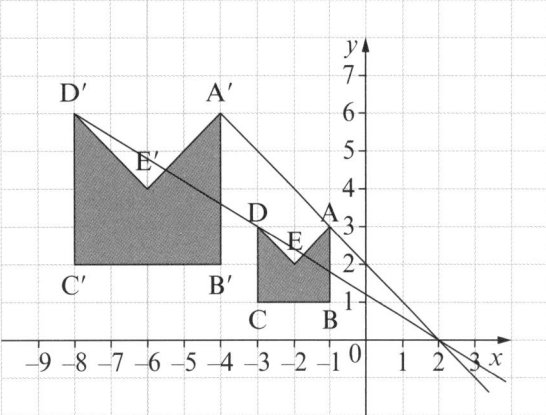

a Write the scale factor of the enlargement.

Read what Zara and Sofia say.

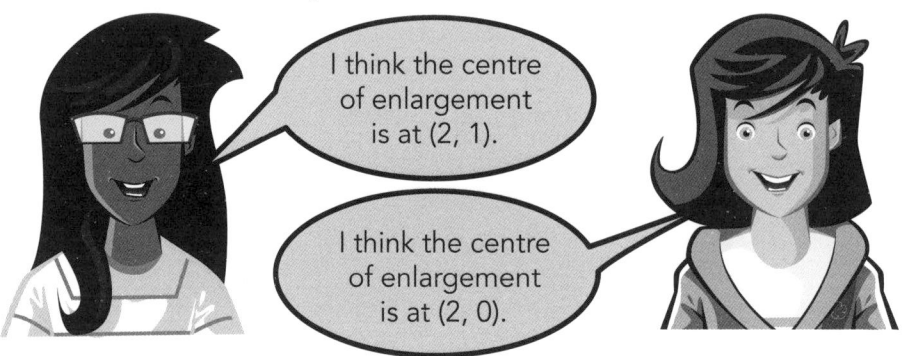

I think the centre of enlargement is at (2, 1).

I think the centre of enlargement is at (2, 0).

b Who is correct? Explain how you worked out your answer.

9 The vertices of rectangle *P* are at (2, 2), (2, 5), (11, 5) and (11, 2).
The vertices of rectangle *Q* are at (2, 2), (2, 3), (5, 3) and (5, 2).

a Is rectangle *P* an enlargement of rectangle *Q*? Explain your answer.

b What are the coordinates of the centre of enlargement?

15 ▶ Distance, area and volume

> 15.1 Converting between miles and kilometres

Exercise 15.1

Focus

Key words

feet
kilometre
mile

1 The table shows the approximate conversion between **miles** and **kilometres**.

Copy the table. Follow the pattern to complete the table.

Number of miles	5	10	15	20	25	30	35	40
Number of kilometres	8	16	24	32				

2 Write true (**T**) or false (**F**) for each statement.

a   3 miles is further than 3 km.

b   70 km is further than 70 miles.

c   12.5 km is exactly the same distance as 12.5 miles.

d   44 km is not as far as 44 miles.

e   In one hour, a person walking at 3 miles per hour will go a shorter distance than a person walking at 3 kilometres per hour.

Tip

Remember that 1 mile is further than 1 km.

3 Read what Sofia says.

> I have to travel 18 km to get to school. My mother has to travel 18 miles to get to work. I have to travel further to get to school than my mother has to travel to get to work.

Is Sofia correct? Explain your answer.

4   This flow chart converts kilometres to miles.

Number of km	÷ 8	× 5	Number of miles

Use the flow chart to copy and complete each conversion.

a   16 km $16 \div 8 = 2$ $2 \times 5 = \boxed{}$ miles

b   48 km $48 \div 8 = \boxed{}$ $\boxed{} \times 5 = \boxed{}$ miles

c   72 km $72 \div \boxed{} = \boxed{}$ $\boxed{} \times \boxed{} = \boxed{}$ miles

5   This flow chart converts miles into kilometres.

Number of miles	÷ 5	× 8	Number of km

Use the flow chart to copy and complete each conversion.

a   15 miles $15 \div 5 = 3$ $3 \times 8 = \boxed{}$ km

b   25 miles $25 \div 5 = \boxed{}$ $\boxed{} \times 8 = \boxed{}$ km

c   40 miles $40 \div \boxed{} = \boxed{}$ $\boxed{} \times \boxed{} = \boxed{}$ km

Practice

6   Convert each distance into miles.

    a   88 km   **b**   72 km   **c**   120 km   **d**   200 km

7   Convert each distance into kilometres.

    a   30 miles   **b**   300 miles   **c**   45 miles   **d**   4500 miles

8   Which is further, 128 km or 75 miles?

    Show your working.

9   Which is further, 180 miles or 296 km?

    Show your working.

10   Use only numbers from the rectangle to complete these statements.

168	65	152
304	190	105

    a   104 km = $\boxed{}$ miles   **b**   95 miles = $\boxed{}$ km

    c $\boxed{}$ miles = $\boxed{}$ km   **d** $\boxed{}$ km = $\boxed{}$ miles

Challenge

11   Work out the missing number in each conversion.

    Give your answer as a mixed number or a decimal.

    a   7 miles = $\boxed{}$ km   **b**   21 miles = $\boxed{}$ km   **c**   39 miles = $\boxed{}$ km

12   Work out the missing number in each conversion.

    Give your answer as a mixed number in its simplest form.

    a   20 km = $\boxed{}$ miles   **b**   34 km = $\boxed{}$ miles   **c**   63 km = $\boxed{}$ miles

13 Every car in the USA has a milometer.

The milometer shows the **total distance** a car has travelled.

When Johannes bought a used car, the milometer read: | 008 935 miles |

When Johannes wanted to sell the car, the milometer read: | 045 605 miles |

Johannes paid $13 995 for the car.

He is told that the value of his car goes down by 5 cents for every kilometre he drives.

Johannes thinks he should get about $10 500 for his car.

Is Johannes correct? Explain your answer. Show your working.

14 Sofia is a delivery driver. She lives in Lydenburg.

On one day, she must deliver parcels to Marble Hall, Ngobi and Sun City.

She can deliver the parcels in any order, but she must start and finish in Oxford.

The table shows the distances between the cities in miles.

The sketch map shows the positions of the cities.

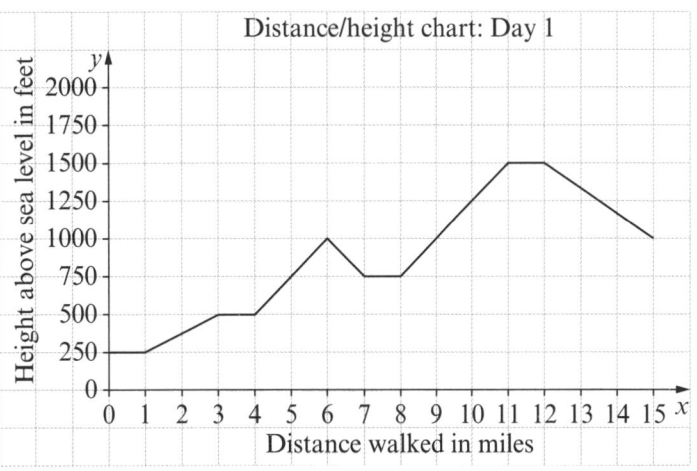

Distances between cities in miles				
Marble Hall				
60	**Lydenburg**			
125	75	**Sun City**		
210	160	85	**Ngobi**	

Work out the shortest route Sofia can take. Give your answer in kilometres.

15 Mia and Shen go on a two-day walk.

They draw graphs to show the distance they walk and their height above sea level each day.

a   How many miles did they walk on
   i   Day 1   **ii**   Day 2?

b   How many kilometres did they walk on
   i   Day 1   **ii**   Day 2?

c   Copy and complete the workings to find the total height, in **feet**, they climbed **up** on Day 1:

From 250 feet to 500 feet = 250 feet

From 500 feet to 1000 feet = 500 feet

From 750 feet to 1500 feet = ☐ feet

Total = 250 + 500 + ☐ = ☐ feet

d   What is the total height, in feet, they climbed **up** on Day 2?

e   An approximate conversion from feet to metres is

   10 feet = 3 metres

   Work out the total height, in metres, they climbed up on
   i   Day 1   **ii**   Day 2.

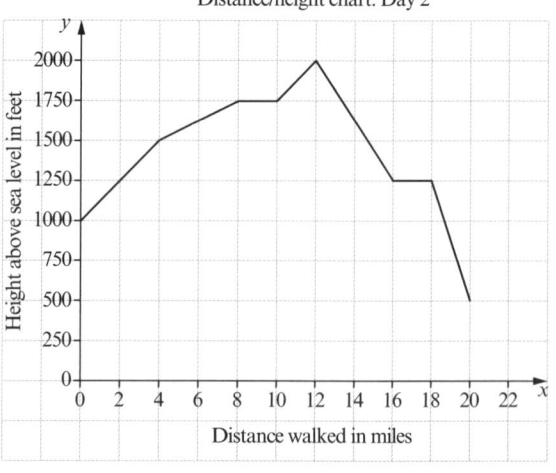

Distance/height chart: Day 2

> **Tip**
>
> Look at the three sections on the graph where the height above sea level increased.

Mia and Shen work out the total time it should take them to do their walk each day using this rule:

Total walk time = 1 hour for every 5 km walked + 1 hour for every 600 m height climbed up

f   Copy and complete these ratios:

   1 hour   :   5 km   1 hour   :   600 m

   ☐ minutes   :   5 km   ☐ minutes   :   600 m

   ☐ minutes   :   1 km   ☐ minutes   :   10 m

g   Use your answers from parts **b**, **e** and **f** to work out the total time it should take them to do their walk on
   i   Day 1   **ii**   Day 2.

> 15.2 The area of a parallelogram and trapezium

Exercise 15.2

Focus

Worked example 15.1

You can work out the area of a parallelogram by making the parallelogram into a rectangle like this:

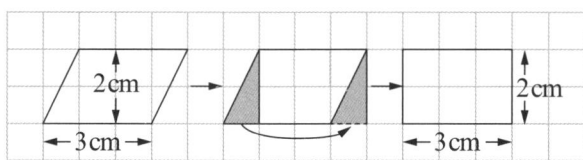

Answer

area = base × height = $3 \times 2 = 6 \, \text{cm}^2$

1   Copy and complete the workings to find the area of each parallelogram.

a
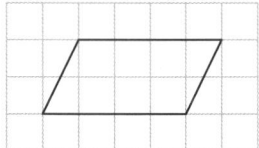

   area = base × height
   $= 4 \times \boxed{}$
   $= \boxed{} \, \text{cm}^2$

b
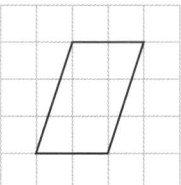

   area = base × height
   $= 2 \times \boxed{}$
   $= \boxed{} \, \text{cm}^2$

c
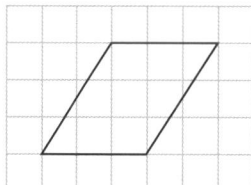

   area = base × height
   $= \boxed{} \times \boxed{}$
   $= \boxed{} \, \text{cm}^2$

2   Work out the area of each parallelogram.

a
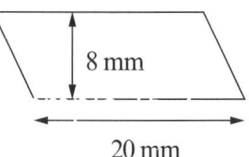
8 mm
20 mm

b
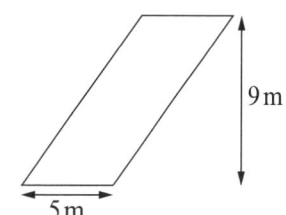
9 m
5 m

Worked example 15.2

You can work out the area of a trapezium in three steps like this:

Answer

Step 1 top + bottom

Step 2 step 1 ÷ 2

Step 3 step 2 × height

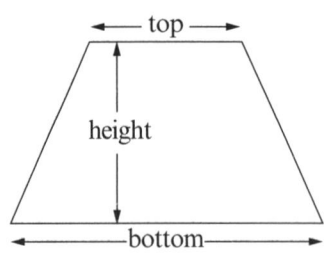

For example:

Step 1 3 + 5 = 8

Step 2 8 ÷ 2 = 4

Step 3 4 × 6 = 24

area = 24 cm²

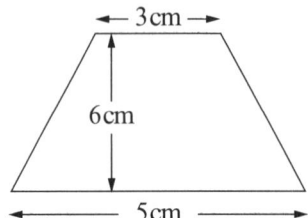

3 Copy and complete the workings to find the area of each trapezium.

a   **Step 1**   4 + 6 = 10
    Step 2   10 ÷ 2 = 5
    Step 3   5 × 3 = ☐ cm²

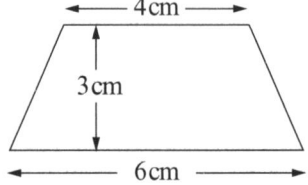

b   **Step 1**   5 + ☐ = ☐
    Step 2   ☐ ÷ 2 = ☐
    Step 3   ☐ × 6 = ☐ cm²

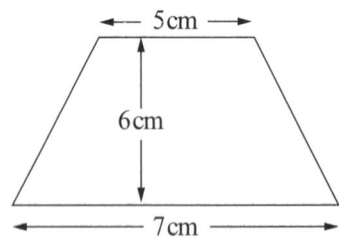

c   **Step 1**   ☐ + ☐ = ☐
    Step 2   ☐ ÷ 2 = ☐
    Step 3   ☐ × ☐ = ☐ cm²

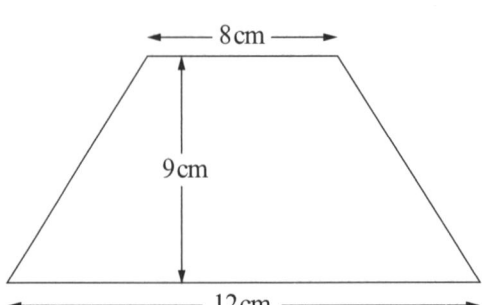

4 Work out the area of each of these **trapezia**.

a

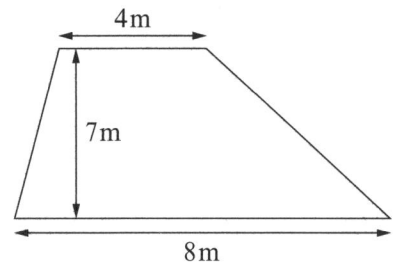

b

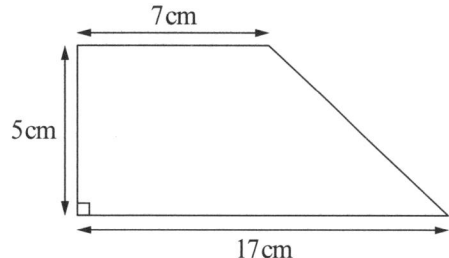

5 This is part of Jen's homework.

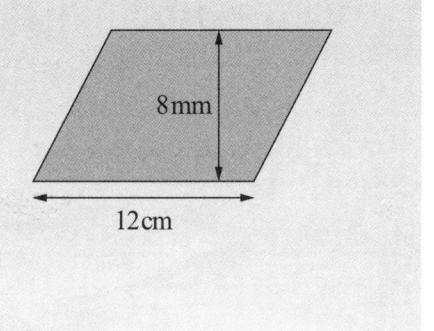

Question
Work out the area of
this parallelogram.
Answer
Area = bh
      = 12 × 8
      = 96 cm²

a Explain the mistake Jen has made.

b Work out the correct answer.

Practice

6 Work out the area of each trapezium. Show all your working.

a

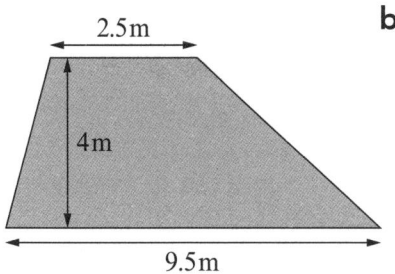

b

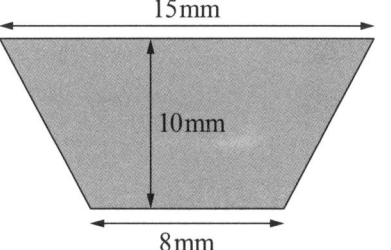

c

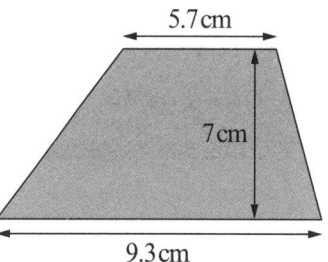

7 The diagram shows a trapezium.

a Work out an estimate of the area of the trapezium.

b Use a calculator to work out the accurate area of the trapezium.

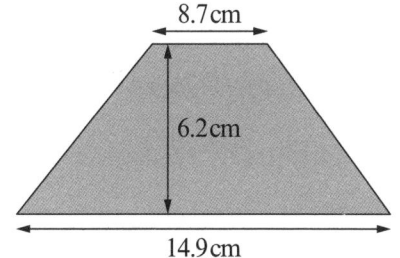

> **Tip**
>
> To work out an estimate, round all the numbers to one significant figure.

8 Here are four shapes, A, B, C and D.

A 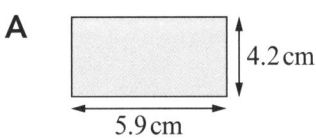 B 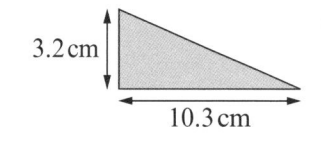 C 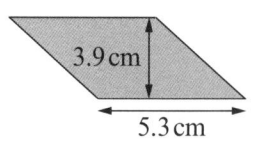 D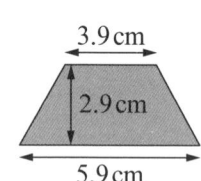

Here are five area cards.

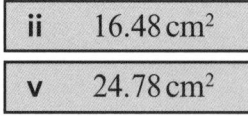

i	14.21 cm²
ii	16.48 cm²
iii	18.41 cm²
iv	20.67 cm²
v	24.78 cm²

a Using only estimation, match each shape with the correct area card. Show your working.

b Use a calculator to check your answers to part **a**.

c Which area card did you not use?

9 This parallelogram has an area of 43.4 cm².

It has a perpendicular height of 28 mm.

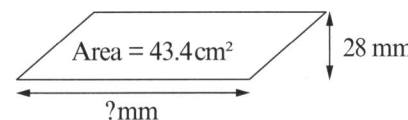

> **Tip**
>
> Remember,
> 1 cm² = 100 mm²

What is the length of the base of the parallelogram?

10 Work out the area of each compound shape.

a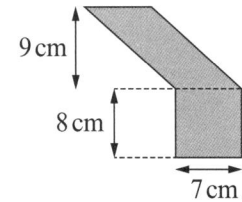

b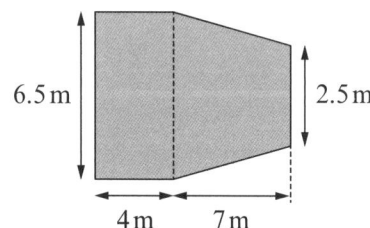

Challenge

11 The diagram shows a trapezium with an area of 7182 mm².

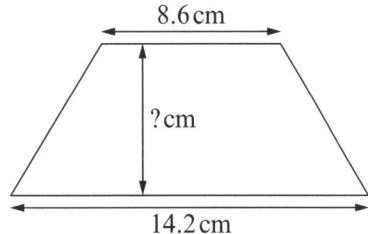

What is the perpendicular height of the trapezium?

12 Kai works out that the shaded area in this diagram is 875 cm².

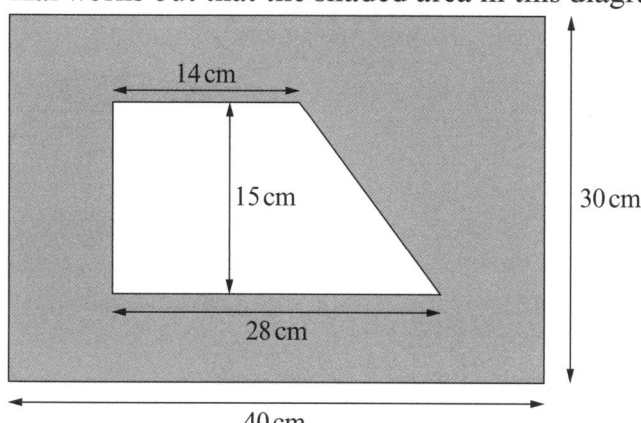

Is Kai correct? Show your working.

13 Work out the area of each shape. Give each answer as a fraction in its simplest form.
Remember to give the units with your answers.

a

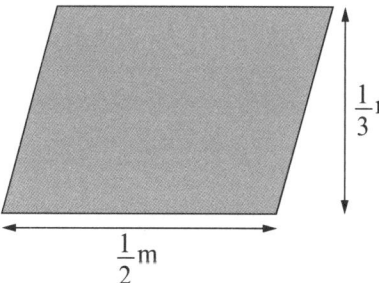

b

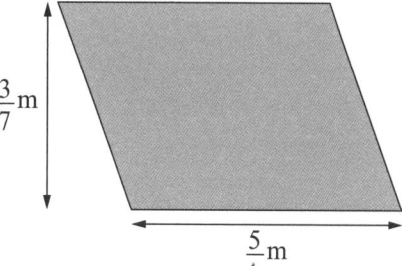

c

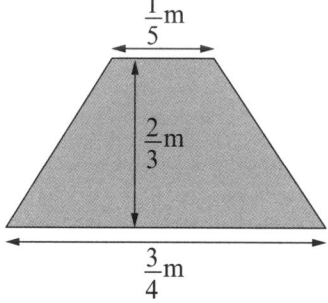

14 Work out the area of this plot of land.
Give your answer in
a square kilometres
b square miles.

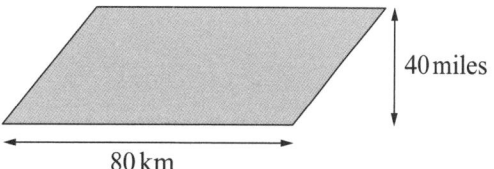

15 Windscreen glass for a van costs $250 per square metre.
The diagram shows a van windscreen in the shape of
a trapezium.
Work out the cost of the glass for the windscreen.

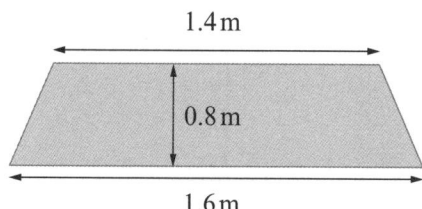

› 15.3 Calculating the volume of triangular prisms

Exercise 15.3

Focus

1   Copy and complete the workings to find the volume of each triangular **prism**.

a

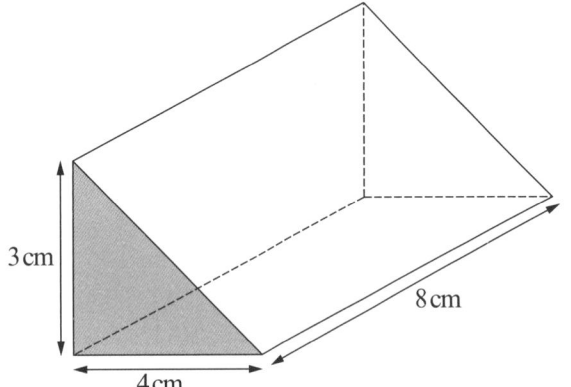

Area of cross-section $= \frac{1}{2} \times b \times h$

$\qquad = \frac{1}{2} \times 3 \times 4$

$\qquad = \boxed{} \, cm^2$

Volume = area of **cross-section** × length

$\qquad = \boxed{} \times 8$

$\qquad = \boxed{} \, cm^3$

b

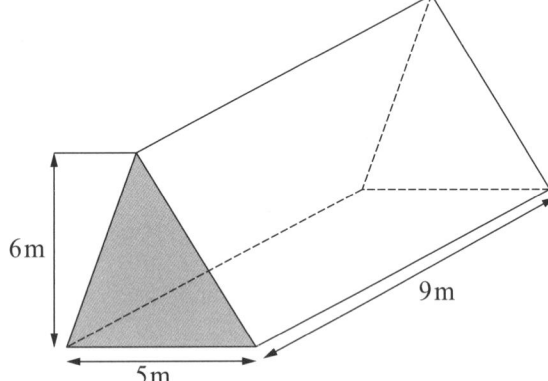

Area of cross-section $= \frac{1}{2} \times b \times h$

$\qquad = \frac{1}{2} \times \boxed{} \times \boxed{}$

$\qquad = \boxed{} \, m^2$

Volume = area of cross-section × length

$\qquad = \boxed{} \times 9$

$\qquad = \boxed{} \, m^3$

2   Work out the volume of each triangular prism.

a

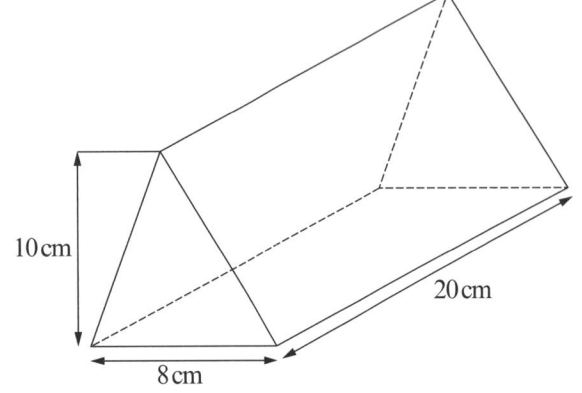

b

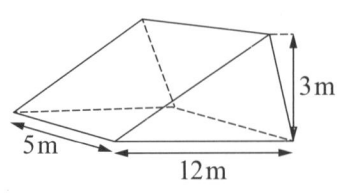

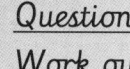 **3** This is part of Anil's homework.

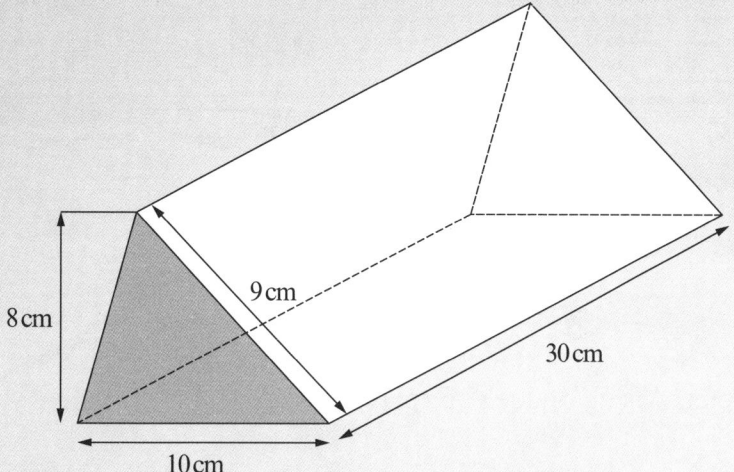

Question
Work out the volume of this triangular prism.

8 cm

9 cm

10 cm

30 cm

Answer
Area of cross-section $= \dfrac{1}{2} \times b \times h$

$= \dfrac{1}{2} \times 10 \times 9 = 45$ cm^2

Volume = area × length $= 45 \times 30 = 1350$ cm^3

Anil has got the answer wrong.

Explain the mistake Anil has made and work out the correct answer.

4 Joe and Alice use different methods to work out the volume of this triangular prism.

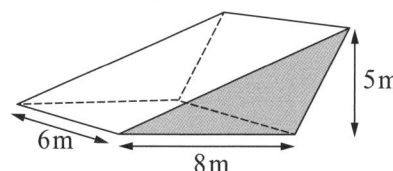

6 m

8 m

5 m

a Copy and complete their methods.

Show that both methods give an answer of 120 m³.

Joe

Area of cross section = $\frac{1}{2} \times b \times h$

$= \frac{1}{2} \times \square \times \square$

$= \square\ m^2$

Volume = area of cross-section × length

$= \square \times \square$

$= \square\ m^3$

Alice

Volume = area of cross-section × length

$= \frac{1}{2} \times b \times h \times l$

$= \frac{1}{2} \times \square \times \square \times \square$

$= \square\ m^3$

b Whose method do you prefer, Alice's or Joe's? Explain why.

Practice

5 The table shows the base, perpendicular height and length of four triangular prisms.

Copy and complete the table.

	Base	Height	Length	Volume
a	6 cm	10 cm	20 mm	$\square$ cm³
b	0.5 cm	12 mm	6 mm	$\square$ mm³
c	1.5 m	6 m	80 cm	$\square$ m³
d	40 mm	4 cm	400 mm	$\square$ cm³

> **Tip**
>
> For each part, make sure the length, width and height are in the same units before you work out the volume.

6 Work out the volume of each compound prism.

a

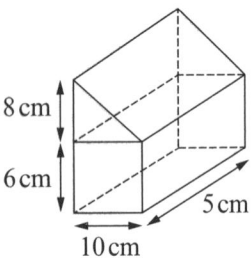

b

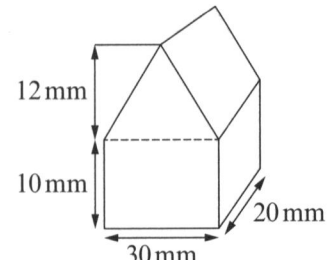

7 Here are three sets of cards.

The white cards show the **volumes** of four triangular prisms.

The grey cards show the **areas** of the cross-sections of the four triangular prisms.

The black cards show the **lengths** of the four triangular prisms.

$V = 72\,cm^3$	$V = 84\,cm^3$	$V = 90\,cm^3$	$V = 108\,cm^3$
$A = 12\,cm^2$	$A = 9\,cm^2$	$A = 18\,cm^2$	$A = 15\,cm^2$
$l = 6\,cm$	$l = 4\,cm$	$l = 12\,cm$	$l = 7\,cm$

Match each white card with the correct grey and black card.

8 The diagram shows a triangular prism.

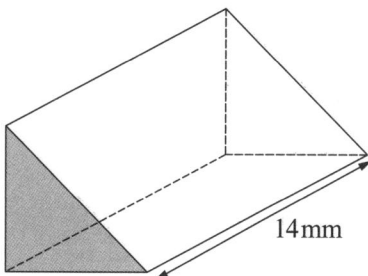

14mm

The volume of the prism is $350\,mm^3$.

Work out the area of the shaded triangle.

Challenge

9 The diagram shows a triangular prism.

The volume of the prism is $224\,cm^3$.

a Work out the area of the shaded triangle.

b Find the base and height of two possible triangular prisms with this volume.

Explain how you worked out your answers.

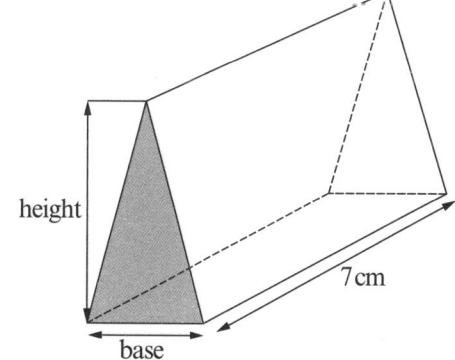

height

7cm

base

10 The diagram shows a triangular prism.

The volume of the prism is $756\,mm^3$.

Work out the base length of the triangle.

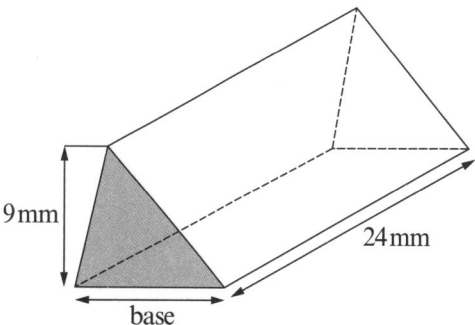

9mm

24mm

base

11 A triangular prism has a base of 8 m, a height of 12 m and a length of 7 m.

    a Work out the volume of the triangular prism.

    b Work out the dimensions of two other triangular prisms with the same volume.

12 The diagram shows a concrete ramp in the shape of a triangular prism.

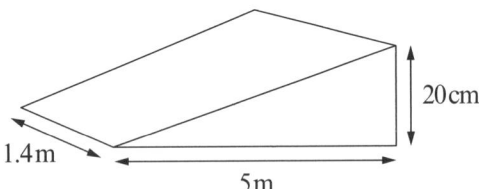

1 m³ of concrete has a mass of 2400 kg.

Hari thinks the mass of the ramp is more than 1700 kg.

Is Hari correct? Explain your answer. Show all your working.

> 15.4 Calculating the surface area of triangular prisms and pyramids

Exercise 15.4

Focus

Key words

net
surface area

1 Complete the workings to find the **surface area** of each solid shape.

    a

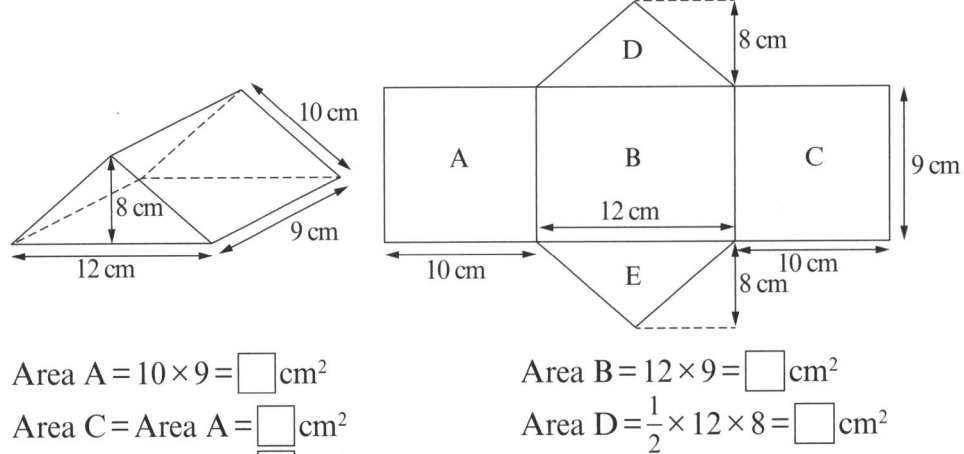

Area A = 10 × 9 = ☐ cm²   Area B = 12 × 9 = ☐ cm²

Area C = Area A = ☐ cm²   Area D = $\frac{1}{2}$ × 12 × 8 = ☐ cm²

Area E = Area D = ☐ cm²

Total area = ☐ + ☐ + ☐ + ☐ + ☐ = ☐ cm²

b

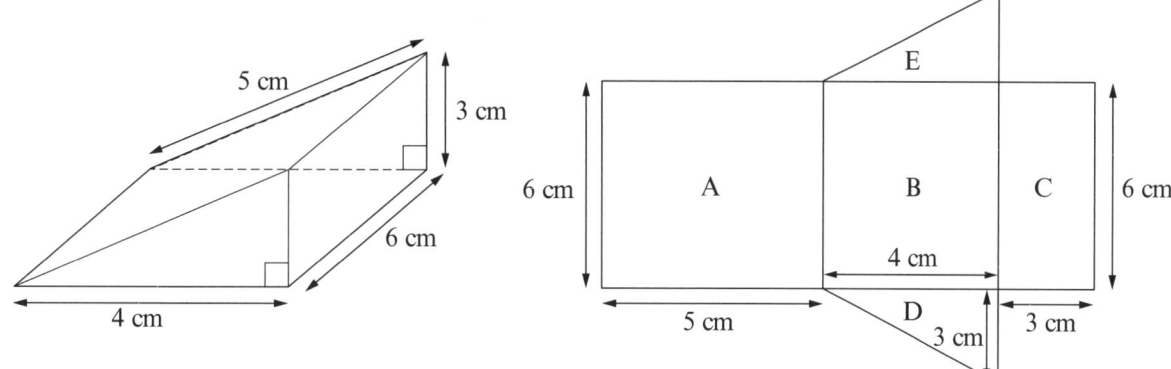

Area A = 5 × 6 = ☐ cm²   Area B = 4 × ☐ = ☐ cm²

Area C = ☐ × ☐ = ☐ cm²   Area D = $\frac{1}{2}$ × 4 × 3 = ☐ cm²

Area E = Area D = ☐ cm²

Total area = ☐ + ☐ + ☐ + ☐ + ☐ = ☐ cm²

c

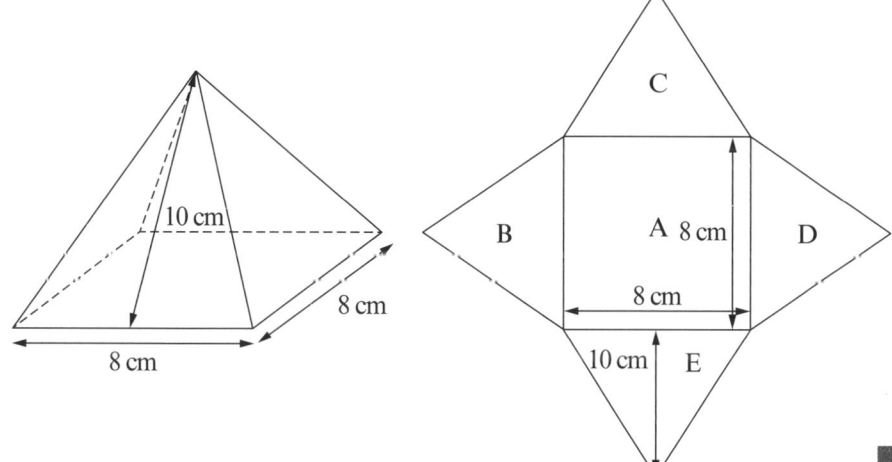

Area A = 8 × 8 = ☐ cm²

Area B = $\frac{1}{2}$ × 8 × 10 = ☐ cm²

Area of all four triangles = 4 × ☐ = ☐ cm²

Total area = ☐ + ☐ = ☐ cm²

> **Tip**
>
> B, C, D and E are identical triangles, so their areas are the same.

2 This is part of Simon's homework.

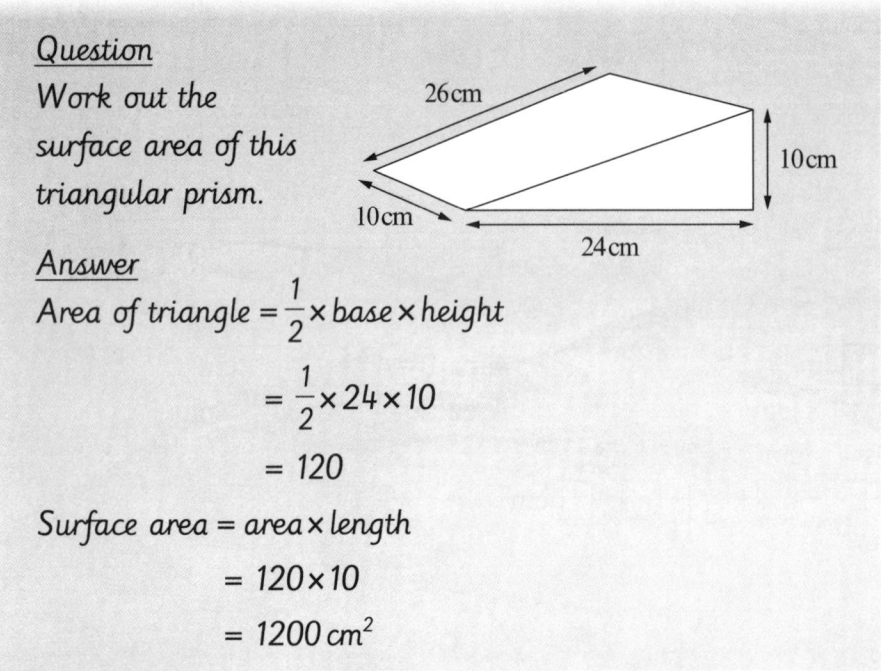

Question
Work out the surface area of this triangular prism.

26cm
10cm
10cm
24cm

Answer
Area of triangle = $\frac{1}{2}$ × base × height

= $\frac{1}{2}$ × 24 × 10

= 120

Surface area = area × length

= 120 × 10

= 1200 cm²

Simon's answer is wrong.

a Explain the mistake he has made.   **b** Work out the correct answer.

Practice

3 For each solid

  i sketch a **net**   **ii** work out the surface area.

  a triangular prism (isosceles)

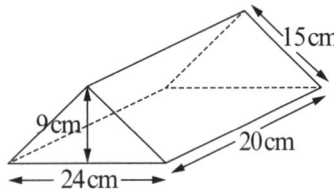

15cm
9cm
20cm
24cm

  b triangular prism (right-angled triangle)

13cm
5cm
10cm
12cm

  c square-based pyramid, all triangles equal in size

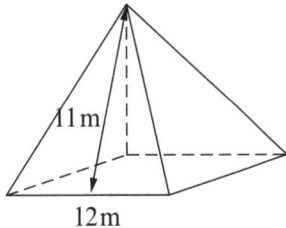

11m
12m

  d triangular-based pyramid, all triangles equal in size

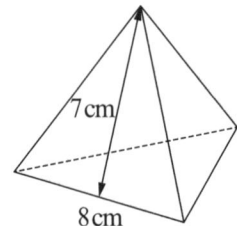

7cm
8cm

4 Mia draws a sketch of a cube of side length 35 mm.

She also draws a sketch of an isosceles triangular prism with the dimensions shown.

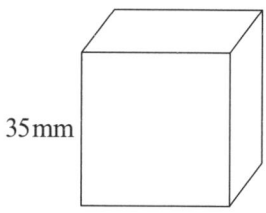 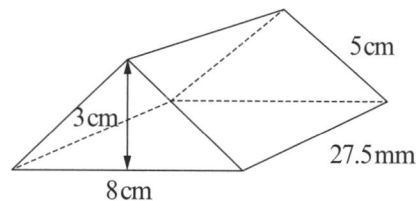

Mia thinks the cube and the triangular prism have the same surface area.

Is Mia correct? Show clearly how you worked out your answer.

5 The diagram shows a triangular-based pyramid and a cuboid.

Show that the surface area of the triangular-based pyramid is more than double the surface area of the cuboid.

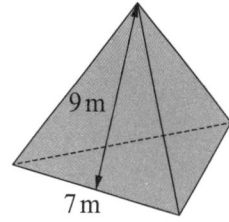 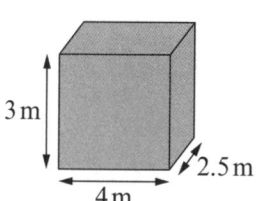

Challenge

6 Look at the diagram.

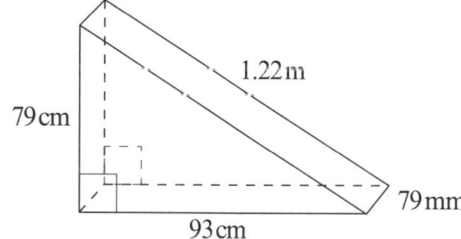 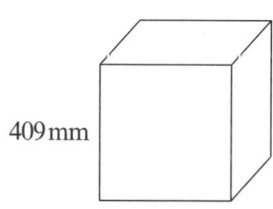

Razi thinks the triangular prism has a smaller surface area than the cuboid.

Use estimation to decide whether Razi is correct.

7 This cuboid has a height of x cm.

The width of the cuboid is twice the height.

The length of the cuboid is three times the height.

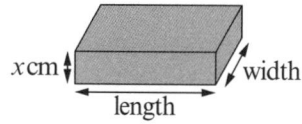

a Work out a formula for the surface area of the cuboid.

b In cuboid **A**, $x = 3$. In cuboid **B**, $x = 5$.

Use your formula to work out the total surface area of the two cuboids (surface area of **A** + surface area of **B**).

8 The surface area of this triangular-based pyramid is the same as the surface area of a cube of side length 12 mm.

Work out the height of the triangular face.

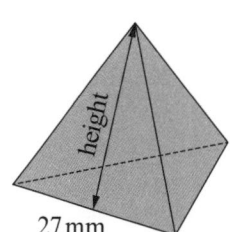

16 ▶ Interpreting and discussing results

> 16.1 Interpreting and drawing frequency diagrams

Exercise 16.1

Focus

1   The **frequency diagram** shows the number of homeworks given to students from class 8B in one week.

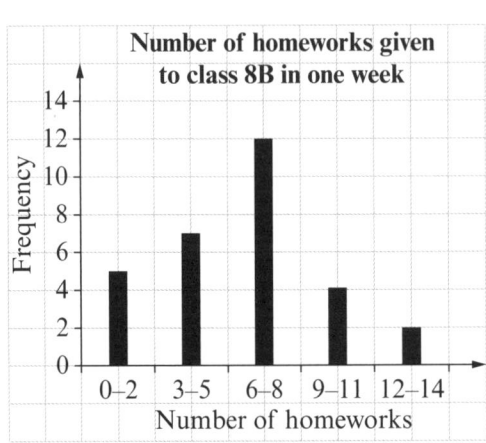

Number of homeworks given to class 8B in one week

a   How many students were given 6–8 homeworks?

b   How many students were given

    i   0–2 homeworks

    ii   12–14 homeworks?

c   How many **more** students were given 0–2 homeworks than were given 12–14 homeworks?

d   How many students are there in class 8B?

2 The frequency table shows the number of bicycles sold by a shop each day during one month.

Copy and complete the frequency diagram to show the data.

Number of bicycles sold	Frequency
0–4	6
5–9	8
10–14	3
15–19	10
20–24	4

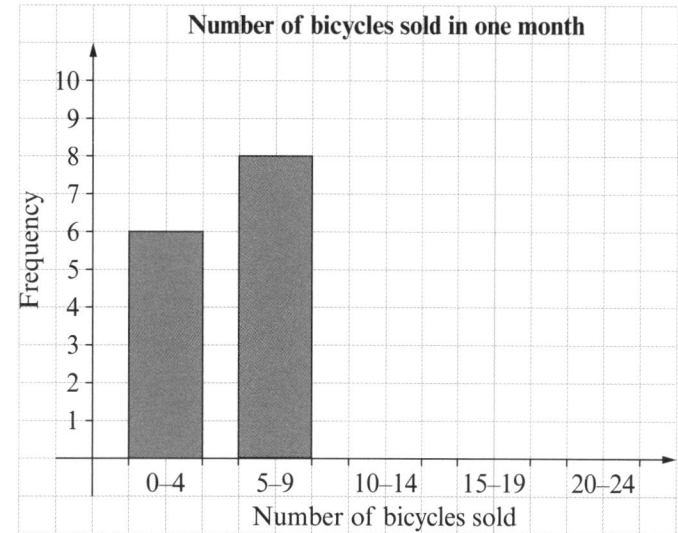

3 The frequency table shows the number of breakfasts sold in a café each day during one month.

a Draw a frequency diagram to show the data.

b On how many days were 10–19 breakfasts sold?

c On how many days were at least 20 breakfasts sold?

Explain how you worked out your answer.

d What is the total of the frequency column in the table?

e How can you tell that the person who made the frequency table has made a mistake?

Explain your answer.

f The manager of the café says:

'The frequency diagram shows that the greatest number of breakfasts sold in one day was 49.'

Is the manager correct? Explain your answer.

Number of breakfasts sold	Frequency
0–9	1
10–19	3
20–29	7
30–39	11
40–49	5

Tip

Compare your answer to part **d** with the number of days in one month.

Practice

4 The frequency table shows the time taken by 30 people to complete a puzzle.

a Explain what the class $0 < t \leqslant 5$ means.

b Explain why you cannot use the **classes** 0–4, 5–9, etc.

c In which class would you include someone who took exactly 15 minutes to complete the puzzle?

Time, t minutes	Frequency
$0 < t \leqslant 5$	3
$5 < t \leqslant 10$	12
$10 < t \leqslant 15$	9
$15 < t \leqslant 20$	6
$20 < t \leqslant 25$	1

d   Copy and complete the frequency diagram
    below to show the data.

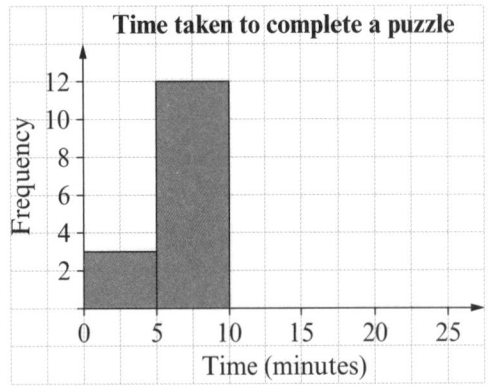

Time taken to complete a puzzle

 5   The frequency table shows the mass of 25 adults.

Mass of adults, m (kg)	Frequency
$65 < m \leqslant 70$	4
$70 < m \leqslant 75$	9
$75 < m \leqslant 80$	7
$80 < m \leqslant 85$	2
$85 < m \leqslant 90$	3

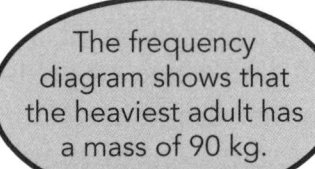

The frequency diagram shows that the heaviest adult has a mass of 90 kg.

a   Draw a frequency diagram to show the data.
b   Read what Zara says.
    Is Zara correct? Explain your answer.
The adults want to go horse riding.
The maximum mass for horse riding is 80 kg.
c   How many of the adults cannot go horse riding?

6   Here are the lengths, in millimetres, of twenty beetles.

12	4	18	16	6	19	15	10	17	12
5	22	7	11	20	14	18	15	3	9

a   Record this information in a frequency table.
    Use the classes $0 \leqslant l < 5$, $5 \leqslant l < 10$, $10 \leqslant l < 15$, $15 \leqslant l < 20$ and
    $20 \leqslant l < 25$.
b   Draw a frequency diagram to show the data.
c   How many of the beetles are at least 10 mm long?
    Explain how you worked out your answer.

Challenge

7 The frequency diagram shows the heights, in centimetres, of some plants.

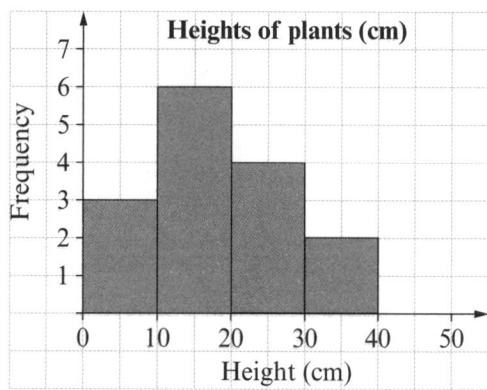

The tallest plant is 40 cm.

Put the information from the frequency diagram into a frequency table.

8 The frequency table shows the heights of sunflowers grown in class 8V's biology lessons.

a Draw a frequency diagram to show the data.

b The tallest student in class 8V is 1.6 m.

How many sunflowers are taller than the tallest student?

c Marcus says: 'The frequency diagram shows that the shortest sunflower was only 1 m high.'

Is Marcus correct? Explain your answer.

d Sofia says: 'The frequency diagram shows that the tallest sunflower was exactly 2 m high.'

Is Sofia correct? Explain your answer.

e How many sunflowers were grown in class 8V's biology lessons?

Height of sunflowers, h (m)	Frequency
$1.0 < h \leqslant 1.2$	2
$1.2 < h \leqslant 1.4$	3
$1.4 < h \leqslant 1.6$	6
$1.6 < h \leqslant 1.8$	12
$1.8 < h \leqslant 2.0$	5

9 40 students were asked to text 'Happy holiday!' on a mobile phone.

The time it took them, in seconds, was recorded. The results are shown below.

10.1	11.2	9.5	7.9	12.8	4.2	17.0	9.3	24.1	13.7
5.1	3.8	12.0	10.5	15.9	14.0	11.6	7.7	9.1	12.5
13.7	15.3	11.4	5.8	10.9	23.5	6.8	14.2	18.5	14.5
11.4	22.4	6.3	10.2	16.0	14.9	12.1	17.8	8.8	16.8

a Draw a frequency table to show the data. Decide on your own **class intervals**.

b Draw a frequency diagram to show the data.

> 16.2 Time series graphs

Exercise 16.2

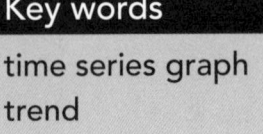

Key words

time series graph

trend

Focus

1 The **time series graph** shows how many drawing pins a company produced over a six-year period.

   a How many drawing pins were made in

      i   2009   ii   2010?

   b In which year did the company make 3 500 000 drawing pins?

   c Between which two years was the greatest increase in production?

   d Between which two years was there no increase in production?

   e Between which two years was the smallest increase in production?

   f Describe the **trend** in the company's production over the six-year period.

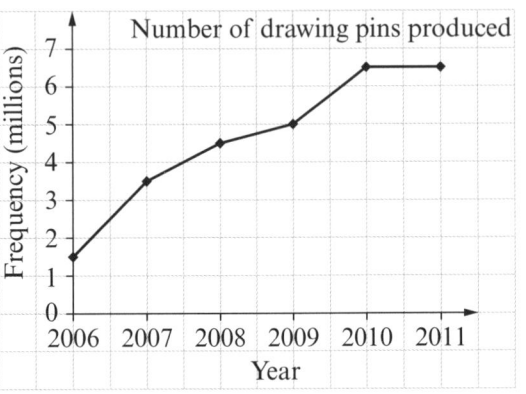

2 Kelly records the number of skis hired at her shop each month for one year.

   The data is shown in the time series graph.

   a Approximately how many skis were hired from Kelly's shop in

      i   March   ii   July?

   b In which month were the most skis hired?

   c Between which two months did the number of rentals triple?

   d Describe the trend in ski hires over the year.

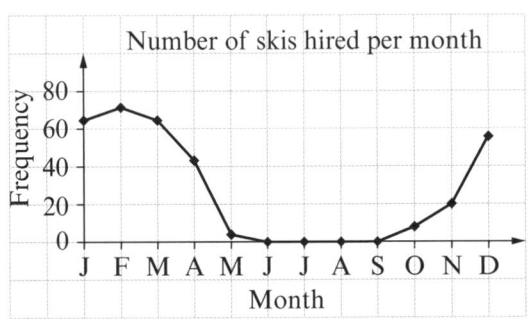

3   Allana invests some money in 2005.
    The time series graph shows the value of her investment from 2005 to 2019.

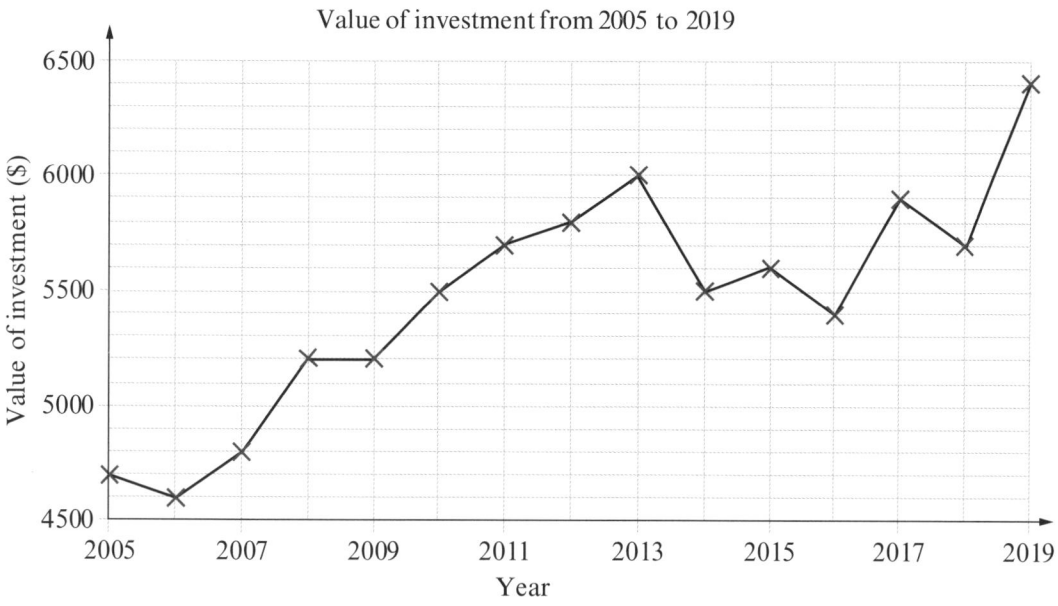

a   How much money did Allana invest in 2005?
b   Between which two years did Allana's investment
    i   stay the same
    ii   increase the most
    iii decrease the most?
c   Describe the trend in the value of the investment from 2005 to 2019.

Practice

4   The table shows the number of skateboards sold by a shop each month
    for one year.

Month	Jan	Feb	Mar	Apr	May	Jun	Jul	Aug	Sep	Oct	Nov	Dec
Number of skateboards	10	13	17	19	22	25	28	23	16	12	9	15

a   Draw a time series graph to show the data.
b   During which two months was the greatest
    i   increase in sales
    ii   decrease in sales?
c   Describe the trend in the data.

5   The table shows the average price of books sold from 'Brendan's Books' over a 20-year period.

Year	1998	2002	2006	2010	2014	2018
Average price of books ($)	11.10	10.80	8.20	7.00	7.30	12.50

a   Draw a time series graph to show the data.

b   In which four-year period did the price of books change the most?

c   Use your graph to estimate the average price of books sold from 'Brendan's Books' in 2004.

d   Describe the trend in the data.

6   The time series graph shows the total number of points scored by two football teams in league two from 2010 to 2018.

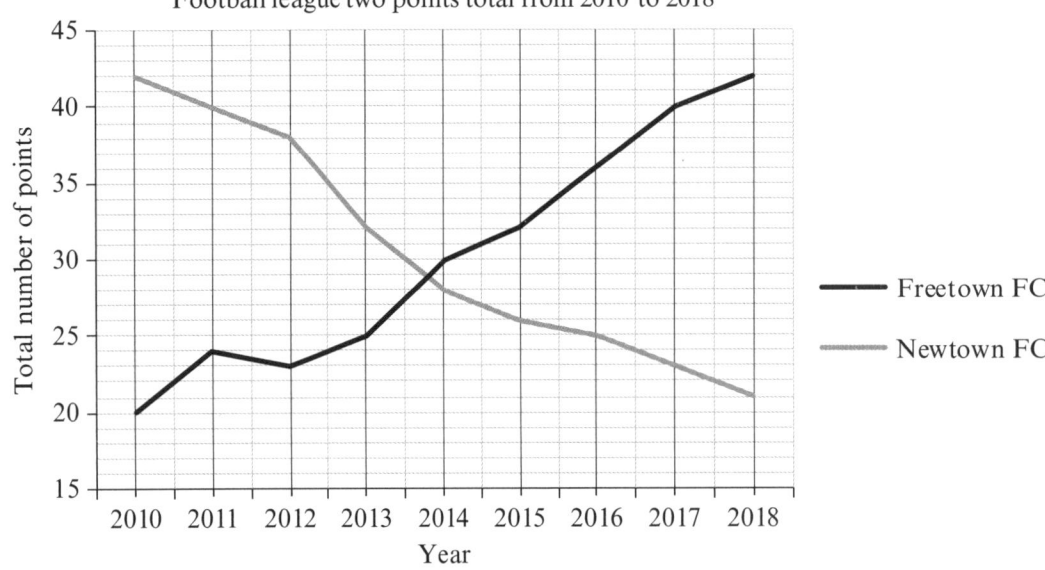

Football league two points total from 2010 to 2018

a   Describe the trend in the points total of
    i   Freetown FC
    ii   Newtown FC.

b   A football team will go up to league one if they have a points total of more than 46 points.

     Do you think Freetown FC will get enough points in 2019 to move up to league one?

     Explain your answer.

c   A football team will go down to league three if they have a points total of fewer than 20 points.

     Do you think Newtown FC will get enough points in 2019 to stay in league two?

     Explain your answer.

Challenge

7 The table shows the number of visitors to a theme park from Autumn 2018 to Summer 2021.

	2018		2019				2020				2021	
	A	W	Sp	Su	A	W	Sp	Su	A	W	Sp	Su
Number of visitors (1000s)	475	400	175	250	450	325	200	250	400	300	150	200

(Key: A = Autumn, W = Winter, Sp = Spring, Su = Summer)

a Draw a time series graph for this data.

b Describe how the number of visitors changes over the seasons during 2019.

c Do similar changes over the seasons that you have noticed in 2019 also happen in the other years? Explain your answer.

d Describe the yearly trend in the number of visitors.

e Use your graph to predict the number of visitors in Winter 2021.

f Explain why your answer to part **e** may be incorrect.

8 The time series graph shows the number of visitors to a riding stable each month from March to October in one year. Some of the points are missing.

a Copy and complete the time series graph using the information below.

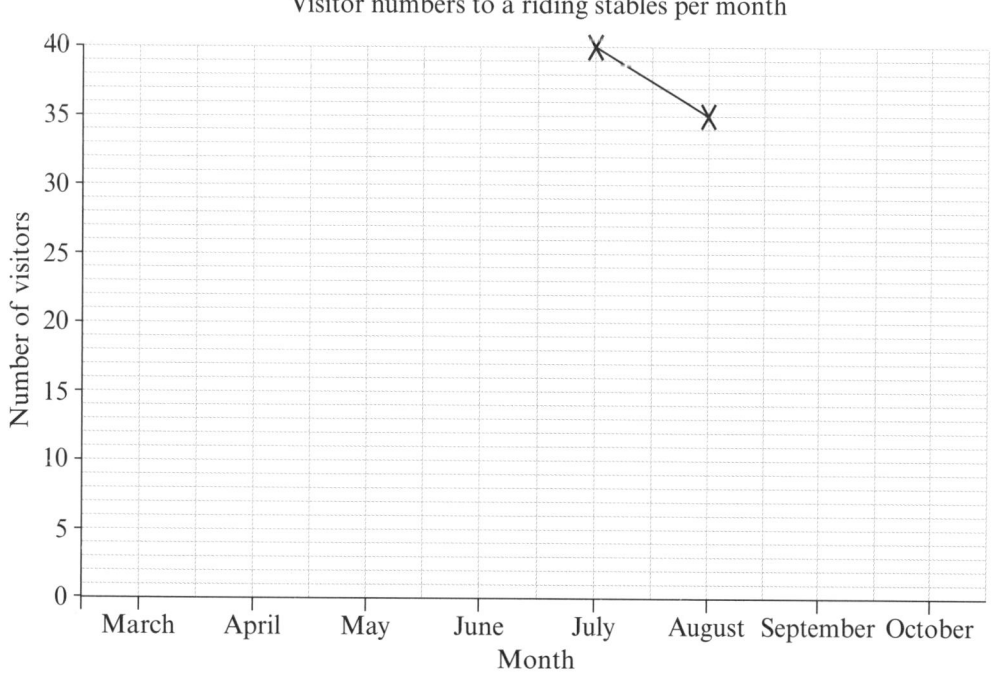

Visitor numbers to a riding stables per month

July had the most visitors and March had the fewest.

The range in the number of visitors was 29.

September had three times as many visitors as March.

August had the same number of visitors as April and May added together.

The ratio of visitors in April : May was 2 : 3.

The number of visitors in June was 80% of the number of visitors in July.

The mean number of visitors per month was 25.

b Describe the trend in the data.

9 The table shows the mean monthly temperatures (°C) in Kangerlussuaq, Greenland and Port Stanley, Falkland Islands over one year.
The temperatures are given to the nearest 1 °C.

	Jan	Feb	Mar	Apr	May	Jun	Jul	Aug	Sep	Oct	Nov	Dec
Kangerlussuaq	−20	−21	−18	−8	3	9	11	8	3	−6	−12	−16
Port Stanley	11	10	9	7	5	3	2	3	5	7	8	10

a Make a copy of the axes below. On the axes, draw a line for each set of data.

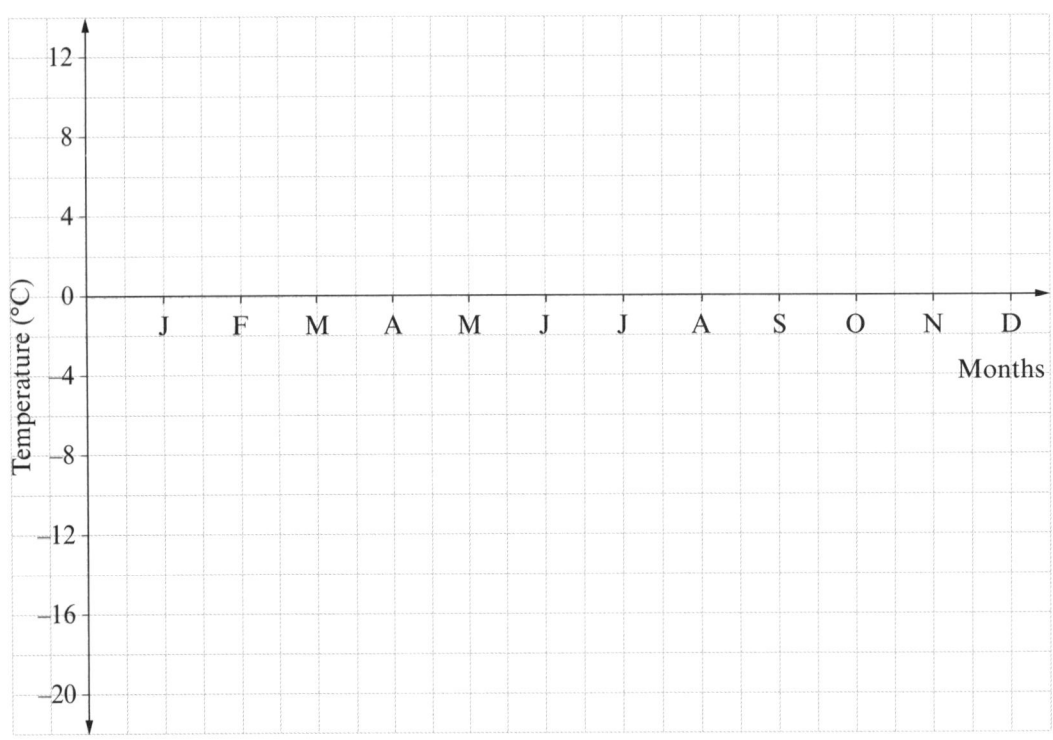

Mean monthly temperature in Kangerlussuaq and Port Stanley

b Describe the trend in the data for

i Kangerlussuaq

ii Port Stanley.

c Write a short paragraph comparing the temperatures in Kangerlussuaq and Port Stanley.

You could use words such as 'maximum', 'minimum', 'warmer', 'colder', 'variation', 'consistent'.

16.3 Stem-and-leaf diagrams

Exercise 16.3

Key words

mean
mode
stem-and-leaf diagram

Focus

1 This **stem-and-leaf diagram** shows the time, in seconds, it takes 10 students to complete a puzzle.

Key: 3 | 0 means 30 seconds

3	0 8 9 9
4	2 4 6 7 7 8

Copy and complete:

The times, in seconds, in order of size, from the fastest to the slowest are 30, 38, 39, …

2 This stem-and-leaf diagram shows the temperature, in °C, each day Fin was on holiday.

Key: 1 | 6 means 16 °C

1	6 7 8 9
2	0 2 2

a Write the temperatures in order, from the coldest to the warmest.

b Work out the

i **mode** ii median iii range.

Tip

Remember, the mode is the most common value, the median is the middle value and the range is the difference between the highest and lowest values.

3 This stem-and-leaf diagram shows the ages of the players in a football team.

Key: 1 | 8 means 18 years

1	8 9 9
2	0 1 2 5 6 9
3	2 5

a Write the ages in order, from the youngest to the oldest.

b Work out the

i mode ii median iii range.

Practice

4 The stem-and-leaf diagram shows how long, to the nearest minute, it took students from class 8U to complete their homework.

Key: 2 | 3 means 23 minutes

2	3 5 7 9
3	0 2 5 5 5 7 8 9 9
4	1 2 4 6 7 9

a How many students timed their homework?

b What was the shortest time taken to complete the homework?

c How many of the students took longer than 30 minutes?

d For this data, work out

i the mode ii the median iii the range.

5   The stem-and-leaf diagram shows the playing times, to the
nearest minute, of some films.

Key: 10 | 2 means 102 minutes

10	5 7 8
11	3 3 3 5 7 8 9
12	0 2 4 5 6 7 8 8
13	3 5 7 7

   a   How many films were timed?

   b   How long was the shortest film, in minutes?

   c   How many of the films lasted less than 2 hours?

   d   How many of the films lasted more than 2 hours?

   e   Why is your total for parts **c** and **d** together not the same as your
answer for part **a**?

   f   For this data, work out

   i   the mode   **ii**   the median   **iii**   the range.

6   These are the masses, in grams, of 25 newborn mice.

6.4   7.3   6.4   8.9   6.9   7.8   6.0   6.2   8.5   7.1   5.9   7.2   8.0

9.5   8.2   5.9   7.5   6.4   7.3   8.6   5.8   9.2   6.9   6.1   9.0

   a   Draw an ordered stem-and-leaf diagram to show this data.

   b   How many of the mice weighed less than 8 g?

   c   What fraction of the mice weighed more than 9 g?

   d   What percentage of the mice weighed between 6.3 and 7.9 g?

   e   Use your stem-and-leaf diagram to work out

   i   the mode   **ii**   the median   **iii**   the range.

Challenge

7   These are the masses, in kilograms, of the motorbikes on sale in a
showroom.

162   180   175   172   198   165   175   208   188   176   166   200

179   208   194   170   180   189   190   173   207   199   209   175

   a   Draw an ordered stem-and-leaf diagram to show this data.

   b   How many of the motorbikes are heavier than 200 kg?

   c   What fraction of the motorbikes are lighter than 180 kg?

   d   What percentage of the motorbikes are 190 kg or heavier?

   e   Use your stem-and-leaf diagram to work out

   i   the mode   **ii**   the median   **iii**   the **mean**.

   f   Which average best represents this data? Give a reason for
your answer.

   g   Tia works out that the range in the masses of the motorbikes
is 45 kg.

   Is Tia correct? Explain your answer.

8   The stem-and-leaf diagrams show the distances, to the nearest metre, that 29 students threw a tennis ball with their right hand and their left hand.

Distance thrown with right hand

Key: 0 | 3 means 3 metres

```
0 | 3 7 8 8
1 | 3 4 4 5 6 6 6 7 9 9
2 | 0 2 3 5 5 6 8
3 | 3 3 4 5 6 7 8 8
```

Distance thrown with left hand

Key: 0 | 3 means 3 metres

```
0 | 2 4 4 5 5 7 8 8 8
1 | 0 1 2 2 4 5 6 7 8
2 | 0 1 1 2 3 4 4 8
3 | 2 5 8
```

a   Copy and complete the table below showing the data for the distances thrown.

	Least distance	Greatest distance	Range	Median distance	Mean distance	Modal distance
Right hand						
Left hand						

b   Make two comments about what the data shows.

c   How many students do you think are left-handed? Explain your answer.

9   The frequency table and the stem-and-leaf diagram show the same information.

They both show the number of emails received by 60 employees of a company on one day.

Anders has spilt tea over the diagrams.

Tip

Use the information to work out all the frequencies first.

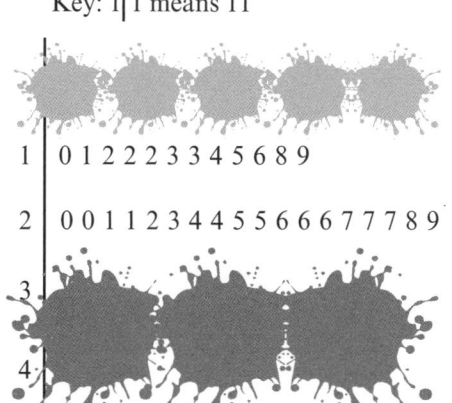

Key: 1 | 1 means 11

```
1 | 0 1 2 2 2 3 3 4 5 6 8 9
2 | 0 0 1 1 2 3 4 4 5 5 6 6 6 7 7 7 8 9
3 |
4 |
```

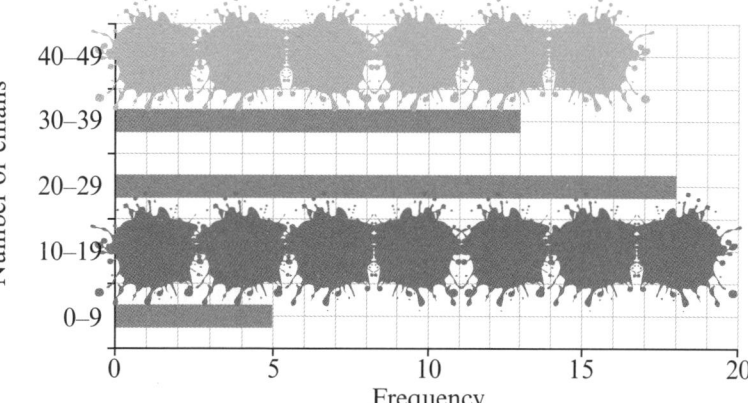

Use the information from the diagrams to draw a pie chart for the data.

> 16.4 Pie charts

Exercise 16.4

Focus

1 The **pie chart** shows the favourite African animal of 45 students.

   a Work out the number of degrees for the Impala section.

   b Copy and complete the workings to write the fraction of students who chose each animal.

   Write each fraction in its simplest form.

   Giraffe: $\frac{120}{360} = \frac{1}{3}$ Zebra: $\frac{40}{360} = \frac{1}{\square}$

   Elephant: $\frac{160}{360} = \frac{4}{\square}$ Impala: $\frac{\square}{360} = \frac{1}{\square}$

   c Copy and complete the workings to find the number of students who chose each animal.

   Giraffe: $\frac{1}{3} \times 45 = 45 \div 3 = \square$ Zebra: $\frac{1}{\square} \times 45 = \square$

   Elephant: $\frac{4}{\square} \times 45 = \square$ Impala: $\frac{1}{\square} \times 45 = \square$

Favourite African animal

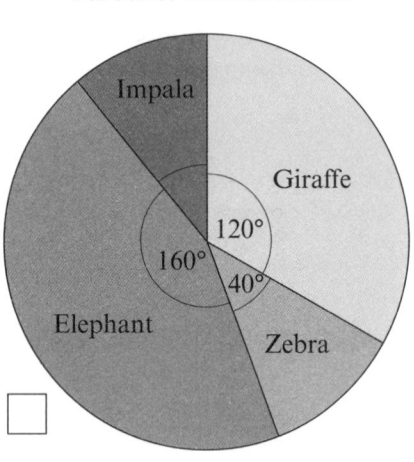

2 The pie chart shows the favourite marine animal of 72 students.

   a Work out the number of degrees for the Whale section.

   b Copy and complete the workings to write the fraction of students who chose each animal.

   Write each fraction in its simplest form.

   Dolphin: $\frac{130}{360} = \frac{13}{36}$ Shark: $\frac{30}{360} = \frac{1}{\square}$

   Turtle: $\frac{110}{360} = \frac{11}{\square}$ Whale: $\frac{\square}{360} = \frac{1}{\square}$

   c Copy and complete the workings to find the number of students who chose each animal.

   Dolphin: $\frac{13}{36} \times 72 = \square$ Shark: $\frac{1}{\square} \times 72 = \square$

   Turtle: $\frac{11}{\square} \times 72 = \square$ Whale: $\frac{1}{\square} \times 72 = \square$

Favourite marine animal

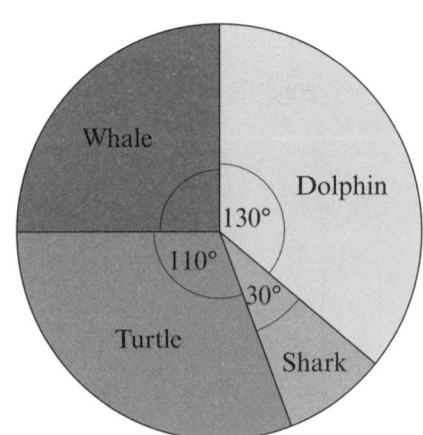

3 Compare the pie charts in questions **1** and **2**.

Copy and complete these sentences. Use either 'greater' or 'less' in each space.

a The proportion of students choosing Elephant was .... than the proportion of students choosing Dolphin.

b The number of students choosing Elephant was .... than the number of students choosing Dolphin.

c The proportion of students choosing Zebra was .... than the proportion of students choosing Shark.

d The number of students choosing Zebra was .... than the number of students choosing Shark.

Practice

4 The pie charts show the proportions of children of different ages in a kindergarten in 2018 and 2019.

Ages of children in kindergarten in 2018   Ages of children in kindergarten in 2019

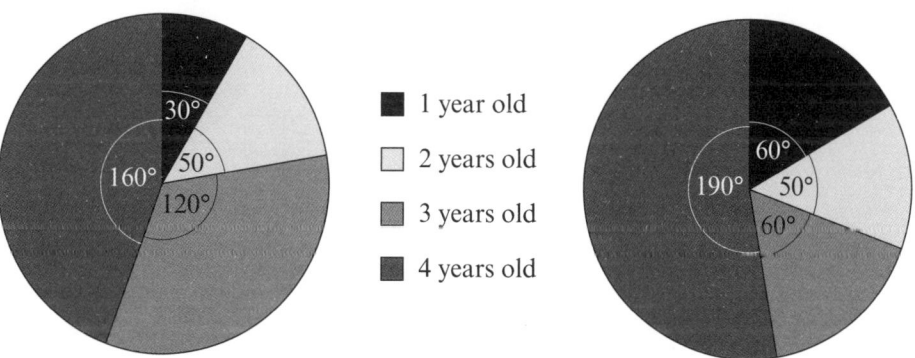

- ■ 1 year old
- □ 2 years old
- ▨ 3 years old
- ■ 4 years old

a What fraction of the children in the kindergarten were 1 year old in

i 2018   **ii** 2019?

b Copy and complete these sentences. Use the words in the rectangle.

doubled	stayed the same	tripled	halved	more than tripled

i In 2019, the proportion of children who were 3 years old had .... compared to 2018.

ii In 2019, the proportion of children who were 2 years old had .... compared to 2018.

iii In 2019, the proportion of children who were 1 year old had .... compared to 2018.

In 2018, the total number of children in the kindergarten was 144.

In 2019, the total number of children in the kindergarten was 72.

c Show that the number of children aged 1 year old in the kindergarten was the same in 2018 and in 2019.

d Show that there were four times as many children aged 3 years old in 2018 than in 2019.

e How many more children aged 4 years old were there in 2018 than in 2019?

> **Tip**
>
> Use the fractions you found in part **a**.

5 A group of men and women took part in a survey about favourite types of holiday.

The group was made up of 180 men and 240 women.

The pie charts show the results of the survey.

Mens' favourite types of holiday

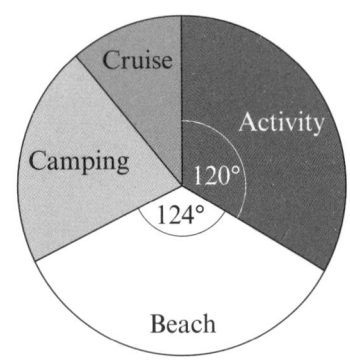

Womens' favourite types of holiday

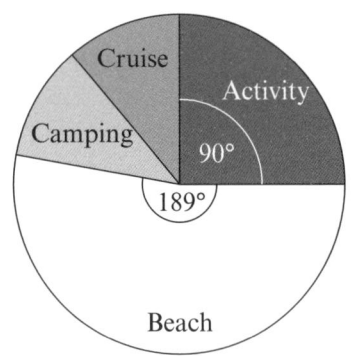

a How many women preferred activity holidays?

b How many men preferred activity holidays?

c How many more women than men said they preferred beach holidays?
Show how you worked out your answer.

d The 'Cruise' sector is the same size in both pie charts.
Without doing any calculations, explain how you know that more women than men preferred cruise holidays.

6 The pie charts show the favourite gym equipment of the members of two gyms.

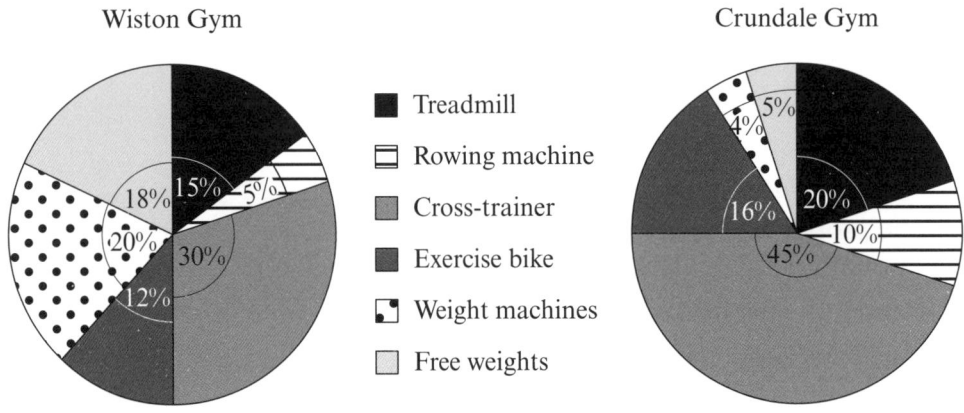

Wiston Gym

Crundale Gym

■ Treadmill
☐ Rowing machine
▨ Cross-trainer
▨ Exercise bike
▨ Weight machines
☐ Free weights

Wiston Gym has 190 members.

Crundale Gym has 120 members.

Which gym had the larger number of members choose cross-trainer as their favourite equipment?

Show your working.

Challenge

7   The pie charts show the percentage of electricity produced from different sources by Argentina, Brazil and Chile.

Argentina electricity production

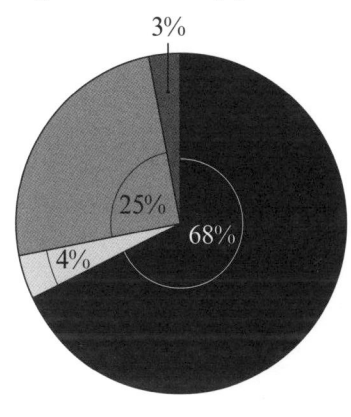

Brazil electricity production

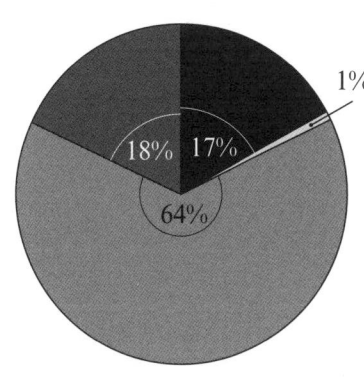

Chile electricity production

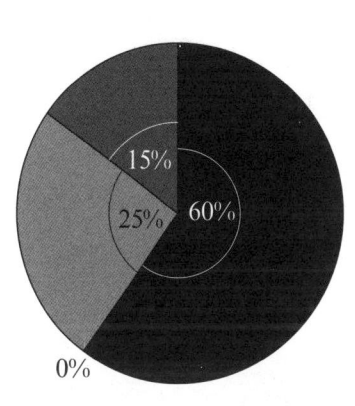

■ Fossil   □ Nuclear   ■ Hydroelectric   ■ Other

Read what Sofia says.

> Looking at the percentages of electricity produced from fossil fuels, the percentage in Argentina is four times the percentage in Brazil, and the percentage in Chile is more than three times the percentage in Brazil.

a   Show that Sofia is correct.

b   Write a statement to compare the percentages of electricity produced from hydroelectric plants in Argentina, Brazil and Chile.

c   Write a statement to compare the percentages of electricity produced from other renewable sources in Argentina, Brazil and Chile.

The table shows the number of kilowatts (kW) of electricity produced each year in Argentina, Brazil and Chile.

Country	Argentina	Brazil	Chile
Number of kilowatts (kW) of electricity produced (nearest million)	40	150	24

d Work out the number of kilowatts of electricity produced from other renewable sources each year in Argentina, Brazil and Chile.

Read what Marcus says.

Looking at the number of kilowatts of electricity produced from other renewable sources, the number in Brazil is more than 22 times the number in Argentina, and the number in Chile is exactly 3 times the number in Argentina.

e Is Marcus correct? Explain your answer.

8 The pie charts show the proportions of different sizes of coat sold in two shops in 2019.

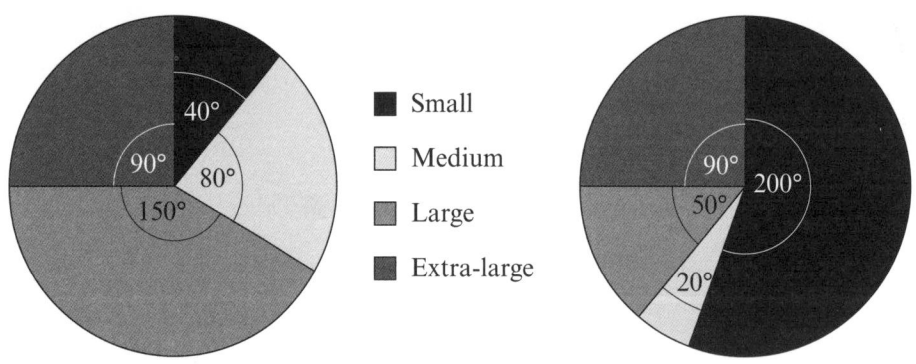

Sizes of coats sold in Outdoor Wear

Sizes of coats sold in Coats-for-all

■ Small
□ Medium
■ Large
■ Extra-large

In 2019, Outdoor Wear sold 900 coats in total.

How many coats does Coats-For-All sell **in total** if they sell

a the same number of small coats as Outdoor Wear

b the same number of medium coats as Outdoor Wear

c the same number of large coats as Outdoor Wear?

9   The pie charts show the proportions of different activities booked
    by people at a water-sports centre on Thursday and Friday.

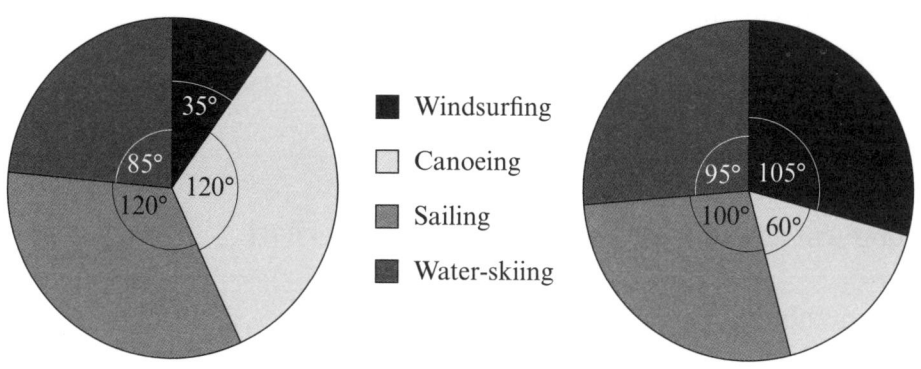

Different activities booked on Thursday   Different activities booked on Friday

■ Windsurfing
□ Canoeing
■ Sailing
■ Water-skiing

On Thursday, 216 people booked activities at the water-sports centre.

On Friday, the same number of people booked for windsurfing as
on Thursday.

a   How many people booked for windsurfing on Friday?

b   How many people altogether booked an activity on Friday?

> 16.5 Representing data

Exercise 16.5

Focus

1   Look at the following sets of data. Which type of diagram, graph
    or chart do you think is best to use to display the data? Choose
    from the options below. Justify your choice for each set of data.

stem-and-leaf diagram	compound bar chart
scatter graph	pie chart

    a   The total numbers of adult and child tickets sold at a cinema
        on two different days.

    b   The proportions of different makes of motorbike sold by one
        shop over a year.

    c   The mass and length of newborn babies in a hospital.

    d   The number of ice creams sold in a shop each day for
        one month.

2 A group of 40 girls play three different sports.

8 of the girls play football, hockey and tennis.

5 girls play football and hockey only, 4 girls play hockey and tennis only, and 7 girls play football and tennis only.

1 girl plays only football, 6 girls play only hockey and 9 girls play only tennis.

a Draw a diagram, graph or chart to represent this data.

b Justify your choice of diagram, graph or chart.

c Make one comment about what your diagram, graph or chart shows you.

 3 The table shows the number of times 50 people exercised in one month.

Number of times people exercised in one month	Number of people
0–4	18
5–9	9
10–14	13
15–19	4
20+	6

a Draw a diagram, graph or chart to represent this data.

b Justify your choice of diagram, graph or chart.

c Make one comment about what your diagram, graph or chart shows you.

Practice

 4 The table shows the number of items of jewellery sold by two shops on one day.

Item	bracelet	necklace	ring	earrings	watch
Shop A	3	14	8	18	2
Shop B	14	8	22	7	9

a Represent the number of items of jewellery sold by each shop on this day using

   i a dual bar chart

   ii a compound bar chart.

Look at your charts in part **a** and answer these questions.

b When you represent this data in a dual bar chart

   i what parts of the data is it easier to compare?

   ii what part of the data is it more difficult to compare?

c   When you represent this data in a compound bar chart
   i   what part of the data is it easier to compare?
   ii   what parts of the data is it more difficult to compare?

d   Copy and complete each statement with either 'dual bar chart'
   or 'compound bar chart'.
   i   When you are comparing individual amounts, it is better
        to use a ....
   ii   When you are comparing total amounts, it is better to
        use a ....

5   Shania measured the mass of 40 eggs laid by her chickens.
    The frequency table shows her results.

Mass, m (g)	Frequency
$45 \leqslant m < 50$	4
$50 \leqslant m < 55$	6
$55 \leqslant m < 60$	12
$60 \leqslant m < 65$	9
$65 \leqslant m < 70$	5
$70 \leqslant m < 75$	4

a   Draw a diagram, graph or chart to represent this data.
b   Justify your choice of diagram, graph or chart.
c   Make one comment about what your diagram, graph or chart
    shows you.

6   These are the number of minutes it took 24 people to solve a puzzle.

25	15	18	40	19	45	25	26	32	22	18	36
41	18	33	19	17	35	21	48	39	42	11	30

a   Draw a diagram, graph or chart to represent this data.
b   Justify your choice of diagram, graph or chart.
c   Make one comment about what your diagram, graph or chart
    shows you.
d   For this data, work out
   i   the mode
   ii   the median
   iii the range.

Challenge

7 A nurse recorded the ages of 12 patients. He also recorded the number of hours of sleep they needed, on average, per night. The table shows his results.

Age (nearest year)	17	32	28	54	80	21	63	50	45	15	76	12
Number of hours of sleep	9	7.5	8.5	6.5	5	8	6.5	7	7	8	6	10

a Draw a diagram, graph or chart to represent this data.

b Justify your choice of diagram, graph or chart.

c Make one comment about what your diagram, graph or chart shows you.

d For this data, work out

  i the mean age of the patients

  ii the mean number of hours of sleep the patients need per night.

e Look at your answers to part **d**. Is the mean a suitable average to use to represent each set of data? Explain your answer.

8 The tables show some information about three Caribbean Islands: Barbados, St Lucia and Grenada.

Population information about Barbados, St Lucia and Grenada								
	Population	Land area (km²)	Land use (%)			Median age (years)		Life expectancy (years)
			agriculture	forest	other	male	female	
Barbados	293 131	430	33	19	48	37.8	40.1	75.7
St Lucia	165 510	606	17	77	6	34.3	36.6	78.1
Grenada	112 207	344	32	50	18	32.0	32.2	74.8

Average weather recorded in Bridgetown (Barbados)												
	Jan	Feb	Mar	Apr	May	Jun	Jul	Aug	Sep	Oct	Nov	Dec
Min (°C)	21	21	21	22	23	24	23	23	23	23	23	22
Max (°C)	28	29	30	30	31	31	30	31	30	30	30	29
Rain (mm)	65	40	35	50	70	105	140	145	170	175	180	95
Days of rain	12	9	7	7	7	14	19	15	15	15	14	13

Average weather recorded in Castries (St Lucia)	Jan	Feb	Mar	Apr	May	Jun	Jul	Aug	Sep	Oct	Nov	Dec
Min (°C)	23	23	24	24	25	25	25	25	25	25	24	24
Max (°C)	29	29	29	30	31	31	31	31	31	31	30	29
Rain (mm)	125	95	75	90	125	200	245	205	225	260	215	160
Days of rain	14	9	10	10	11	15	18	16	17	20	18	16

Average weather recorded in St Georges (Grenada)	Jan	Feb	Mar	Apr	May	Jun	Jul	Aug	Sep	Oct	Nov	Dec
Min (°C)	22	22	22	23	24	24	24	24	24	24	23	23
Max (°C)	30	30	31	31	31	31	31	31	31	31	31	30
Rain (mm)	115	80	65	70	115	220	230	220	200	245	245	175
Days of rain	14	9	10	7	13	17	20	18	17	20	20	18

Decide which diagrams, graphs or charts are best to use to represent this data.

Make a poster to show some of the information above to describe facts about the three Caribbean islands.

> 16.6 Using statistics

Exercise 16.6

Focus

1   In a hockey competition, Catalonia won and Andalucia was knocked out in the semi-finals.

The numbers of goals they scored in their matches are shown in the box.

Catalonia	5, 6, 3, 2, 3, 4, 3, 3
Andalucia	2, 1, 1, 3, 1, 6, 0

a   Work out the mean score for each team.

b   Use the means to state which team scored more goals, on average, per match.

c   Work out the range for each team.

d   Use the ranges to state which team's scores were more varied.

2 A scientist measured the masses of some male and female mice. Here are the results.

> **Males** 22 g, 28 g, 21 g, 27 g, 24 g, 29 g, 28 g, 27 g, 23 g
> **Females** 32 g, 20 g, 30 g, 18 g, 21 g, 19 g, 22 g, 24 g

a For each group
   i write the masses in order of size
   ii write the median mass
   iii work out the range in masses.
b Use the medians to state which group is heavier, on average.
c Use the ranges to state which group's masses are less varied.

3 The number of school days missed by each member of class 8T in one month was recorded.
Here are the results.

> **Boys** 1, 3, 0, 0, 0, 2, 1, 1, 1, 3, 2, 4, 1
> **Girls** 0, 0, 2, 3, 1, 0, 2, 0, 5, 0, 0, 1, 0, 0, 3

a For each group
   i write the number of school days missed, in order, from most to least
   ii write the modal number of school days missed
   iii work out the range in the numbers of school days missed.
b Use the modes to state whether boys or girls missed more school days, on average.
c Use the ranges to state which is more varied, the number of school days missed by the boys or by the girls.

Practice

4 A science teacher recorded the total test scores of the boys and girls in his class.
The 12 girls had a total score of 276. The 15 boys had a total score of 315.
Who did better on average, the boys or the girls? Give a reason for your answer.

5 In a college, there are three adult language classes. Here is some information about the ages of the adults in each class.

Class	Number of people	Mean age (years)	Age range (years)	Age of oldest person (years)
Japanese	16	35	20	44
Spanish	28	37	33	65
English	34	26	45	64

Use the information in the table to answer these questions. Give reasons for your answers.

a Which class has the highest average age?

b Which class has the greatest variation in ages?

c Work out the age of the youngest person in each class.

Explain how you worked out your answer.

6 Pablo and Carlos play golf. They record their scores on the same golf course each week for 8 weeks. Here are their results.

> **Pablo**   73, 64, 74, 64, 72, 75, 64, 74
> **Carlos**   73, 69, 70, 72, 71, 70, 72, 72

a Copy and complete this table to show Pablo's and Carlos's golf scores.

	Mean	Median	Mode	Range
Pablo				
Carlos				

b **i** Who do you think did better on average, Pablo or Carlos?

ii Which average did you use to compare the scores?
Why did you use this average?
Why did you not use the other averages?

c Who do you think had more consistent scores, Pablo or Carlos?
Explain how you worked out your answer.

> **Tip**
>
> When you play golf, the lower your score the better. It is always the person with the lowest score who wins a competition.

> **Tip**
>
> 'More consistent scores' means scores that are less varied.

7   Serena recorded the number of lengths of the swimming pool she swam on each visit for two months.

> **March**   40, 62, 30, 65, 40, 64, 42
> **April**   42, 55, 44, 47, 52, 40, 46, 43, 45

    a   Work out the mean, the median and the range for each month.

    b   State whether each of the following statements is True (T) or False (F). Justify your answers.

        i   The number of lengths she swam per visit in March was higher, on average, than the number of lengths she swam per visit in April.

        ii   The numbers of lengths she swam per visit in March were more varied than the numbers of lengths she swam per visit in April.

    c   Is it possible to work out the modal number of lengths for each month? Explain your answer.

Challenge

 8   The table shows the number of goals scored in each match in the Men's Football World Cup in 2010 and the Women's Football World Cup in 2011.

Goals scored		0	1	2	3	4	5	6	7
World Cup	Men 2010	7	17	13	14	7	5	0	1
	Women 2011	1	8	4	9	8	1	1	0

    a   Copy and complete this table for the number of goals scored by the men and women.

	Mean	Median	Mode	Range
Men 2010				
Women 2011				

    b   Which average is the best one to use to compare the number of goals scored by men's teams and women's teams in these two World Cups?

    c   Use the average you selected in part **b** to decide whether more goals were scored in men's matches or women's matches in these two World Cups.

    d   Were the numbers of goals scored per men's match more or less varied than the numbers per women's match?

    Explain how you worked out your answer.

9   Here is some information about the ages of the men and women
    working for a company.

	Men	Women
Number of employees	43	72
Median age	38	29
Mean age	39.1	30.8
Modal age class	36–45	26–35
Youngest person	16	18
Oldest person	64	52

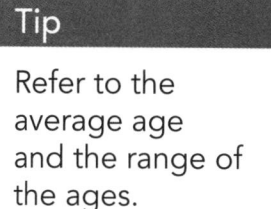

Tip

Refer to the
average age
and the range of
the ages.

Describe the differences between the ages of the men and women.

10 The users of two websites were asked to grade them for ease-of-use.
    They used a scale of 1 to 5.

1 was poor and 5 was excellent. The results are shown in this table.

Grade		1	2	3	4	5
Frequency	Website A	4	18	11	16	11
	Website B	35	5	8	25	27

Use averages to decide which website is better.

Justify your choice.